Maybe I've loved you
Since before the mountains were hills
And ached for the sky
And we can remember
what it's like
To be green
And rolling
And fall in love
Again and again.
—*Kirsten Bergh*
1979–1996

In loving memory of
Jack Heckelman
1923–2005

Cosmo Doogood's

URBAN ALMANAC

Celebrating Nature & Her Rhythms in the City

FOR THE YEAR

2006

Includes:
Secular and Religious Festivals, Important Birthdays and Deathdays,
a Dream Journal, Urban Survival Strategies, Living Urban Treasures,
Urban Sanctuaries: Sacred Places and Spaces in the City,
Urban Legends, Jokes, Quotes, and Poems,
The Wisdom of the Ages, and a Weather Journal,

INCLUDING AN

εPHEMERIS

OF THE

MOTIONS of the SUN and MOON,

AND THE TRUE

Places and Aspects of the Planets

FEATURING

A Daily Calendar and Organizer,
A Field Guide to Urban Flora and Fauna,

&

Weather Predictions for the Entire United States,
for Twelve Months
{ *January 2006 – December 2006* }

By C O S M O   D O O G O O D – Philom.

MINNEAPOLIS

PRINTED AND SOLD BY ERIC UTNE :: DESIGN: BOSSENOVA.COM

*The definition of insanity is doing the same thing
over and over and expecting different results.*
– Benjamin Franklin

THANKS TO:
Eli, Oliver, Sam, Leif & Cilla Utne,
Mark, Dana, and Aaron Bossen, Lizzie and Sally Coventry Holzapfel,
Kathleen Melin, Elizabeth Larsen, Andi McDaniel, Michael Bader,
Sarah Haberman, Molly Gaines, Theresa Wolner, Sonya Burke, Bettina Gordon,
Lexy Adams, John Poore, Kathy Kinzig, Brinkley Prescott, John Miller,
Kerry Miller, Jennifer Fox, Linda Bergh, Jack Heckelman, Christina Beck,
Gene Gollogly, John Alexandra, Claus Sproll, Magda Lissau, Alexander Cameron,
Rick Spaulding, Kaiulani Lee, Kim Knutson, Lisa Ringer, Louise Erdrich, Brian Baxter,
Susan White, Will Winter, Jim Lenfestey, Dave Astin, Shivon Robinsong, Marko Pogačnik,
Win Phelps, Gigi Coyle, Arthur Zajonc, Chris & Signe Schaefer, Marion Bornschlegel,
Sharon Koukkari, Tove Borgendale, David Tresemer, Laura Lea Cannon, Karen Cross,
Tawana Robertson, Marc Allen, Sarah Rosenberg, Charlie Winton, Horst Rechelbacher,
Theresa Marquez, John Fuller, Susan Lantz, Kim Corrigan, Andrea Tintle, Mary Adams,
Kasey Arnold-Ince, Mary Christianson, Fonda Black, Peter Buckley, Lisa Proctor, Judy
Rudrud, Tim Morgan, Chris Dodge, Kristin Brabec, Talya Schaefer, Sally Bickford,
Lynn Jericho, Jeff Linzer, Cara Schneider, Brenda King, Marion Leon, Jane Barrash,
Cal Appleby, Faith Hess, Eva Marie Bittleson, Reinoud Meier, Kevin Kane, Margot Adler,
Seth Sutel, John Dramgoole, Bec Kageyama, Michael Toms, Mary Utne O'Brien,
And most of all to Nina Utne, whose faith and love warm the Cosmos.

Cover illustration, *Hangin' with the Homies* by Christopher Zacharow
Logo woodcut by Nick Wroblewski

Cosmo Doogood's Urban Almanac:
Celebrating Nature & Her Rhythms in the City
Copyright © 2005 by Eric Utne

www.cosmosurbanalmanac.com

Published by Cosmo's Urban Almanac
4025 Linden Hills Blvd.
Minneapolis, Minnesota 55410 USA

Founder, Cosmo Doogood
Editor, Eric Utne
Managing Editor, Martha Coventry
Associate Editor, Danielle Maestretti
Designer, Margaret Bossen
www.bossenova.com

Cosmo Doogood's Urban Almanac is neither a book nor a magazine – it's both!
Magazine retailers, please scan the UPC code on the front cover. ISSN 1552-4671
Booksellers, please scan the bar code on the back cover. ISBN 0-9761989-1-6
Printed on New Leaf Good News Offset paper
100% Recycled, 40% Post-Consumer Waste, Processed Chlorine Free
Printed and bound in Canada by Webcom

COSMO DOOGOOD'S

URBAN ALMANAC

Celebrating Nature & Her Rhythms in the City

CONTENTS

FRANKLIN

UELAND

"Start slow and taper off..."

– Brenda Ueland

"If you wou'd not be forgotten
As soon as you are dead and rotten,
Either write things worth reading,
or do things worth the writing."

– Benjamin Franklin

COURTEOUS READER...

Cosmo Doogood's Urban Almanac has two guiding spirits—Benjamin Franklin, the patron saint of almanacs, and Brenda Ueland, Cosmo's poetic muse and personal trainer. Though Ben and Brenda never met—he was born 185 years before she was—and neither is currently living, both are very much present in all our deliberations at the almanac.

Ben and Brenda would have appreciated each other. I keep seeing them floating together (both were life-long swimmers) in a great, meandering river somewhere over yonder, swapping quips and generally keeping each other chortling while bobbing merrily along.

Brenda could match wits with Ben any day. She used to say, "If something's worth doing, it's worth doing poorly," and that she had "three husbands and a hundred lovers," but she "never had a love affair with a married man unless he brought a note from his wife." She actually got one once. Her third husband was my grandfather, Sverre Hanssen.

Like Ben, Brenda was a writer. By her count she published six million words in her lifetime—mostly in magazine articles, a column in the Minneapolis newspaper, and a few books. Carl Sandburg called her book *If You Want to Write* "the best book ever written about how to write." Graywolf Press reprinted the book 15 years ago and has sold more than 300,000 copies to date.

Also like Ben, Brenda was an athlete. Every day, until well into her late 80s, Brenda ran twice around the three-mile lake near her home, "once for the body and once for the soul." She said the worst thing about falling off a stepladder and breaking her hip while changing the storm windows of her Minneapolis home (at 91 years old) was that she could no longer "dart from

between parked cars in the middle of city blocks and dodge on-coming traffic." She explained setting three AAU swimming records for over 80-year-olds by saying that it simply took her "longer to sink than the competition." She lived until she was 93 years old.

One of Brenda's favorite admonitions was to, "Start slow and taper off." Her secret for healthy living was the same as for good writing—it was all about slowing down: "long, inefficient, happy idling, dawdling and puttering." And this: "...inspiration does not come like a bolt, nor is it kinetic, energetic striving, but it comes slowly and quietly and all the time, though we must regularly and every day give it a little chance to start flowing, prime it with a little solitude and idleness. I learned that you should feel when writing not like Lord Byron on a mountaintop, but like a child stringing beads in kindergarten —happy, absorbed, and quietly putting one bead on after another."

Brenda's advice to moodle and doodle is a nice complement to Ben's more urgent, "Lost time is never found again," and, "...do not squander time, for that's the

stuff life is made of." But the pace of life today is all movement, all energetic striving, no down time, no rest.

WHAT'S INSIDE
How can we navigate these rapids and get more time for moodling and doodling? This year's edition of *Cosmo Doogood's Urban Almanac* offers several strategies to help you create more resilience and flow in your life by connecting with nature's rhythms, including a revolutionary new exercise program and a set of lunar rhythm charts.

Paying attention to nature's rhythms can have enormous health benefits. According to a new book by award-winning science writer Roger Lewin, the key to stress-free living and optimum health is getting in synch with nature's rhythms. Lewin reports on the findings of heart specialist Irving Dardik, who claims that long-distance running, biking, and swimming are more likely to kill you than to cure you. The real key, Dardik says, is to "make waves," movement *and* rest. See page 31. It may change your life.

This year we introduce a new feature to the almanac—Lunar Rhythm charts. Austrians Johanna Paungger and Thomas Poppe are two of the most popular writers in Europe. Their books *Moon Time* and *Guided by the Moon* have been translated into 22 languages and have sold more than 13 million copies. Cosmo, Johanna, and Thomas collaborated to bring you the charts that begin on page 68. The charts not only tell you the most advantageous times to plant, tend, and harvest your garden, but they also indicate the best days to clean your house, get a haircut, have dental surgery, and quit a bad habit. Don't believe it? Suspend your disbelief and give it try this year. What have you got to lose?

It gives me an unseemly amount of pleasure to announce that Doc Weather's "pretty good" weather predictions are much more accurate than those of the *Old Farmer's Almanac.* You'll find Doc's predictions for 2006 and his comparative analysis for the first six months of 2005, beginning on page 18.

Since January 17, 2006, marks the 300th birthday of Benjamin Franklin, we pay a special tribute to our patron saint in this year's almanac. Ben's ideas and worldview are as relevant today as they were in his day. According to best-selling Franklin biographer Walter Isaacson, "We can easily imagine having a beer with him after work, showing him how to use a Palm Pilot, sharing the business plan for a new venture....He would laugh at the latest joke about a priest and a rabbi, or the one about the farmer's daughter." He would also have a great deal to say, as would his fellow founders, about the inflammatory mix of politics and religion that's tearing the world apart these days. We turn to the founding fathers' surprisingly contemporary words for counsel, starting with Isaacson's essay on page 49.

May your year be blessed with a harmonious flow of movement and rest. ✄
— *Eric Utne*

P.S. What's wrong with this year's cover image *Hanging with the Homies,* by NYC artist Christopher Zacharow? The painting depicts a group of birds gathered on a Manhattan antenna. We will give a three-year subscription to the person who comes up with the most convincing explanation for why the scene *could not* possibly occur in real life, and another three-year subscription for the most convincing rationale for why the scene *could* happen in real life. The birds pictured are (clockwise from top)

1. Northern Cardinal
2. Ruby-Throated Hummingbird
3. Baltimore Oriole
4. Hairy Woodpecker
5. American Goldfinch
6. Indigo Bunting
7. Painted Bunting

Send your answer to *info@cosmosurbanalmanac.com*

LOOK UP

The Moon
Queen of heaven, ruler of the night sky
By Norman Davidson

The word *month* is derived from an Old English word for moon, so we are effectively saying *moonth*. It takes the Moon 29½ days to pass from new, through its phases, and back to the invisible new Moon again. In early times the calendar month kept to these phases. The beginning of the month was announced when the waxing crescent first appeared, or was calculated to appear, in the evening sky. This moment also started the first day of the month, which began at sunset and ended at the next sunset. Today's generally used calendar no longer follows the movement of the Moon, but that of the Sun (dividing 365¼ days into 12 months), though some religions, like Islam and Judaism, still use the old system.

Sun and Moon had a special importance for people of earlier times, and their positions were well known and carefully recorded. The full Moon's positions appear to have been built into the layout of ancient stone circles. It is thought that Stonehenge, for example, was constructed to show, among other things, the positions of the rising and setting of Sun and Moon.

The Moon's phases vary from night to night. In one part of the month, the lit area of the Moon grows larger or waxes; in another it grows smaller or wanes until it disappears altogether, only to be reborn a few days later. The basic picture of this is shown below.

Figure 1 represents the Moon's changing position in the sky at the moment of sunset over a period of two weeks, half of its monthly motion. The Sun is below the western horizon, just after sunset. As the sky darkens on the first day of the lunar month, the crescent Moon becomes visible. About a week later we have the first quarter Moon, which rises in the east around noon and is at the peak of the sky at sunset. The full Moon rises at sunset and is up all night. The last quarter Moon rises around midnight.

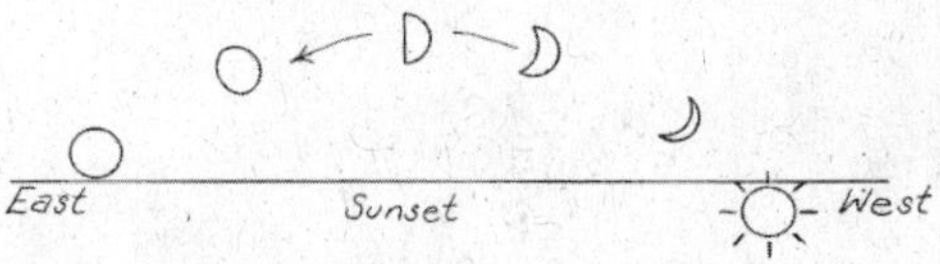

Fig. 1

Figure 2 shows the position of the Moon at dawn over the next two weeks. Throughout the month the Moon rises about 51 minutes later each night, until at last, at new Moon, the Sun and Moon rise and set together and the cycle begins anew.

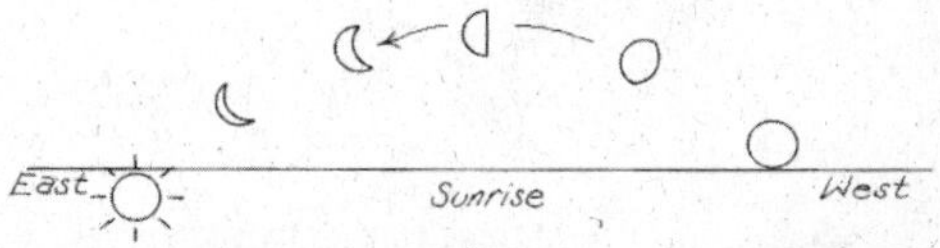

Fig. 2

Figure 1 shows the Moon waxing during evenings, and Figure 2 shows it waning during mornings. It should be noted that the lit edge nearest the Sun is always directed along the path of a curve (approximately the ecliptic). This is the picture from day to day in the course of a month. But during each day the whole sky, with Moon and Sun, turns from left to right, or east to west. This means that one particular phase, say half Moon, makes a daily movement as in Figure 3.

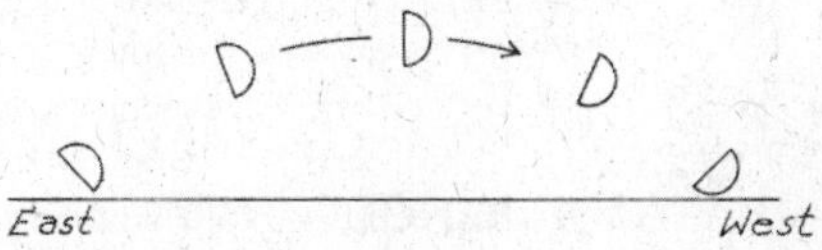

This applies to all the other phases, so when the evening crescent Moon is first seen at sunset, it is in the act of setting and is only briefly visible. The full Moon, on the other hand, is visible all night because it takes the whole night to travel the arc of the sky.

Fig. 3

The evening half Moon is called first quarter, since the Moon has completed the first quarter of its monthly cycle. Seen from above the Earth, the Moon's movement and shadow would appear as in Figure 4 (inner ring). The phases in Figure 4 appear as if you are standing on the earth looking toward the Moon.

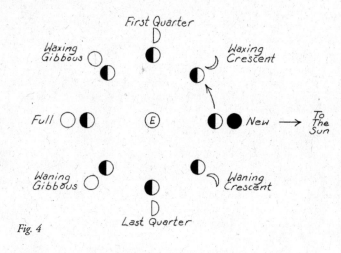

Fig. 4

MOON LITERARY REFERENCES

Literature includes many references to the Moon. Astronomical references in Shakespeare's works include act 2, scene 1, of *Macbeth*, in which Banquo and Fleance set the lunar scene for the murder of King Duncan. The scene opens:

(Enter Banquo, and Fleance, with a torch before him.)

BANQUO: How goes the night, boy?

FLEANCE: The moon is down; I have not heard the clock.

BANQUO: And she goes down at twelve.

FLEANCE: I take't, 'tis later, sir.

BANQUO: Hold, take my sword. There's husbandry in heaven; Their candles are all out.

On a starless evening a bright phase of the Moon could shine through thin cloud or mist and still be seen before it sets. So Fleance could observe it "go down" or set. When King Duncan arrived at the castle earlier that evening, Banquo noted "This guest of summer, the temple-haunting martlet" or martin. So we can assume it was a summer night (the historical King Duncan was killed in battle on August 14, 1040). At midnight in summer the ecliptic would lie low across the horizon from east to west, and the Moon phase to "go down" at midnight is first quarter. It would set as in Figure 5.

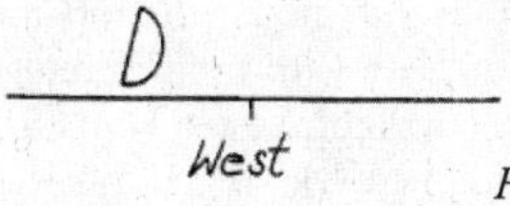

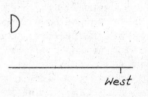

Fig. 5

At sunset that evening, near when the King arrived at the beginning of act 1, scene 6, the Moon would have been "upright" and higher to the left (Figure 6). So we know the phase of the Moon on the night King Duncan was murdered, and stage set designers may well use such information in depicting the sky above Macbeth's castle.

Fig. 6

A lunar phenomenon that often appears in literature is the Harvest Moon. The Harvest Moon is the full Moon that falls nearest the date of the autumn equinox. Shortly before and after it is full, the Moon rises close to the moment of sunset on several consecutive nights. This allows the farmer taking in the harvest to have the fields still lit after sunset.

THE TIDES

As mentioned above, the Moon passes due south above the horizon about 51 minutes later each day. It can be noticed that tides on the seashore can have this same time delay of about 51 minutes on consecutive days. Tides differ from place to place, but 51 minutes is a fair average. For example, if there is a high tide at noon, then the next day it will occur around 12:50 p.m. In between there will have been another high tide at about 25 minutes after midnight.

What is called a tidal bulge of ocean is pulled toward the Moon on one side of the Earth and falls away from it on the other (Figure 7). The Earth rotates inside this and experiences periods of high tide at the bulges and low tide 90 degrees from the bulges. But by the time the Earth has rotated once, the Moon has moved on eastward against the background of the stars, the bulge has moved round with it, and the Earth has to rotate further to catch up.

Theoretically, the period of 51 minutes for the Earth's rotation to catch up with the tidal bulge each day is correct at times of full Moon, new Moon, first quarter, and last quarter. At other times (because of the influence of the

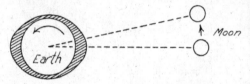

Fig. 7

Sun), the tidal bulge is either displaced westward clockwise (shortly after new and full Moons) or displaced eastward counter clockwise (shortly before new and full Moons). This is a theoretical and oversimplified picture, and the tides at different coastlines on the Earth have their individual rhythms, which cannot be explained so easily. Suffice it to say the Earth and the Moon respond to each other (with the Sun involved, too), and the tides express a link, even if complicated, between their rhythms.

MOON TO EARTH

Finally, since human beings have set foot on the Moon, one might ask what the sky looks like from there. During the Moon's orbit of the Earth, it keeps the same face turned toward us. Therefore, someone standing on the Moon would experience the Earth shining like a large Moon but never rising or setting. The Earth will remain fixed above the horizon and its diameter will be about four times that of the Moon seen from Earth. In its almost stationary position in the lunar sky, the Earth will go through all phases from new to full and back again in the space of a lunar day. A day on the Moon lasts a synodic month (29.53 days) of Earth time. During the lunar night on its Northern Hemisphere the stars will slide past the gibbous or full Earth from left to right. The lunar year (marked by the return of the Sun to the same zodiacal constellation) will have no more than 12 complete lunar days. The Sun will rise in the lunar morning with a flash of light transforming night to day in a moment, because there is no atmosphere to create dawn. Sunset will quickly plunge the lunar landscape from day into starlit night. During

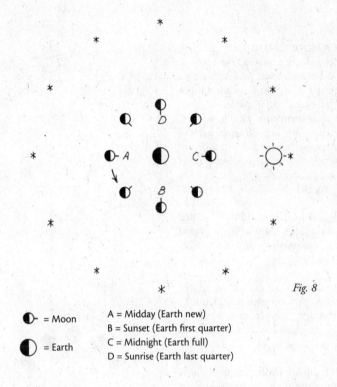

Fig. 8

◖ = Moon

◗ = Earth

A = Midday (Earth new)
B = Sunset (Earth first quarter)
C = Midnight (Earth full)
D = Sunrise (Earth last quarter)

the day the Sun will shine in a black sky, again because there is no atmosphere. But the Earth's atmosphere and oceans will cause the Earth to shine out in white and blue color.

Also, whatever phase the Moon appears at from Earth, the Earth will appear in the opposite (complementary) phase seen from the Moon. When we see a crescent Moon (less than half full) in the sky, the lunar inhabitant in the grey-blue ashen-light area (where it is night) will experience the Earth as gibbous (more than half full). In fact, the shape of the ashen-lit area seen on the

Moon from Earth is the shape of the Earth's phase seen at that moment from the Moon. So the crescent Moon with ashen light shows two realities in our sky. The unlighted part of the Moon, when seen from the Earth, is still slightly visible because some light from the Sun reflects off the Earth onto the part of the Moon that is facing us. This phenomenon was called the old Moon in the new Moon's arms. Figure 8 shows the basic situation for a point on the lunar surface facing Earth. The far side of the Moon never experiences the Earth in the sky at all.

MAKE A MOON CALENDAR

A Moon calendar showing the approximate dates for Moon phases during a particular month can be made simply. Cut out two circular pieces of cardboard of different sizes. Divide the edge of the larger one into 30 equal parts of 12 degrees each. Number the divisions counter-clockwise to represent dates (Figure 9), disregarding for the moment those months with 28, 29, or 31 days.

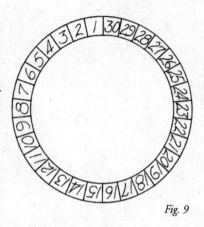

Fig. 9

Divide the smaller disk into 12 equal parts and place a phase of the Moon at each, also proceeding anticlockwise, as in Figure 10.

The smaller disk is placed on top of the larger, perhaps with a split pin to pass through their centers. Find the date of any phase (say new Moon) and place that phase beside that date.

The other phases will then be indicated beside the dates when they occur during a lunar month. If a month has, say, 31 days, then an adjustment can be made at the end of the 30th day by moving the smaller disk back a day and counting 30 as 31. If the month has 28 days, then at the end of the 28th day the smaller disk can be moved forward two days. A month of 29 days should have the phase disk moved forward one day at the end of the 29th. This keeps the calendar close to the 29½ day lunar month. ☆

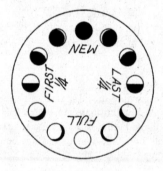

Fig. 10

Adapted from *Sky Phenomena: A Guide to Naked-Eye Observation of the Stars* by Norman Davidson (Lindisfarne Press, Great Barrington, MA). Davidson is also author of *Astronomy and the Imagination* (Penguin Books). He writes, lectures, and consults at Sunbridge College in Spring Valley, New York. For more information on naked-eye astronomy, see Acknowledgements, p. 273.

LOOK OUT:
2006 SKY SUMMARY

Mercury has four good appearances this year: two in the evening sky—in late February and mid-June—and two more in the mornings of early August and late November. On August 7 it lies just below Venus in the morning sky; on December 5 it takes part in a predawn gathering with Jupiter and Mars.

Venus is the main attraction of the morning sky in early 2006, but it never gains the prominence we usually expect of it. Even at its best, in late February, Venus rises less than three hours ahead of the Sun. The main event happens the morning of August 27, when it is joined by the much fainter Saturn. You'll probably need binoculars to actually detect Saturn in the glow of twilight.

Mars, between oppositions this year, can best be found almost stationary against the stars in the evening sky while the constellations pass behind it. On June 17 it meets with Saturn at about the best time to see Mercury during its pop-up in the evening sky—a nice planetary trio.

Jupiter has made its way to the stars of Libra, a fairly nondescript part of the sky. It's a morning object the first third of the year, reaches its first stationary point on March 5, swirls into opposition in early May, and concludes its loop on July 6.

Saturn reaches opposition in late January and begins the year with a completion of its retrograde loop. In the last week of January and the first week of February it lies near the Beehive star cluster in Cancer. Saturn switches to the morning sky in August.

Meteor showers: It's a good year for the January Quadrantids, but early-morning viewing of the August Perseids and the December Geminids is partly spoiled by the Moon. Moonlight will not be a problem for any surprise the November Leonids may still try to throw our way—a small outburst has been predicted to occur at the normal peak.

Eclipses: This year's four solar and lunar eclipses all favor the eastern hemisphere. The March total solar eclipse favors Africa, Europe, and Asia, with the Moon's shadow crossing the Mediterranean coast of Africa and the eastern Black Sea.

Excerpted from *Celestial Delights: The Best Astronomical Events Through 2010.* For more information, see Acknowledgements, p. 273.

DOC WEATHER 2006
Doc's "pretty good" general weather forecast

Doc Weather is a scientist, artist, and instructor at a California college. He has been studying and predicting the weather, using his own well-kept, secret methods, for 25 years. Two Chicago commodities traders have been using his long-range forecasts for years to predict crop yields and swear they are more accurate, and make them more money, than those of the National Weather Service. Doc was reluctant to let us print predictions that he'd have to make a year and a half in advance (due to publishing deadlines), knowing most people would compare them to the 5- and 10-day forecasts on the nightly news. But when we told him we'd call them "pretty good" predictions, he agreed.

With a year of prognostications under his belt, we asked Doc how he did for the first six months of 2005 compared to the Old Farmer's Almanac. You'll find the results on page 21. Cosmo Doogood would like to point out that the observant reader can come to only one incontrovertible conclusion on reviewing the following data:

Doc Weather's weather predictions, for the first six months of 2005, were significantly more accurate than those of the Old Farmer's Almanac. So, for future gardening, travel, and special-event planning, like weddings, vacations, and so forth, who you gonna trust, that other almanac or Doc Weather? – Cosmo

OVERVIEW FOR 2006

Watch for a cold turbulent center in the Dakotas in early **January** with tracks into the mid-Atlantic states. Venus, Moon, and Mercury transiting the Mountain states early in the first week should trigger strong storms from the Northern Plains to the mid-Atlantic states. Look for a nor'easter late in the week on the East Coast.

Watch for temperate, seasonal weather due to horizontal jet stream patterns accompanied by mild weather for most of the continent except northwest and northeast corners for the first two weeks of **February**. Colder in the west with storms in the Great Lakes as the result of a Denver to Great Lakes storm track in the second half of the month.

In **March** very seasonal temperatures should dominate the continent except for the northeast corner. Look for clear and mild conditions over the western third of the continent at midmonth. In the latter half of the month look for clear and colder conditions from the Mississippi eastward with storms centering in the northeast.

© PhotoDisc

In **April**, the new eclipse points should shift the jet stream to a blocking pattern over the High Plains for most of the month. Look for high pressure over the southern High Plains to keep the jet stream to the north on western third of the continent. Low-pressure centers should form over the Pacific Northwest (PNW) and the northeast and be moderately active most of the time and very active in the middle of the month.

May will be unsettled in the first week with moderate warm fronts in the east. Cold in the High Plains will accompany wet in the Corn Belt at midmonth returning to moderate temperatures but wet east of the Mississippi and hot and dry conditions in the western states.

Most of **June** should be warm and dry to the Continental Divide. The Great Lakes to mid-Atlantic states should be the preferred storm track most of the month with intermittent fronts dominating most weeks, but intensifying in the second week, with dryness in the East late in the month. Look for regular rains in the Corn Belt with a late heat surge.

A hot and dry pattern for most of the continent from the West Coast to the Mississippi Valley should dominate **July**. Respite from the dryness and heat should come in the third week in the High Plains and Gulf Coast but this should be short lived as dry conditions with above average temperatures rule the month in most section.

Hot and dry weather in the Corn Belt in the first two weeks of **August** will yield to wetter and cooler conditions there in the third week. The PNW and the Northeast should be unseasonably cool with moisture in the Northeast most of the last three weeks of the month. The area around Denver looks to be very active with thunderstorms in all but the third week.

September should see a shift to storm activity in the Great Basin with a strong block over the Mississippi Valley. Cool and wet conditions for the eastern third of the country should dominate the rest of the month. Cool and wet in the Corn Belt and the mid-Atlantic states should be the dominant pattern with the storm jet on the West Coast dropping south in some early rain patterns after the 23rd.

October weather should be mild for the first week across the nation. This pattern should turn colder for the West and Northeast for the remainder of the month. Look for warm conditions from the southern High Plains to the southeast for the last three weeks of the month, with early cold into the two northern corners of the U.S. Watch the Northeast for storms moving up the coast.

November should start on a dry note for the West with unseasonable cold in the eastern third of the country, with mild temperatures in the West. This should be the pattern for weeks one and three. This should alternate with mild Pacific maritime influences in weeks two and four for northern sections of the continent, with rains across the West Coast and the central states.

In **December**, week one should continue the pattern of western rains and continental mildness. In week two expect temperatures on the continent to fall as mildness covers the West. In week three a strong shift should bring storms across California into the central states. After the 23rd look for colder in the West and for citrus threatening freezes in the Southeast. ✂

— *Dennis Klocek, aka Doc Weather*

LOOK UP:
DOC WEATHER 2006
A Weather Challenge

The *Old Farmer's Almanac* (OFA) claims to have a traditional 80 percent accuracy in its forecasts. Cosmo Doogood wanted to know if Doc Weather could do better. The challenge was on. However, the OFA uses 16 micro-sections of the U.S. for its forecasts. Doc Weather uses four longitudinal climatic divisions and then includes indications on the northern or southern track in each division for a given week. These differences make it difficult to compare the two systems directly. So it was finally agreed to compare the number of forecasts made in only the comparable sections of the two publications and then assess the number of right and wrong forecasts for January to July of 2005.

The comparison between the OFA and Doc Weather was not easy to do. The OFA bases much of its forecasts on climatology. It includes the average mean temperatures and precipitation amounts at the beginning of each month. Rather than using this kind of abstract climatology, Doc Weather tries to give dynamic weekly pictures of the way the jet stream will move into your locale. As a result, Doc Weather uses weak, moderate, and strong as values to characterize storm force and tracking in a given week. The OFA, using the more statistical approach, rarely assesses individual storm strength. In order to level the playing field the comparison counted indications of dry/wet and cold/mild for both publications. Vague terms like seasonable were not counted as a forecast hit or miss. Seasonable can mean many things to many people.

In the last analysis, both sets of predictions were evaluated primarily on the exactness of the timing of significant weather events as stated in the two publications. Due to the fluid nature of weather, a grace period of one day on either side of a date given in either publication was considered a hit.

The following results were obtained:

For a total of 338 weather forecasts in the OFA, 174 forecasts were correct and 164 were incorrect— a 51 percent accuracy.

During the same months Doc Weather made a total of 191 predictions. Out of the 191 forecasts, 135 were correct and 56 were incorrect, yielding a 71 percent accuracy.

While Doc's number is not the traditional 80 percent accuracy claimed by the OFA, it is "pretty good" given the year and a half lead-time. Doc Weather hopes that the courteous reader will find this comparison worth contemplating.

– Doc Weather

WEST COAST / PACIFIC MARITIME

SUMMARY: JAN. cool 1st week PNW then storms N and S. FEB. clear, mild then cold and storm. MAR. weak fronts N, mild S, early; then storms N and S mid-month to late. APR. Cool, unsettled w/fronts to N: mild below Mt. Shasta. MAY. fronts to N early and midmonth otherwise dry; dry to S. JUNE. warm and dry, N and S. JUL. cool to N, hot to S early; hot and dry N and S late. AUG. cool with fronts to N mid-month and late. SEPT. Clear and seasonal early; cooler with fronts to N, late. OCT. unsettled N and S with fronts N early until 3rd week then clearing. NOV. clear and cool early turning rainy N and S after 10th. DEC. rain, clear, rain, clear N and S.

JAN. 2006 · Week 1: Cool to N with fronts; temperate and clear to S.
Week 2: Temperate to N with early fronts; wet fronts to S. **Week 3:** Storms PNW with fronts below Mt. Shasta week's end. **Week 4:** Unsettled then moderate storm PNW at week's end.

FEB. 2006 · 1: Clear seasonal, N and S. **2:** Clear, mild to S; moderate fronts PNW after 10th. **3:** Colder with fronts PNW and N CA early and late in week. **4:** Storm track to N, cooler, clear to S, warmer.

MAR. 2006 · 1: Weak intermittent fronts PNW and N CA; mild to the S. **2:** Moderate fronts PNW early in the week. **3:** Winter storm PNW / N CA 16–18. **4:** Strong storms N and S to Sacramento, 22–24.

APR. 2006 · 1: Fronts to N, midweek; dry and warm to S. **2:** Fronts PNW to Mt. Shasta, 13–14. **3:** Cool with dynamic, moderate fronts PNW to Mt. Shasta 17–19. **4:** Cool and unsettled PNW; seasonable to the S.

MAY 2006 · 1: Weak lows PNW after 3rd. **2:** Clear, warmer N and S. **3:** Moderate to strong fronts PNW to Mt. Shasta, 16–18. **4:** Warm, clear to S; moderate fronts N of Mt. Shasta.

JUN. 2006 · 1: Clear to S, moderate fronts PNW. **2:** Warm and dry N and S. **3:** Warm and dry, N and S. **4:** Warm and dry, N and S.

JUL. 2006 · 1: Cool PNW and N CA after 3rd. **2:** Cool PNW; warm and dry to S. **3:** Dry and hot N and S. **4:** Hot and dry N and S; cool fronts late in N.

AUG. 2006 · 1: Cooler PNW, unsettled; temperate to the S. **2:** Cooler N and S; fronts PNW midweek **3:** Cold fronts PNW 14–20; cooler S. **4:** Temperate N and S; unsettled PNW.

SEPT. 2006 · 1: Seasonal N and S, then clearing and warmer. **2:** Warm S, seasonal with fronts N. **3:** Clear and warm, N and S. **4:** Cold fronts PNW to N CA after 23rd.

OCT. 2006 · 1: Clear, mild S; unsettled N after the 3rd. **2:** Unsettled S; fronts N. **3:** Cold, wet PNW and S; early. **4:** Cold PNW and N CA early; warmer, clearing late

NOV. 2006 · 1: Cold fronts PNW and N CA early. **2:** Moderate, good rains PNW and N CA after 10th. **3:** Clear, dry N and S then strong rains late. **4:** Rain N and S early and late.

DEC. 2006 · 1: Persistent rains N and S all week. **2:** High, mild N and S. **3:** Widespread rains early. **4:** Cold N, mild S after 23rd.

A

MOUNTAIN REGION / BASIN & RANGE

SUMMARY: JAN. very cold early, then stormy. FEB. temperate High Plains, fronts midmonth, then colder late. MAR. temperate until mid-month, then storms, cold late in N; dry, mild to S. APR. dry, warm early; fronts to N, late. MAY unsettled first 3 weeks, then clearing. JUN. hot, dry N and S early; cool with fronts to N last week. JUL. warm, dry N and S early; storms midmonth S High Plains, then hot and dry. AUG. cool with fronts the 2nd, 3rd and 4th week. SEP. clear, warm to S with fronts to N at mid-month.

OCT. unsettled with fronts N and S. NOV. storm to N early, then settled until stormy last week. DEC. unsettled with fronts until strong storm near Christmas.

JAN. 2006 · Week 1: Cool with fronts early; then milder and settled. **Week 2:** Very cold to N with fronts 9–11; temperate to the S. **Week 3:** Strong storms N mountains 18–20. **Week 4:** Watch for strong mountain storms after the 25th.

FEB 2006 · 1: Weak fronts to N, temperate over High Plains. **2:** Cold fronts into Great Basin 12th–14th. **3:** High over N mountains and High Plains, temperate. **4:** Cold storms PNW to Denver 23–25.

MAR. 2006 · 1: Weak intermittent fronts and seasonal temperatures N and S. **2:** Fronts with rain in the N, midweek. **3:** Winter storm midweek in the N, high to S. **4:** Look for a major storm in the northern Rockies 23–25.

APRIL 2006 · 1: Dry, warm High Plains and mountains. **2:** Dry, warm to the S. moderate, late fronts N. **3:** Moderate fronts N and S. **4:** Warm and dry, Denver to Central States, fronts Dakotas, 22–23.

MAY 2006 · 1: Weak lows in N mountains after the 3rd. **2:** Cold with flurries N, 8–10. **3:** Unsettled with moderate fronts 17–19. **4:** Warmer, clear, mountains and S High Plains.

JUN. 2006 · 1: High, dry mountains and High Plains. **2:** Hot, dry mountains and High Plains. **3:** Hot, dry mountains to High Plains. **4:** Hot to the S; cool and moist Dakotas.

JULY 2006 · 1: Warm then cold fronts at mid-week in Dakotas. **2:** Warm and dry N and S. **3:** Storms S high Plains; dry N mountains. **4:** Hot and dry N and S early; Denver monsoon late.

AUG. 2006 · 1: Thunderstorms High Plains, N and S. **2:** Fronts in High Plains; N and S, 9–10. **3:** Cold fronts northern mountains to Denver. **4:** Dry, cool High Plains to N; Wet, warm to S.

SEPT. 2006 · 1: Fronts to S early, then clearing and warmer. **2:** Clear, warm S Plains; fronts to N after 11th. **3:** Clear and warm SW. **4:** Dry N and wet S in the Plains.

OCT. 2006 · 1: Cold N; fronts Denver; midweek. **2:** Cold, dry N; fronts S. **3:** Cold, wet to N; dry to S. **4:** Fronts N early; warmer late.

NOV. 2006 · 1: Storms, N Plains; late. **2:** Wet, mild N, dry S; end of week. **3:** Dry, mild, settled all week. **4:** Storm into Denver; early.

DEC. 2006 · 1: Unsettled, fronts, into High Plains; all week. **2:** Mild to S; cold to N, late fronts. **3:** Cold N High Plains, storms Denver. **4:** Cold surge N mountains; midweek.

TO LEARN MORE ABOUT DOC WEATHER'S FORECASTS GO TO <WWW.DOCWEATHER.COM>

MID-CONTINENT / CORN BELT & GULF

SUMMARY: JAN. very cold first 2 weeks then strong storms. FEB. temperate until fronts midmonth, then storms late. MAR. clear, mild until last week, then storms. APR. moderate fronts N of Corn Belt dry to S; cold fronts 3rd week Denver to Chicago. MAY cool with intermittent fronts early, Dakotas to Central states, strong rains late. JUN. cool and wet Great Lakes to Ohio; dry Iowa and S. JUL. cool, wet to N; hot dry Gulf coast; then shift in last week. AUG. hot, dry turns cool N and S with rains in Corn Belt at mid-month then dry. SEP. hot, dry until mid month; fronts Great Lakes. OCT. wet S, cool N turns wet N, dry warm S at midmonth. NOV. early cold N and S then milder until 3rd week storms. DEC. unsettled with moderate fronts until strong storm near Christmas, then clearing.

JAN. 2006 · Week 1: Very cold with storms 3–4; OK to VA. **Week 2:** Very cold with fronts OK to PA 10–12. **Week 3:** Strong storms, High Plains to Great Lakes 19–21. **Week 4:** Expect late and strong storms in the Central States.

FEB. 2006 · 1: Temperate W, cooler in Ohio Valley. **2:** Temperate S, midweek cold fronts Great Lakes/Ohio Valley. **3:** Moderate fronts OK to TN, track to S. **4:** Storm track intensifies 25–27 Chicago to OH.

MAR. 2006 · 1: High pressure Gulf Coast into Mississippi Valley, weak fronts N. **2:** Seasonal temperatures in the S, disturbances Ohio Valley early. **3:** High-pressure Denver to the Mississippi, warmer. **4:** High pressure to S, warmer, cool to N with strong fronts Mississippi Valley 25–27.

APR. 2006 · 1: Dry and warm S, showers and cool Great Lakes late. **2:** Moderate fronts NE Corn Belt, dry and warm W and S. **3:** Dynamic cold fronts Denver to Great Lakes, 19 to 21. **4:** Cool weak fronts, Great Lakes and E 22-24, warmer to the S..

MAY 2006 · 1: Weak lows, cooler Central states. Dry to south. **2:** Cold fronts Dakotas to Central states, 10–12. **3:** Widespread, moderate rains, Corn Belt, 18–20. **4:** Cooler with moderate fronts Minnesota to Central states.

JUN. 2006 · 1: Cool and wet Great Lakes to Ohio Valley. **2:** Hot and dry IA and S, cooler to N. **3:** Hot and dry, IA and S; cool N. **4:** Hot with moderate rains Corn Belt.

JULY 2006 · 1: Storm across N tier into Great Lakes, much cooler. **2:** Hot, dry Gulf Coast, Central states; turbulent Great Lakes. **3:** Dry, cool Central states, fronts CO to OK. **4:** Mid-Continent hot and dry Central states and N; fronts Gulf Coast.

AUG. 2006 · 1: Hot ,dry Central states and Corn Belt. **2:** Moderate/ good rains, Corn Belt, Gulf coast 10–11. **3:** Cool and wet central and N Corn Belt. **4:** Cool N and dry S; weak fronts Corn Belt.

SEPT. 2006 · 1: Strong block Rockies to OH; dry and hot. **2:** Cool Great Lakes with fronts. **3:** Wet and cool, whole Corn Belt. **4:** Dry, cool N; wet Gulf coast and Central states.

OCT. 2006 · 1: Wet to S; cool to N. **2:** Dry, warm Corn Belt; Fronts Gulf Coast. **3:** Cold, rains in Corn Belt; dry to S. **4:** Dry, clear to S; fronts N midweek.

NOV. 2006 · 1: Cold N to S, weak fronts late. **2:** Wet, mild N; dry to S after 10th. **3:** Clear, mild turning colder, unsettled; late. **4:** Storm into Central states; midweek.

DEC. 2006 · 1: Unsettled, fronts, Dakotas to Central states; all week. **2:** Moderate rains, Great Lakes; late. **3:** Storms Dakotas to Central and N Central states. **4:** Mild S, cold N after midweek.

C

TO LEARN MORE ABOUT DOC WEATHER'S FORECASTS GO TO <WWW.DOCWEATHER.COM>

EAST COAST / ATLANTIC SEABOARD

SUMMARY: JAN. cold with storms mid-Atlantic states. FEB. Cold, fronts into NE early moving S midmonth then back into NE, late. MAR. cold, wet NE to mid-Atlantic most of month. APR. cool, wet NE to mid-Atlantic coast, most of month. MAY weak fronts NE, dry to S early; cool with rains 3rd week N and S. JUN. cool , moist to N; dry and warm to S, wet to S in last week. JUL. hot, dry to S; fronts and cooler to. N. AUG. Dry to N early then temperate to cool with fronts, NE and mid-Atlantic states. SEPT. Hot, dry early turning cooler at mid month with wet to the S. OCT. wet to S turns wet to N with cold at mid-month. NOV. early cold N and S, then milder until late month storm up the coast. DEC. unsettled until widespread rains around Christmas, then colder S .

JAN. 2006 · WEEK 1: Very cold with storms mid-Atlantic states 4-7. **WEEK 2:** Very cold with fronts all week NE and mid-Atlantic states. **WEEK 3:** Wet storms mid-Atlantic states late or early next week. **WEEK 4:** Watch for dry in the SE and wet and wild in the NE

FEB. 2006 · 1: Cold with fronts OH to NJ. **2:** Possible fronts NE, late in week or early next week. **3:** Moderate fronts early in the week mid-Atlantic states. **4:** Wet fronts into the NE at month's end.

MAR. 2006 · 1: Cold trough Northeast down to mid-Atlantic states, weak to moderate fronts. **2:** Wet into Northeast, early and late. **3:** Late week cold fronts mid-Atlantic states and north. **4:** Cool and wet mid-Atlantic states and north, 26 to 28.

APR. 2006 · 1: Cool and wet mid-Atlantic to NE , late. **2:** Cool with unsettled weather in NE, week's end. **3:** Cool and wet, Northeast at the end of the week. **4:** Cool with moderate fronts NE, 26 to 28, weak to moderate rains SE.

MAY 2006 · 1: Weak lows northeast, dry to S. **2:** Cool with rains NE, week's end, dry to S. **3:** Moderate fronts into mid-Atlantic states, late. **4:** Cool with fronts Northeast and Mid Atlantic states.

JUN. 2006 · 1: Cool and wet Northeast to mid-Atlantic states. **2:** Hot and dry Mid Atlantic, cool in Northeast. **3:** Hot and dry Mid Atlantic states, cool, moist Northeast. **4:** Clear early then rain in the S late

JUL. 2006 · 1: Warm to S; cool/unsettled to the N, late. **2:** Dry S; cool and moist N, week's end. **3:** Wet and cool NE. **4:** Hot dry to S, cooler, late fronts N.

AUG. 2006 · 1: Dry to S; cool, unsettled to N. **2:** Fronts to SE; dry to N. **3:** Cool and moist; N and S. **4:** Wet and cool Northeast and mid-Atlantic states.

SEPT. 2006 · 1: Hot and dry early; moderate late, look for hurricanes in Gulf of Mexico. **2:** Cool mid-Atlantic to Northeast after 11th. **3:** Cool and moist Mid Atlantic seaboard. **4:** Wet SE and Mid Atlantic; dry, cold N.

OCT. 2006 · 1: Wet Mid Atlantic states and S; late. **2:** Fronts NE ; clear/ warm S. **3:** Cold NE with fronts down to Mid Atlantic coast; late. **4:** High to S; fronts mid Atlantic states, late.

NOV. 2006 · 1: Cold N to S, weak fronts late. **2:** Wet, mild Mid Atlantic states; dry to S. **3:** Mild then cooler; rain mid-Atlantic states, late. **4:** Nor'easter up the coast; late.

DEC. 2006 · 1: Unsettled, fronts, mid-Atlantic; all week. **2:** Possible moderate rains mid-Atlantic coast. **3:** Widespread late rains, OH to mid-Atlantic coast **4:** Cold, OH to FL (freeze) after midweek and late.

TO LEARN MORE ABOUT DOC WEATHER'S FORECASTS GO TO <WWW.DOCWEATHER.COM>

Cirrus radiatus

Cirrostratus fibratus

Cirrocumulus undulatus

Altocumulus stratiformis

Altostratus translucidus

Altocumulus undulatus

Stratocumulus undulatus

Stratus opacus

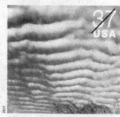

Cumulus humilis

Cumulonimbus mammatus

Cumulonimbus incus

Cumulus congestus

Altocumulus castellanus

Altocumulus lenticularis

Cumulonimbus with tornado

26

About Clouds

Learn more about cloud formations

By Mark Bossen

Hamlet: Do you see yonder cloud that's almost in shape of a camel?

Polonius: By the mass, and 'tis like a camel, indeed.

Hamlet: Methinks it is like a weasel.

Polonius: It is backed like a weasel.

Hamlet: Or like a whale?

Polonius: Very like a whale.

– William Shakespeare

As with many things, learning to name clouds is the first step in understanding them. Clouds are named and classified using a Latin system to describe their appearance as seen from the ground.

The Latin suffix strato (meaning *layer*) describes clouds with a flat, wide appearance, and cumulo (meaning *heap*) indicates puffy, piled-up clouds.

More precise classification is achieved by indicating the height of the cloud base.

HIGH–LEVEL CLOUDS (CIRRO)

The prefix "cirr-", as in cirrus clouds, indicates clouds that are located at high levels, forming above 20,000 feet (6,000 meters). At these altitudes clouds consist mainly of ice crystals and are often thin in appearance.

MID–LEVEL CLOUDS (ALTO)

Names containing the prefix "alto-", as in altostratus, describe mid-level clouds, with their base between 6,500 and 20,000 feet (2,000 to 6,000 meters). Mainly composed of water droplets, they will contain ice crystals at colder temperatures.

LOW–LEVEL CLOUDS (NO PREFIX)

Low-level clouds have a base below 6,500 feet (2000 meters) and are primarily water droplets.

The examples below can help you remember these naming conventions:

	FLAT	PUFFY
LOW	Stratus	Cumulus
MED	Alto stratus	Alto cumulus
HIGH	Cirro stratus	Cirro cumulus

Nimbo as a prefix (meaning "rain") or nimbus added as a suffix, indicates that the cloud can produce precipitation. A thunder cloud is therefore a *cumulonimbus* cloud.

There are also a number of cloud types with more specific, descriptive names that do not fit these conventions. **Contrails** (condensation trails) and **mammatus** clouds (pouchlike, puffy, descending clouds) are examples of this type. ✯

CUMULUS

Cumulus clouds are some of the most commonly seen, and also a good example of vertically developed clouds. They can reach altitudes over 40,000 feet. The condensation of water vapor releases enormous amounts of energy within the cloud.

FAIR WEATHER CUMULUS

Fair weather cumulus have a lifespan of 5-40 minutes. They have flat bases and sharp outlines. Occasionally, fair weather cumulus can develop into towering cumulonimbus clouds, bringing thunderstorms.

ALTOCUMULUS

Altocumulus clouds are often shaded, a making them distinguishable from the high-level cirrocumulus. They commonly indicate an advancing cold front. Altocumulus clouds in the morning are often followed by thunderstorms later in the day

CUMULONIMBUS

Among the most readily identified cloud formations, a really big cumulonimbus formation will sometimes assume the "anvil" shape that is a strong predictor of heavy rain accompanied by lightning and severe weather.

CIRROSTRATUS

Cirrostratus are high-level clouds composed of ice crystals. They have a sheet-like appearance, are fairly transparent, and the Sun or Moon can easily be seen through them.

MAMMATUS

One of the few formations to occur in descending air, mammatus clouds are often seen after a tornado. They do not indicate coming severe weather, but rather, that the worst of the storm has passed.

CONTRAIL

A contrail (condensation trail) is a vapor trail that often forms behind jet aircraft. The contrail forms from the water vapor contained in the jet's engine exhaust.

PILEUS

Pileus clouds are smooth in appearance and occur over the top of a geological feature large enough to have a significant effect on the flow of air, such as a mountain.

Making Waves

A revolutionary approach to health maintenance and healing based on harmonizing with nature's rhythm.

By Roger Lewin

"Heard melodies are sweet, but unheard ones are sweeter."
So wrote John Keats in Ode on a Grecian Urn. *It's true that we find melodies sweet, but the unheard melodies–the rhythms of nature–influence our lives in so many more ways. Rhythms in nature are ubiquitous, from the universe itself, through seasonal, monthly, and daily rhythms of organisms, down to DNA, the molecule of life. Nature is rhythm.*

Modern exercise theories have got it all wrong—upside down, backwards, and inside out. Sustained exertion, such as in long-distance running, biking, swimming, and other endurance sports and exercise regimens, is actually more likely to lead to disease than to optimum health, more likely to kill you than to cure you. So claims Irving Dardik, a gifted maverick who just may be a 21st-century Einstein, a discoverer of the Holy Grail of science, the theory of everything. He calls it the "SuperWave Principle."

As a youth, Dardik was a world-class competitive sprinter. In college he studied to become a physician, specializing in vascular surgery. Eventually he combined his interests by becoming the founding chair of the U.S. Olympic Sports Medicine Council. There he began a friendship with Jack Kelly, who was president of the U.S. Olympic Committee. When Kelly, an Olympic rower, collapsed and died after a running workout, Dardik was shocked and despondent—Kelly was not supposed to die. He was doing everything conventional Western medicine says leads to high-level health: he rowed three or four times a week, and then ran five miles back to his apartment.

Dardik threw out everything he thought he knew about health and disease and started from scratch, doing his own research. He soon noticed that countless highly trained athletes develop various forms of chronic disease like cancer and heart disease. Could these athletes' exercise regimens actually be causing their disease? He knew from his own experience with Olympic athletes that marathon runners, for instance, were constantly getting sick, while sprinters were

We live in a universe of rhythms:
the daily, or circadian, rhythms
of light and dark, sunrises
and sunsets.

a healthy bunch. "Could there be something wrong, something unnatural about pushing yourself too hard for too long?" he wondered.

Dardik dove into the scientific literature for clues to an answer to this question. In the animal realm, sustained exertion is the exception, he found. Everyone knows that cheetahs are the fastest creatures on Earth. But what most people are unaware of is that they run in short, heart-pounding bursts. And then they stop and rest. "I found that all animals do that, a burst of exertion, then rest; a burst of exertion, then rest," says Dardik. "You see this in whales when they dive, sharks when they hunt, birds in flight. Everywhere I looked, no matter what kind of animal is involved, it was the same pattern: a burst of exertion, followed by rest, and so on."

But what does that kind of activity mean on the level of heart physiology? "Think about when you exercise. Your heart rate rises. And when you rest, the heart rate falls," says Dardik. "That's not intermittent spikes of activity on a straight line, like on an electrocardiogram. Nature's not like that. That's a wave! And, further, when you plot the individual heartbeats along that wave—contracting, relaxing, contracting, relaxing—you have a series of little waves riding within the big wave of the heartbeat pattern. That's what I call the HeartWave. It's waves waving within waves."

The image of the HeartWave entranced Dardik. It resonated with all the reading he had done in quantum mechanics, where waves are fundamental. He soon found that waves are everywhere in nature.

We live in a universe of rhythms: the daily, or circadian, rhythms of light and dark, sunrises and sunsets; the monthly rhythms of the lunar cycle; the yearly rhythms of the seasons; and more. So basic is this milieu that some rhythms are encoded in our genetic being.

© PhotoDisc

We see the cyclic rise and fall through daily fluctuations in, for instance, blood pressure, body temperature, enzyme activity, hormone output, mental acuity, physical abilities. Menses in women and testosterone levels in men cycle with the lunar month. Reproduction, migration, and hibernation cycles track the yearly seasons. Local ecosystems are a symphony of cycles, in close resonance with each other. Even our own galaxy, the Milky Way, pulsates rhythmically, pushing out huge volumes of gas, and then sucking it back in. Rhythms in nature, nature as rhythms.

Dardik eventually came up with what he calls the SuperWave principle, which he says is the explanation for the natural universe at all levels. Simply stated, the SuperWave Principle is HeartWave writ large—in other words, there is no starting and stopping, no straight lines in any organism, anywhere. Everything is continually rhythmically cycling, from a single heart cell to the Milky Way. Waves waving within waves.

The core of Dardik's SuperWave Principle, as it applies to health, is that health depends on a balanced relationship—a wave—between stress and recovery, each of which is unhealthy by itself. From his explorations and his observations of the natural world, he devised a cyclic exercise protocol.

"Dardik speculates that when a person makes large waves of energy expenditure and recovery, the body's immune chemistry and repair processes are activated," wrote journalist Tony Schwartz in a 1991 cover story for *New York* magazine. Those processes, in turn, produce their own trickle-down healthy waves

Health depends on a balanced relationship—a wave—between stress and recovery, each of which is unhealthy by itself.

as they carry out their work—waves waving within waves. Schwartz noted that Dardik drew support from the work of Nobel Prize winner Ilya Prigogine, who argued that living systems, at every level, are healthier when they are oscillating, or making waves.

Someone who does cyclic exercise—exertion and rest, exertion and rest—is spending as much time training the body's recovery physiology as training

the exertion physiology. "That was new," says Dardik. "No one had thought about that. All they thought about was getting the heart rate up there, and keeping it up there. And then when you are finished, you keep moving, keep jogging, to cool off. God forbid that you should stop! God forbid that you should actually think about the physiological processes of recovery!"

Someone who does cyclic exercise is spending as much time training the body's recovery physiology as training the exertion physiology.

"I got a couple of top athletes, put a heart monitor on them, and then had them do a sprint, then have them sit down," explains Dardik. "Sometimes their heart rate would plummet from one-fifty, down to forty, to thirty, to twenty-five. I said, 'My God, what is going on?' That's why people can be in danger of dying after sustained exertion. That's what happened to [running guru] Jim Fixx (who died suddenly of a heart attack). And that's what happened to my friend Jack

Kelly." These athletes had been training for exertion and not for recovery.

Dardik has worked with scores of people with chronic diseases of various kinds, putting them through the exercise protocol, and in many cases witnessing remarkable reversals of disease symptoms, in diabetes, chronic fatigue syndrome, hypertension, multiple sclerosis, even cancer. And in a clinical trial on healthy women, run in collaboration with researchers from Harvard Medical School and Columbia University in New York, Dardik found all measures of health and well-being improved significantly after doing just eight weeks on his cyclic exercise protocol.

In 1995, a friend sent Dardik a photocopy of an article from the journal *Circulation*, titled, "Reduced Heart Rate Variability and Mortality Risk in an Elderly Cohort." Dardik remembers reading the article and experiencing "an absolutely Eureka moment!" He knew his exercise protocol increases heart rate variability in a way that sustained exercise does not.

The heart-rate variability that the authors talked about is a simple insight into the way the heart really works—like a

© PhotoDisc

wave—and its association with health. When a nurse takes your pulse at the doctor's office, he or she will give you a number, 60 beats a minute, for example. But that, in fact, is just an average. If you were to plot each beat throughout that minute you would find that your heart might be beating at an average of 70 beats a minute, say; and at another point, it might be an average of 50. Heart-rate variability, then, is a measure of how much the inter-beat interval varies between consecutive heartbeats when you are at rest.

The authors had surveyed 736 elderly people over a period of years, and found that those with high heart-rate variability lived considerably longer compared to those with low heart-rate variability, "I see chronic diseases as a disorder of a person's wave pattern," says Dardik. "When you increase heart-rate variability you are re-normalizing the wave pattern, and you reverse the disease." Re-normalizing the wave pattern also helps us to deeply reconnect with our ancient, natural rhythms.

For 80,000 generations, we followed the cycles of hunting and gathering and then, for the last 400 generations, an agriculturalist lifestyle. People woke,

slept, and pursued the food quest according to nature's daily, monthly, and seasonal cycles. These cycles are impressed in our DNA and the physiology and behavior it orchestrates. The Industrial Age began just 10 generations ago. The press of modern living is barely two generations old. We now live in a world whose pace and rhythm is completely foreign to our fundamental biology. With our natural rhythms and cycles disrupted, or, more precisely, flattened, chronic diseases are the inexorable outcome, the "diseases of civilization."

The authors had surveyed elderly people over a period of years, and found that those with high heart-rate variability lived considerably longer compared to those with low heart-rate variability.

"When you come from the SuperWave perspective, ill health happens when there is a dissociation between the internal rhythms and the external rhythms in nature," says Dardik. "I

© PhotoDisc

therefore prefer not to talk about what causes disease, but instead to ask, how do you cause health?"

Causing health is not about trying to live the life of hunter-gatherers; it is about tuning your body to the rhythms that orchestrated their lives, the rhythms that shaped us as human beings. When we are in sync with these natural rhythms, we are at our healthiest.

"Imagine the impact in terms of personal suffering, premature death, and the economies in industrialized nations if collectively we could embrace the holistic view of individual health that flows from the SuperWave Principle," says Dardik. "Imagine a society where people took charge of their own health, by reconnecting with the rhythms of nature, becoming in harmony with the rhythms of nature, as our ancestors were. What a triumph of the human spirit that would be!" ⚡

Roger Lewin, Ph.D. is a prize-winning author of 20 popular science books. His book Complexity: Life at the Edge of Chaos *holds the honor of being voted one of the top 100 science books for the 20th century. For 10 years he was News Editor of* Science Magazine. *This article was adapted from his book,* Making Waves: Dr. Irving Dardik's SuperWave Principle, *published by Rodale Press in the fall of 2005.*

The Cyclic Exercise Protocol
Nature's program for fitness and health

Dardik's Cyclic Exercise Protocol is akin to interval training, in that it involves short bursts of intense exercise, followed by recovery. A key difference is that the recovery period is not through exercising at a slower rate, as in interval training, but through stopping completely. The protocol is natural, tuning the human body to the way other animals exert themselves, and recover, in nature. In short, the Cyclic Exercise Protocol restores the waves that have been obliterated by our modern life styles. And in restoring natural rhythms in the body, it restores health.

THE TECHNIQUE
A typical exercise cycle starts with a relaxed jog, raising one's heart rate from a resting rate of say 70 beats per minute to around 100. This may involve running for a minute or two, covering one or two city blocks. The exerciser then stops completely and ideally finds a place to sit down until his or her heart rate comes down to near the resting rate. The cycle is then repeated at greater intensity, raising the upper limit by 10-20 beats each cycle, with complete rest in between, until the last cycle goes for the person's maximum heart rate (about 175 beats per minute for a 200 lb. 50 year-old, and 200 beats per minute for a 150 pound 30-year-old).

The effect of the Cyclic Exercise Protocol can be enhanced by varying one's activity according to the time of day and phase of the moon. In the week going into the new moon, the lowest energy segment of the lunar cycle, exercise cycles are done in the early morning, between 6 and 9, close to the lowest energy segment of the day, in terms of the body's circadian rhythm. The cycles themselves are also low energy, very gentle, maybe just three or four moderate bursts of exertion and recovery, three times a week. These cycles are designed to kick start the metabolism, to help people pull out of the energy trough they've gone into during the night and early morning.

The week after the new moon, a time of rising energy in the lunar cycle, the exercise cycles are done later in the day, between 9 and noon, a time of rising energy in the body's circadian rhythm. These cycles are kicked up a notch in terms of intensity and heart-rate targets. Again, it is three or four bursts of exertion and recovery, three times a week.

Finally, in the week leading to up the full moon, the time of maximum energy in the lunar cycle, the exercise cycles are done between 3 and 6 in the afternoon, the time of maximum energy in the circadian cycle. Tracking this pattern, the exercise cycles are now done at maximum intensity, reaching the highest heart-rate target that is appropriate for the individual.

The week immediately following the full moon is a period of recovery, of no exercise, leading down toward the trough of low energy, and then the exercise cycling starts over again.

Mapping the intensity with which the cycles are done onto the circadian energy wave, and mapping that onto the lunar energy wave, brings us as close to reconnecting to the rhythms of nature as we can while still living in the "civilized" world. – R.L.

A MONTH OF CYCLES *On each "x" day do 3 or more cycles per day*

	1	2	3	4	5	6	7	8	9	10	11	12	13	14	15	16	17	18	19	20	21	22	23	24	25	26	27	28	29	30	31
Intensive cycles (3–6pm)																							×	×	×	×					
Medium cycles (9–12pm)																×	×	×													
Gentle cycles (6–9am)								×	×	×	×																				
Rest	–	–	–	–	–	–																							–	–	–

Living Urban Treasures
Embodying the spirit of their dwelling places
By Elizabeth Larsen and Andi McDaniel

For decades the Japanese have honored individuals who have mastered one of the nation's traditional arts and crafts, such as pottery making, textile dyeing, theater arts, and kimono design, as Important Intangible Cultural Properties, more commonly known as Living National Treasures.

Inspired by the Japanese example, *Cosmo Doogood's Urban Almanac* initiated a new, North American tradition by honoring six individuals, who embody the spirit of the places where they dwell, as Living Urban Treasures. These are individuals whose lives have helped create and shape the cultural identity of their communities. They are writers, artists, entrepreneurs and activists. Their very presence enhances the quality of life for all who live around them. Additionally, this year we asked each honoree the same question:

"How can people connect with and celebrate nature, wherever they are?"

JEAN M. GARDNER

Imagine a New York City architecture professor whose driving inspiration isn't the poetry of steel and glass, but rather the interdependence between the human species, the built environment, and the earth. An art historian by training and the author of *Urban Wilderness: Nature in New York City*, Gardner retrains people to think of the Big Apple not only as the home of the icons of industrialization, but also a thriving wildlife metropolis blessed with parklands, freshwater marshes, and evergreen stands. These are the places where we find "a sense of well-being. . . a feeling that this is where one belongs," she writes. The toads, fish, frogs, snakes, turtles, butterflies, hawks, and pigeons of

Jean Gardner photo by Brian Livezey

"Wherever you are, go outside your door. Take in a deep breath. Pause. Engage all your senses. Slowly let your breath out. Connection complete! Celebration started!" – JMG

the quintessential American city couldn't agree more.

Photo courtesy of Gary Nabhan

"Take your five favorite friends or neighbors out on a wild foraging excursion, to sustainably harvest native plants with edible roots, shoots, or fruits in your area. Then collectively prepare them for a wild-foraged feast that allows an even larger group of people to "taste the landscape" in which you live." – GPN

GARY PAUL NABHAN

Subsistence hunter, ethnobiologist, environmental activist, MacArthur Genius Fellowship recipient. From his post at the Center for Sustainable Environments at Northern Arizona University, Nabhan applies his gift for cross-cultural interpretation to an almost impossible breadth of topics—from Native American agriculture to the desert plants of the Southwest to the need of wild places for children to the plight of the Middle East. His book *Coming Home to Eat: The Sensual Pleasures and Global Politics of Local Foods* is a classic on why eating from our food-shed naturally makes us more passionate about the fate of the environment.

SHEILA WATT-CLOUTIER

An Inuit leader who was born in Nunavik in northern Quebec and now lives in Iqaluit—the capital of the new territory of Nunavut—Watt-Cloutier puts a human face and a human rights perspective to the crisis of melting ice in the world's polar regions. "The Arctic is the world's barometer of climate change, and Inuit are the mercury in that barometer," she says. "We are the early warning system for the world." A nurturer of traditional wisdom and environmental activist, Watt-Cloutier entered Canadian politics in 1995. Her urgent mission propelled her up the ranks to her current position as a member of the Canadian Roundtable on Environment and Economy, which will guide Canada in its follow-up commitments to the Kyoto agreements.

Photo courtesy of Sheila Watt-Cloutier

"Connect with and celebrate nature by being one with nature and you will never feel disconnected from yourself or from others." – SWC

RICHARD C. WHEELER

In our current mania for testing and monitoring every ounce of the school experience, it's almost impossible to imagine an educator canceling classes so that students can get outdoors and explore their relationship to nature. But as the headmaster of the Catalina Island School in the late 1970s, Richard C. Wheeler did just that. Today Wheeler writes and speaks about the importance of seeing the marine environmental crisis as a crisis of the spirit. In his role as environmental evangelizer he has paddled his kayak along the 1,500-mile migratory path of the Great Auk—an extinct flightless bird who used to thrive on the coast of Maine—and circumnavigated Cape Cod in a rowboat. Along the way, he visited 66 classrooms and raised $60,000 for the Cape Cod Museum of Natural History's Naturalist in the Schools program.

Suggested by Richard Andrew Swanson

Photo courtesy of the Cape Cod Museum of Natural History

"Open your eyes...notice things. Make sketches of what you see. The vegetation as it comes to life again each year. The little wildflowers that somehow find a place to grow. The ant that opens the peony in the spring." –RCW

ROALD TWEET

A writer, lecturer, and storyteller, this bard of the Mississippi River is also a public radio personality whose "Rock Island Lines" program on Public Radio WVIK in Rock Island, Illinois, tells the stories of the people and places that make up this westward bend in the mighty river. A semi-retired English professor at Augustana College, Tweet's spirited scholarship is rooted in his lifelong enthusiasm for traveling the river. From railboats to riverboats to the engineering feats along the Upper Mississippi, Tweet carves his stories into details as fine as the grooves on the woodcarvings he whittles in his spare time.

Suggested by Arden Cody

Roald Tweet photo by Mariusz Matoga

"You don't have to travel to find nature. I used to ask the students in our Arts and Regional Studies Program, "What is the Midwest? Where is the heartland?" As you get people talking about the heartland, gradually they realize that the center of the heartland is on their own front porch." –RT

ANNA MARIE CARTER

In a city where air pollution warnings are a way of life and residents are advised not to drink the water, there is rarely a cause for environmental celebration. Thankfully, The Seed Lady of Watts wasn't about to let her Los Angeles neighborhood go totally to pot. A master gardener, Carter practices direct action by building free, organic gardens for people who suffer from HIV/AIDS, cancer, diabetes, high blood pressure, obesity, and other illnesses. "The majority of people here eat food that is bagged, bottled, canned, boxed, or frozen," she explains. "A majority of this food comes from South America and Mexico through free-trade agreements. We do not even get food grown in California. DDT is still widely used in Latin America." Thanks to Carter, Watts now boasts pockets of green that enrich both body and soul.

"Go out and celebrate this earth. Go and contribute to the quality of the air. Go plant something and create oxygen and create beauty. Just go do it, and believe me, people will come join you." – AMC

DO YOU KNOW A LIVING URBAN TREASURE?

Last year we asked you, our readers, to nominate people as Living Urban Treasures and we're pleased to include several of your suggestions in this book. All our Urban Sanctuaries and Essential Places also came from you (see page 275). You weighed in on Civilizing Ideas, Urban Survival Strategies, Phenological Sightings, and the almanac itself.

Please continue to send us your ideas for these categories, as well as your thoughts, inspirations, poems, cartoons, etc., and tell us why these things mean something to you. Our e-mail address is nominate@cosmosurbanalmnac.com or you can reach us through the Web at www.cosmosurbanalmanac.com.

Illustrations by Nora Widgen

Basic Biodynamics
On the farm, in the garden
By John Miller

To help us reclaim and enjoy our connection with food and eating, the Slow Food movement challenges us to consider how we prepare and consume our food. Biodynamics asks us to look deeply at how we grow it. Our relationship with food, now so rushed and dehumanized, was once profoundly sacramental (echoed still in grace before meals). The farmer or gardener, whose deep knowledge and loving practice bring health to others and the Earth, does truly holy work.

Biodynamics is an advanced form of organic agriculture (or care of the earth) based on a science of the life forces at work in nature. It strives to bring about balance and healing. Biodynamics began in 1924 when a group of farmers asked Rudolf Steiner to address the degeneration that they noticed in certain seed strains and cultivated plants. The need to counteract the increasing toxicity and pollution deriving from chemical fertilizers was a crucial issue affecting the soil, human health, and nutrition. But underlying these, Steiner recognized an even greater need: to heal the earth herself. Thus was born the first ecological farming system to develop as a grassroots alternative to chemical agriculture.

Biodynamics sees the farm or garden or vineyard as a living, complex organism with its own individuality.

Biodynamic agriculture goes beyond organic agriculture in many different ways. First, there is a profound understanding of the interdependence of the various elements that make up a particular farm (soils, plants, livestock, weather). These are treated as an integrated system, and the working together of each aspect is optimized. Next, there is an understanding of the subtle interconnections between the earth and the heavens (lunar cycles, planetary movements). Third, there is the use of preparations—herbal stimulating agents inoculated into compost or sprayed on the land. These increase the vitality of the soil and the health of plants and animals raised on the farm. Biodynamics offers a form of sustainable agriculture that can actually heal nature.

Biodynamics sees the farm or garden or vineyard (some of France's greatest wines are biodynamically grown) as a living, complex organism. Its rich diversity of plants and animals each contribute a unique presence and add up to a self-contained entity with its own individuality. Plants bring vital or etheric (Earth-bound) forces; animals add soul or astral (cosmic) forces. (For a feeling of the two, first imagine walking through a clovery meadow, glittering with dew in the morning sun. Then picture evening milking in a barn full of quietly ruminating cows, with cats curled in the hay and mice skittering in the loft overhead.) Crops and pastures are rotated; companion planting is extensively used. Hedges provide windbreaks and homes for wild creatures.

Underlying all is the soil. Rich humus is nourished by carefully prepared composts of plant and animal wastes and harmoniously balanced in terms of the classical elements: earth, water, air, and fire (the sun's warmth and light). The elements are imbued by the activities of elemental beings, working in accord with the rhythms of day and night, planets and stars, and the seasons of the earth (whose soul breathes in during winter, out in summer).

Here are some practical suggestions for biodynamic gardening in suburb or city.

MAKE COMPOST

So what if you don't have a cow! Kitchen and yard waste make excellent compost, blended with layers of soil and sprinkled with lime if too wet and sloppy. Mix in fireplace ashes, too. Keep a good balance of air and water, the right mix of green plants and dried materials (such as autumn leaves, which should be moistened first and shredded if possible). Avoid meat scraps and pet and human waste. If you can get some farm manure (preferably organic), great! (But make sure it is mixed with ample straw to absorb the wet and to balance the carbon/nitrogen ratio.) There's a whole lore of compost preparations in biodynamics. These are complicated to make, so order them (available online) and add them to your compost pile.

PROMOTE DIVERSITY

Even on a small plot—or in an apartment window—you can utilize companion planting and crop (or bed) rotation. Biodynamic gardeners often use a rotation of root crops (radishes, beets, carrots), leaf crops (spinach, chard, cabbage), fruits (cucumbers, tomatoes, peppers), and flowers. A balance of

these in a single bed is also good. Fruit trees can go around the garden. You can also create a temenos or sacred space, by letting some land go wild. This provides a home for wildlife, bringing astrality to your garden's etheric energy. In smaller spaces, the biodynamic/French intensive method maximizes productivity. It uses double digging (to break up hardpan and keep topsoil on top) and raised beds. Each bed is a vibrant plant community, attracting (or repelling) its own insect life. (Insects also bring astrality.)

BUY QUALITY COMPOST

When first making your beds, you may want to bring in lots of compost to create a fertile soil and help raise the level of the bed. Whether you start with a sandy or clay-based soil, good compost is the key to building living humus. You can even mulch with compost, if you have enough. (Be careful about dry or acidic mulches like straw or wood chips, which tie up nitrogen if incorporated into the soil.)

READ ABOUT BIODYNAMICS

Go online, (www.biodynamics.com), and explore the variety of biodynamic literature. You'll find detailed explanations of and directions for things that have only been hinted at here.

DEVELOP YOUR INTUITION

This is most important of all! Feel yourself mediating between earth and heaven, harmonizing the *ens vitale* (earthly, life-giving entity) and *ens astrale* (cosmic, soul-filling entity). Feel the sun on your back, the rain in your face. Walk barefoot on the soil, and look upwards with wondering eyes. ⚡

RESOURCES: The Biodynamic Farming and Gardening Association (BDA), a nonprofit organization open to the public, was formed in the U.S. in 1938 to foster, guide, and safeguard the biodynamic method of agriculture. Its activities include organizing conferences, workshops, and seminars; stimulating and supporting research; publishing and distributing literature, including a bimonthly journal *Biodynamics*; and advising farmers and gardeners and the general interest public. In addition, the BDA supports 11 grassroots regional groups, as well as many Community Supported Agriculture (CSAs) groups springing up all over the country. The BDA now has more than 1,000 members, though many more use biodynamics in a less formal way. www.biodynamics.com

© PhotoDisc

The Art and Science of Phenology

By David Lukas

Phenology is the study of recurring natural phenomena. Whether you are a backyard gardener deciding when to plant seeds, or a scientist studying global climate change, you can contribute to our understanding of the world through the practice of phenology.

Ultimately the study of phenology is a personal story about your own relationship to nature. How do you connect with plants and animals? What is it that you notice or are curious about? Phenology is one of many ways to learn about your own spirit and love for life.

The study of phenology is more important than ever. Detailed, repeated observations are an immensely valuable tool that will help us decide how to approach the challenges of global climate change. Develop a calendar of natural events for your own neighborhood. These observations are limited only by your imagination, and you'll find that the more attention you pay to the natural world, the more connected you start feeling to Nature and her seasonal rhythms as they unfold around you.

(Editor's Note: : *In our 2005 debut issue, we introduced many of our readers to phenology (a portion of the essay is reprinted above). Other readers, as we discovered, have been tracking the patterns of the natural world for years. They sent us their observations on backyard birds, the relationship between climate and nature, and how phenology can be a family affair.*

In Britain there is now a network of more than 13,000 people reporting their phenological observations. We were eager last year to start the North American Phenology Network—or NAPN. We even created a logo. But like most big and wonderful ideas, it's taking us a while to get it off the ground. We would still love to give people a way to share with others what they learn about the natural world and provide needed data on bird and animal habits and climate change. So, please be patient. Someday NAPN will be reality.

In the meantime, record what you see, hear, and smell in the world around you and check www.cosmosurbanalmanac.com periodically for updates on our progress toward the North American Phenology Network.) – *Cosmo*

PHENOLOGY: CHECKLIST

DATE OBSERVED   **SPRING**

- ____ Look for restless flights of geese & ducks.
- ____ Fields green up with new grass shoots.
- ____ Flies land on the side of the house on a warm day.
- ____ Hungry squirrels and chipmunks show up at bird feeders.
- ____ Early forest flowers bloom.
- ____ Enthusiatic tree frogs trilling in neighborhood ponds.
- ____ Sap moves in the trees.
- ____ Long-forgotten flowers in the backyard.
- ____ The weather turns briefly cold again.
- ____ Ice disappears from lakes.
- ____ Daylight savings begins.
- ____ Fields are plowed.
- ____ Newly arriving warblers sing.
- ____ Apple trees flower.
- ____ Butterflies fly on warm days.
- ____ Spring is in full bloom by late April.

FALL

- ____ Leaves turn glorious colors.
- ____ Flocks of small birds head south.
- ____ Squirrels very actively make ready for winter.
- ____ Hawks and eagles soar over high ridges.
- ____ Rake fallen leaves.
- ____ Pine cones start dropping seeds.
- ____ Look for butterfly cocoons.
- ____ Gulls on the beach hunker in the wind.
- ____ Pumpkins are ready.
- ____ Forests echo with the cries of elk.
- ____ Antlered deer spar.
- ____ Bears move into hibernation.
- ____ First frost appears one morning.
- ____ Snowbirds head for Florida.
- ____ Ring-necked pheasants scurry across bare cornfields.
- ____ Ice appears on small puddles.

DATE OBSERVED   **SUMMER**

- ____ Sun-warmed tomatoes fresh off the vine.
- ____ Lots of berries for cobblers and pies.
- ____ Days get longer.
- ____ Turtles sun on logs.
- ____ Birds nest or feed young.
- ____ Mosquitoes come out as the sun goes down.
- ____ Nights fill with the hum of crickets.
- ____ Thunderstorms billow up on hot days.
- ____ Hurricane season starts!
- ____ Salamanders retreat under damp logs.
- ____ Young raccoons tag after their mothers.
- ____ Tadpoles turn into tiny frogs.
- ____ Bats dart in twilight skies.
- ____ Kids search for monarch caterpillars.
- ____ Dragonflies hunt over ponds.
- ____ Hawks circle on thermals.
- ____ Sandpipers show up again on mudflats.

WINTER

- ____ Animal tracks appear in the snow.
- ____ Ice-fishing season begins.
- ____ Chickadees and finches flock to feeders.
- ____ Morning mist hangs over open fields.
- ____ Woodstove smoke lingers.
- ____ Ducks gather in huge groups on open bays.
- ____ Northern birds arrive after bad storms.
- ____ Holly adds cheer to the season.
- ____ Annual Christmas Bird Count.
- ____ Squirrels sneak out for a quick bite.
- ____ Birds already nest in the far south.
- ____ Great Horned Owls hoot on chilly nights.
- ____ Days are very short now.
- ____ Snow sounds squeaky on extremely cold nights.
- ____ Full moon is especially bright.

What Would Ben Do?

What Benjamin Franklin means for our times

By Walter Isaacson

What leadership lessons can we learn from our founders? What qualities and personality traits make a leader great? There is not, I think, one answer. What made the era of the founders so successful was that there was a group of leaders who each had different talents and who together complemented one another.

It was critical to have someone like George Washington, who was revered by all and could command authority. We also needed men like John Adams and his cousin Samuel, who were unflinching and unbending and uncompromising in pursuit of principle. Then, too, we needed bright young philosophers like Thomas Jefferson and James Madison.

But equally important, the aborning nation needed a Benjamin Franklin: someone who was sage yet sensible and very pragmatic, who could bring people together and calm their passions, who could understand that it was possible to uphold core values while also seeking to find common ground with others.

Indeed, these are the traits, I think, that account for Franklin's recurring popularity. Ben Franklin, that ambitious urban entrepreneur, seems made of flesh rather than marble; addressable by nickname, he turns to us from his-

tory's stage with eyes that twinkle from behind those new-fangled spectacles. He speaks to us, through his letters and hoaxes and autobiography, not with orotund rhetoric but with a chattiness and clever irony that is very contemporary, sometimes unnervingly so.

Franklin helped invent the type of middle-class meritocracy that informs the American dream today. Jefferson's idea of a meritocracy, expressed in his founding documents for the University of Virginia, was to take the cream of the naturally young men and elevate them from the masses to become part of a new "natural aristocracy." But Franklin, though he loved young Jefferson, had a less elitist ideal. In his document launching the academy that became the University of Pennsylvania, he talked of helping all "aspiring" and "diligent" young men (alas, not women) from any stratum or of any natural endowment, for he felt that society was helped by elevating people from all levels who strove to improve themselves.

He believed in a new political order in which rights and power would be based not on the happenstance of heritage but on merit, virtue, and hard work. He rose up the social ladder from runaway apprentice to royal dinner guest in a way that would become

Franklin wowed the French through a combination of idealism, diplomacy, humor, and folksy charm. Ladies of the court wore their hair to look like his fur cap and medallions with his image bearing the inscription: "He snatched the lightning from the skies and the scepter from the tyrants."

quintessentially American. Yet in doing so he resolutely resisted, as a matter of principle—sometimes to a fur-capped extreme—aristocratic pretensions. More than almost any other founder (certainly more than Washington and Adams) he held firm to a fundamental faith that the New World should avoid replicating the hierarchies of the Old. His aversion to elitism and his faith in a new order built on the virtues of common people are among his most lasting legacies.

Indeed, the roots of much of what distinguishes the nation can be found in Franklin: Its cracker-barrel humor and wisdom. Its technological ingenuity. Its pluralistic tolerance. Its ability to weave together individualism and community cooperation. Its philosophical pragmatism. Its celebration of meritocratic mobility. The idealistic streak ingrained in its foreign policy. And the Main Street (or Market Street) virtues that serve as the foundation for its civic values. Franklin was egalitarian in what

became the American sense: he approved of individuals making their way to wealth through diligence and talent but opposed giving special privileges to people based on birth.

The aborning nation needed someone who could uphold core values while also seeking to find common ground with others

The way he built his own media empire foreshadowed the strategies of media tycoons today. He had a printing press, so he decided he needed something to print, such as a newspaper or magazine or Poor Richard's Almanack. Next he franchised his operations up and down America with relatives and former apprentices, and then he created the first media distribution system, the colonial post office, to tie them together.

Franklin began each day contemplating the question: "What good shall I do this day?" and ended with, "What good have I done today?"

Portrait medallion of Benjamin Franklin, by Jean Baptiste Nini after a drawing by Anne Vallayer-Coster, 1779. Terra cotta. Collection of Stuart E. Karu. Photo: Peter Harholdt.

At the height of his success, Franklin did something unusual. He stepped back from his businesses to devote himself to philanthropy, community projects, and civic works. His mother, back in Boston, disapproved of his lack of focus on his earthly calling. She was a good Calvinist Puritan who believed in the doctrine of salvation through God's grace alone. Her son, on the other hand, had rejected this doctrine and espoused instead the covenant of works. He believed that salvation came through good works, that the only religious doctrine he could be sure of was that if God loved all his creatures then the best way to serve God was to serve your fellow men. He explained this in a letter to his mother, which ended with the wonderful line "I would rather have it said, 'He lived usefully,' than, 'He died rich.'"

When it came time for a declaration to be written explaining why the colonies had asserted their independence, the Continental Congress appointed a committee to draft it. It included, among others, Thomas Jefferson, Benjamin Franklin, and John Adams.

They were clear, in their first sentence, about the purpose of the declaration. "A decent respect to the opinions of mankind" required the signers to explain their actions. It was, in short, a propaganda document or, to put it more politely, a piece of public diplomacy designed to enlist others to their cause.

Jefferson wrote the first draft and sent it down Market Street to Franklin. He had begun his famous second paragraph with the words, "We hold these truth to be sacred." Franklin took his heavy black printer's pen—you can see the rough draft in the Library of Congress—crossed out sacred, and made it: "We hold these truths to be self-evident." His point was that our rights come from rationality and reason and depend on the consent of the governed, not the dictates or dogmas of a particular religion.

Jefferson went on to say that by virtue of their equal creation people are endowed with certain inalienable rights. Here we see the probable influence of that old Massachusettes Puritan John Adams. The committee added the phrase "endowed by their Creator." The final sentence became the perfect balance of fealty to divine providence tempered with an understanding that our rights are guaranteed by the consent of the governed.

Americans have long struggled to come to grips with the role of religion and divine providence in our politics and society. But our founders were sensible enough to realize that whatever each of us believes about the place of religion in public life—whether the words "under God" should appear in the Pledge of Allegiance or the Ten Commandments be displayed in public buildings—invocations of the Lord should be used to unite rather than divide us.

On June 11th, 1776 Thomas Jefferson, Roger Sherman, Benjamin Franklin, Robert J. Livingston and John Adams were appointed by Congress to draw up a Declaration resolution. On July 4th, 1776, the thirteen colnies were declared Free and Independant States, under the name of the United States of America.

The complex interplay among various facets of Franklin's character—his ingenuity and reflective wisdom, his Protestant ethic divorced from dogma, the principles he held to and those he was willing to compromise—means that each new look at him reflects and refracts the nation's changing values. He has been vilified in romantic periods and lionized in entrepreneurial ones. Each era appraises him anew, and in so doing reveals some aspect of itself.

Franklin has a particular resonance in 21st century America. A successful publisher and consummate networker with an inventive curiosity, he would have felt right at home in the information revolution, and his unabashed striving to be part of an upwardly mobile meritocracy made him, in social critic David Brooks's phrase, "our founding Yuppie." We can easily imagine having a beer with him after work, showing him how to use a Palm Pilot, sharing a business plan for a new venture, or discussing Bill Clinton's foibles and George Bush's foreign policy. He would laugh at the latest joke about a priest and a rabbi, or the one about the farmer's daughter. We would admire both his earnestness and his self-aware irony. And we would relate to the way he tried to balance, sometimes uneasily, a pursuit of reputation, wealth, earthly virtues, and spiritual values.

Franklin represents one side of the American character: pragmatism versus romanticism, practical benevolence versus moral crusading. He was on the side of religious tolerance rather than evangelical faith. The side of social mobility rather than an established elite. The side of middle-class virtues rather than aristocratic aspirations.

Whichever view we take, it is useful to engage anew with Franklin, for in doing so we are grappling with a fundamental

Franklin tried to balance, sometimes uneasily, a pursuit of reputation, wealth, earthly virtues, and spiritual values.

issue: how can we live a life that is useful, virtuous, worthy, moral, and spiritually meaningful? For that matter, which of these attributes is most important? These are questions just as vital for a self-satisfied age as they were for a revolutionary one.

During his lifetime, even though he was not a member of a particular church, Franklin contributed to the building fund of every church in Philadelphia. And at one point, when the people of Philadelphia were trying to raise money for a hall for visiting preachers, he wrote the fundraiser's prospectus. Even if the Mufti of Constantinople, he said, were to come here to preach Muhammad to us and teach us Islam, we should offer him a pulpit, we should be open and listen, for we might learn something. And on his deathbed, he was the largest individual contributor to the Mikveh Israel synagogue, the first synagogue built in Philadelphia. So at his funeral all the ministers, preachers, and priests of Philadelphia, along with the rabbi of the Jews, linked arms and marched together, accompanying his casket to his burial place.

Franklin did not embody every transcendent, poetic ideal, but he did embody the most practical and useful ones. That was his goal, and a worthy one it was. The most important of these ideals, which he held from the age of 21 when he first gathered the Junto (his philosophical discussion club), was a faith in the wisdom of the common citizen that was manifest in an appreciation for the possibilities of democracy. It was a noble ideal, transcendent and poetic in its own way.

And it turned out to be, as history has proven, practical and useful as well. ✒

BEN FRANKLIN: IN SEARCH OF A BETTER WORLD

Walter Isaacson's essay, from which this article is adapted, appears in *Benjamin Franklin: In Search of a Better World*, edited by Page Talbott and published by Yale University Press in November 2005. The book, which includes essays by nine other prominent historians of Franklin, is a companion to an exhibition of the same name opening at the National Constitution Center in **Philadelphia** in December 2005 and running through April 2006. It then travels to the Missouri Historical Society in **St. Louis** (June–September 2006), the **Houston** Museum of Natural Science (October 2006–January 2007), the **Denver** Museum of Nature and Science (March–May 2007), the **Atlanta** History Center (July–October 2007), and the Musée des Arts et Métiers in **Paris** (December 2007–March 2008). To find out more, visit http://www.benfranklin300.org/.

LOOK BACK:
THE FOUNDING FATHERS
Reflecting upon religion and politics

DEAR READER...
January 17, 2006, marks the 300th anniversary of the birth of Benjamin Franklin, patron saint of almanacs. With religiously motivated acts of terrorism and civil disobedience, controversial Supreme Court rulings, and inflammatory debate about the proper balance of politics and religion a regular fixture of the daily news, we thought it timely to turn to Franklin and his peers for counsel. How did the founders of our nation reconcile their spiritual beliefs with their democratic values? Are their ideas relevant to our lives and the issues we face today?

As the following quotes from Franklin, Thomas Jefferson, John Adams, Thomas Paine, and James Madison clearly demonstrate, the Foundering Fathers were spiritual men who believed in God and the principles of Christianity. Yet they were highly skeptical of organized religion and took great care to separate the workings of government from the influence of religion. Would they have supported the display of the Ten Commandments on government property, or the teaching of both evolution and intelligent design in public schools, or compulsory prayer in the military, or allowing faith-based organizations to teach abstinence in public schools? You decide.

— *Cosmo Doogood*

Ben Franklin

I have lived, Sir, a long time, and the longer I live, the more convincing proofs I see of this truth—that God governs in the affairs of men. And if a sparrow cannot fall to the Ground without his Notice, is it probable that an Empire can rise without his Aid?

How many observe Christ's birthday! How few his precepts! O! 'tis easier to keep holidays than commandments.

Freedom is not a gift bestowed upon us by other men, but a right that belongs to us by the laws of God and nature.

Be in general virtuous, and you will be happy.

Beer is proof God loves us and wants us to be happy.

And yet, he also said...

Lighthouses are more helpful than churches.

*Man will ultimately be governed
by God or by tyrants.*

— *Ben Franklin*

Religion which I found to be without any tendency to inspire, promote, or confirm morality, serves principally to divide us and make us unfriendly to one another.

I wish it (Christianity) were more productive of good works ... I mean real good works ... not holy day keeping, sermon-hearing ... or making long prayers, filled with flatteries and compliments despised by wise men, and much less capable of pleasing the Deity.

If we look back into history for the character of the present sects of Christianity, we shall find few that have not in turns been persecutors and complainers of persecution. The primitive Christians thought persecution extremely wrong in Pagans, but practiced it on one another. The first Protestants of the Church of England blamed persecution on the Roman church, but practiced it on the Puritans. They found it wrong in Bishops, but fell into the practice both here (England) and in New England.

Thomas Jefferson

The doctrines of Jesus are simple, and tend to all the happiness of man.

Of all the systems of morality, ancient or modern which have come under my observation, none appears to me so pure as that of Jesus.

*I am a real Christian,
that is to say, a disciple
of the doctrines of Jesus.*

— *Thomas Jefferson*

God who gave us life gave us liberty. And can the liberties of a nation be thought secure when we have removed their only firm basis, a conviction in the minds of the people that these liberties are a gift from God? That they are not to be violated but with His wrath? Indeed I tremble for my country when I reflect that God is just, and that His justice cannot sleep forever.

And yet, he also said...

The legitimate powers of government extend to such acts only as are injurious to others. But it does me no injury for my neighbor to say there are 20 gods, or no God. It neither picks my pocket nor breaks my leg.

...our civil rights have no dependence on our religious opinions, any more than our opinions in physics or geometry.

I am for freedom of religion and against all maneuvers to bring about a legal ascendancy of one sect over another.

I have recently been examining all the known superstitions of the world, and do not find in our particular superstition [Christianity] one redeeming feature. They are all alike, founded on fables and mythology.

The clergy converted the simple teachings of Jesus into an engine for enslaving mankind ... to filch wealth and power to themselves... these clergy, in fact, constitute the real Anti-Christ.

—*Thomas Jefferson*

History I believe furnishes no example of a priest-ridden people maintaining a free civil government. This marks the lowest grade of ignorance, of which their political as well as religious leaders will always avail themselves for their own purpose.

All persons shall have full and free liberty of religious opinion; nor shall any be compelled to frequent or maintain any religious institution.

I contemplate with sovereign reverence that act of the whole American people which declared that their legislature should 'make no law respecting an establishment of religion, or prohibiting the free exercise thereof,' thus building a wall of separation between Church and State.

John Adams

We Recognize No Sovereign but God, and no King but Jesus.
(with John Hancock, April 18, 1775)

The general principles upon which the Fathers achieved independence were the general principals of Christianity... I will avow that I believed and now believe that those general principles of Christianity are as eternal and immutable as the existence and attributes of God.

We have no government armed with power capable of contending with human passions unbridled by morality and religion. Avarice, ambition, revenge, or gallantry, would break the strongest cords of our Constitution as a whale goes through a net. Our Constitution was made only for a moral and religious people. It is wholly inadequate to the government of any other.

(July 4th) ought to be commemorated as the day of deliverance by solemn acts of devotion to God Almighty.

— *John Adams*

I have examined all religions, as well as my narrow sphere, my straightened means, and my busy life, would allow; and the result is that the Bible is the best Book in the world. It contains more philosophy than all the libraries I have seen.

And yet, he also said…

I almost shudder at the thought of alluding to the most fatal example of the abuses of grief which the history of mankind has preserved—the Cross. Consider what calamities that engine of grief has produced!

But how has it happened that millions of fables, tales, legends, have been blended with both Jewish and Christian revelation that have made them the most bloody religion that ever existed.

The divinity of Jesus is made a convenient cover for absurdity. Nowhere in the Gospels do we find a precept for Creeds, Confessions, Oaths, Doctrines, and whole carloads of other foolish trumpery that we find in Christianity.

Thomas Paine

The cause of America is in a great measure the cause of all mankind. Where, some say, is the king of America? I'll tell you, friend, He reigns above.

And yet, he also said…

I would not dare to so dishonor my Creator God by attaching His name to that book (the Bible).

Of all the tyrannies that affect mankind, tyranny in religion is the worst.

—*Thomas Paine*

Whenever we read the obscene stories, the voluptuous debaucheries, the cruel and tortuous executions, the unrelenting vindictiveness with which more than half the Bible is filled, it would be more consistent that we call it the word of a demon than the word of God. It is a history of wickedness that has served to corrupt and brutalize [hu]mankind.

I do not believe in the creed professed by the Jewish Church, by the Roman Church, by the Greek Church, by the Turkish Church, by the Protestant Church, not by any Church that I know of. My own mind is my own Church.

All national institutions of churches, whether Jewish, Christian, or Turkish, appear to me no other than human inventions, set up to terrify and enslave mankind, and monopolize power and profit.

The age of ignorance commenced with the Christian system.

Persecution is not an original feature in any religion; but it is always the strongly marked feature of all law-religions, or religions established by law.

Here it is that the religion of Deism is superior to the Christian Religion. It is free from all those invented and torturing articles that shock our reason or injure our humanity, and with which the Christian religion abounds. Its creed is pure, and sublimely simple. It believes in God, and there it rests.

James Madison

At the Constitutional Convention of 1787, James Madison proposed the plan to divide the central government into three branches. He discovered this model of government in Isaiah 33:22, from which he read, "For the Lord is our judge, the Lord is our lawgiver, the Lord is our king; He will save us."

We have staked the whole future of American civilization, not upon the power of government, far from it. We've staked the future of all our political institutions upon our capacity...to sustain ourselves according to the Ten Commandments of God.

And yet, he also said...

Who does not see that the same authority which can establish Christianity, in exclusion of all other religions, may establish with the same ease any particular sect of Christians, in exclusion of all other sects?

During almost fifteen centuries has the legal establishment of Christianity been on trial. What has been its fruits? More or less, in all places, pride and indolence in the clergy; ignorance and servility in the laity; in both, superstition, bigotry and persecution.

Ecclesiastical establishments tend to great ignorance and all of which facilitates the execution of mischievous projects. Religious bondage shackles and debilitates the mind and unfits it for every noble enterprise, every expanded project.

Religion and Government will both exist in greater purity, the less they are mixed together.

— James Madison

The Civil Government, though bereft of everything like an associated hierarchy, possesses the requisite stability and performs its functions with complete success, whilst the number, the industry, and the morality of the priesthood, and the devotion of the people have been manifestly increased by the TOTAL SEPARATION OF THE CHURCH FROM THE STATE.

Ben Franklin's
13 VIRTUES

© Dover Books

Around 1730, while he was in his mid-20s, Benjamin Franklin developed his own self-improvement program, listing 13 virtues that he felt were an important guide for living. Mastering all these virtues at once was "a task of more difficulty than I had imagined," so he decided to tackle them one at a time. For most of his life he kept a small journal with a separate page for each virtue, evaluating himself regarding each one daily. He also focused on one virtue per week, four times per year. These virtues were frequently featured in *Poor Richard's Almanack*. In one edition he advised: "Be temperate in eating, wine, girls, and cloth, or the Gout will seize you and plague you both."

So how virtuous was Ben? Franklin was known to relish his food, womanize, and sometimes dress to impress people. His food and wine-drinking habits led him to be plagued with the gout for much of his life. To which he might say, "Search others for their virtues, thy self for thy vices." – *C.D.*

Temperance
Eat not to dullness; drink not to elevation.

Silence
Speak not but what may benefit others or yourself; avoid trifling conversation.

Order
Let all your things have their places; let each part of your business have its time.

Resolution
Resolve to perform what you ought; perform without fail what you resolve.

Frugality
Make no expense but to do good to others or yourself; i.e., waste nothing.

Industry
Lose no time; be always employed in something useful; cut off all unnecessary actions.

Sincerity
Use no hurtful deceit; think innocently and justly, and, if you speak, speak accordingly.

Justice
Wrong none by doing injuries, or omitting the benefits that are your duty.

Moderation
Avoid extremes; forbear resenting injuries so much as you think they deserve.

Cleanliness
Tolerate no uncleanliness in body, cloths, or habitation.

Tranquility
Be not disturbed at trifles, or at accidents common or unavoidable.

Chastity
Rarely use venery but for health or offspring, never to dullness, weakness, or the injury of your own or another's peace or reputation.

Humility
Imitate Jesus and Socrates.

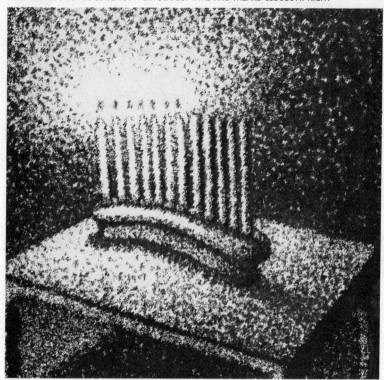

The Twelve Holy Nights
Awakening your hidden spiritual wisdom
By Lynn Jericho

Long before modern calendars, ancient folk traditions around the world provided rituals to deepen peoples' experience of the year. The cycle of the year is a magical procession for the human soul. At summer solstice, the soul sweeps out of itself into the earthly delights of nature. At winter solstice, while nature sleeps in darkness, the soul turns inward seeking its spiritual core.

Age-old mystery traditions throughout the northern hemisphere spoke of the time following the winter solstice as a period when the spiritual world is more perceptible than at any other time of year. The same is true for the period following the summer solstice for people in the southern hemisphere. The time between sunset on Christmas Day, December 25, and sunrise on Epiphany, January 6, was called by early Christians the Twelve Holy Nights, a time when you can awaken the hidden spiritual wisdom of your own self.

No matter what your beliefs, you can use the time of the Holy Nights to contemplate your relationship to nature, to spirit, and to other human beings. Since con-

No matter what your beliefs,
you can use the time of the Holy Nights
to contemplate your relationship
to nature, to spirit, and to
other human beings.

templative work during this special time of the year can be subtle, you need to come with both the warm, sweet openness of a simple shepherd and the intelligent discernment of a wise king. Then, on Epiphany, the 13th day, you will awaken to find gifts of inspired thought, feeling, and intention surrounding your soul.

Here are some guidelines for a Holy Nights practice. They invite you to bring your awareness to certain aspects of your soul and to reflect on how your soul perceives and is perceived.

Just before bedtime go to a quiet place in your home. Candlelight will provide a softer mood than electric lighting. Sitting still, establish a gentle breathing rhythm and settle comfortably into your body. Now begin your contemplation with a meditative verse such as the one below by Rudolf Steiner. Opening to your heart, consider the soul perception exercise for the corresponding night. Spend as much time as you need with yourself. Close the contemplation with your starting verse. If you wish you can write down your experiences, either immediately following the contemplation or the next morning.

If you want to continue this nocturnal work beyond the Twelve Holy Nights, there are natural rhythms that mirror the period from Christmas to Epiphany—the four seasons and the lunar cycles. Each season lasts 13 weeks and there are 13 lunar months in each year. Contemplate each soul perception for one week each season or one lunar month each year. During the thirteenth week or lunar month receive the gifts of spiritual self-development. The rhythms of nature and the cosmos are powerful.

Destiny

The wishes of the soul are springing
The deeds of the will are thriving
The fruits of life are maturing.

I feel my destiny,
My destiny finds me.
I feel my star.
My star finds me.
I feel my goals in life.
My goals in life are finding me.
My soul and the great World's are one.

Life grows more radiant about me.
Life grows more arduous for me.
Life grows more abundant within me.

– *Rudolf Steiner*

DEC. 25: FIRST HOLY NIGHT
Soul Perception—Inner Touch

Tonight imagine your beginning. Not necessarily your conception or your birth, but the heart of who you are and why you are here.

Look inside your skin to find your heart's beginning, your manger. Can you touch with your imagination this holiest part of your soul? This is the part of you that is always innocent, never feels lonely and has so much light and warmth that it is like a small sun inside of you. You will not find words here, just the sparkling glimmer of pure light. Let yourself shine here for a few silent moments before you fall asleep.

Dream of sweet self and sunlight.

DEC. 26: SECOND HOLY NIGHT
Soul Perception—Well-being

Consider the well-being of your soul. Well-being is the absence of "the sins of the world" in body and soul. What is significant about well-being is that when "all is well" we do not notice it; we are just in the blessed moment. We notice well-being only when it is not wholly present. Be still and sense the presence of your well-being. Seek the glad tidings in your soul.

Then let the parts of your soul's inner being where you find hunger, thirst, weariness, or pain begin to speak of your needs for nourishment, quenching, rest, and healing. Write these needs down in your holy heart center (and on paper if you wish.). Make your true Christmas list.

Feel well and lively.

Are there things you see, that you are longing to share with others? If you did not worry about how you would be seen, would you be free to give your vision to others?

DEC. 27: THIRD HOLY NIGHT
Soul Perception—Self Movement

Sit still and sense your inner movement—the ease of your journey toward your goals. This is the reflection of your path of growth and development. There is a dance of destiny in every area of your outer and inner lives. The earth and the planets and the stars are never still and always sensitive to each other. Likewise, the constant movements in your soul life are mutually sensitive to the movements in your daily life of work and relationships.

How are you and your life moving differently tonight than last night or last year? What movement will you develop tomorrow and over the course of the coming year?

Enjoy your dance.

DEC. 28: FOURTH HOLY NIGHT
Soul Perception—Balance

There is a wonderful Latin word that has special significance during these reflective Holy Nights—fulcrum. Fulcrum is the point of purchase that allows for the support of a revolving object. It is the core experience of balance in your soul and on it all the activity of your inner life orients itself.

Consider the balance of your life. Find one or two polarities like thinking and willing, giving and receiving, joy and suffering, or speaking and listening. Which end of the pole are you closer to? Where do you find your creative center?

Feel your balance.

DEC. 29: FIIFTH HOLY NIGHT
Soul Perception—Smell

Imagine the spirit world breathing you in as if you were giving it life. What scent would you offer?

And nature, how does she know your odor? Do you make her glad at your presence in her varied world? Do you remind her of winter, spring, summer, or fall?

Are your thoughts, feelings, and deeds like a baby's breath or lily of the valley, fresh-fallen snow or rich compost?

Breathe deeply, exhale gently.

DEC. 30: SIXTH HOLY NIGHT
Soul Perception—Taste

Our tongue perceives and our soul responds to four tastes:

Sweet tastes give us an immediate sense of being special and good.

Sour tastes wake us up and get our juices flowing.

Salty tastes enhance and intensify our attention.

Bitter tastes chase desire away and indicate purification or healing property.

What have you tasted of nature and spirit that has given your soul these feelings? In the coming year if nature is to taste your deeds and spirit is to taste your thoughts, what in you will they savor?

Taste all things deeply.

DEC. 31: SEVENTH HOLY NIGHT
Soul Perception—Vision

A dear friend once asked me to meditate on two possible gestures behind my deeds in the world. He wondered if my inner experience was "See me" or "I see." The first is a needy gesture and the second a gesture of generosity. Most of us need to be seen before we can see.

How do you need or want to be seen by others? Is it your thoughts, your feelings, or your deeds that long for recognition?

Are there things you see, that you are longing to share with others? If you did not worry about how you would be seen, would you be free to give your vision to others?

See and be seen from infinite perspectives.

*In the stillness and silence of
your soul, recall a conversation
you had during the day.
Forget the words. Focus on the
voice and tone of the other.*

JAN 1: EIGHTH HOLY NIGHT
Soul Perception—Warmth

Our interactions with the world and others can feel heartwarming or chilling. Recognize what warms you and feel gratitude.

Can you redeem the cold with your inner warmth? Radiating warmth into the shadows of our world is a great challenge these days.

A woman was walking to a concert in NYC on a cold, bitter night and was approached by a homeless person asking for money. She gave him some change and looked him in the eye. "What is your name?" she asked. He looked at her and answered, "It's Daniel...no one has asked me my name in years."

Warm chilled hearts.

JAN. 2: NINTH HOLY NIGHT
Soul Perception—Hearing

Consider the voice and tone of those close to you. Ask yourself questions about who is speaking and find answers by paying attention to the echoes that resonate within your being. In the stillness and silence of your soul, recall a conversation you had during the day. Forget the words. Focus on the voice and tone of the other. There is a wonderful Irving Berlin song with the lyric "The song is ended, but the melody lingers on."

Listen to what lingers on in your soul.

JAN. 3: TENTH HOLY NIGHT,
Soul Perception—Language

Each of us has our own idiosyncratic language. These are the little phrases that are unconsciously included in our speaking. Because they are spoken so frequently, they seem meaningless, perhaps irritating, but they reveal so much, and if we were to give an impersonation of a person, these phrases of theirs would be essential.

Choose someone you are very close to and recall one of his or her idiosyncratic phrases. What do you learn about this person if you reflect on this phrase? This task of reflection is not about analyzing the speaker; rather it is to feel the hidden personality revealed in his or her oft-repeated words.

Listen well to all words.

JAN. 4: ELEVENTH HOLY NIGHT,
Soul Perception—Thought

We all share a vast store of universally known ideas and ideals but what makes us individual and unique is the way they evolve in us and how we interpret and express them.

Find in your heart a universal concept such as love, freedom, courage, trust, longing, fulfillment, wonder, etc. Then bring into your heart someone you know well. Recall how this person's words and deeds uniquely reveal their particular reflection of this universal ideal.

Through this contemplation you will find in yourself a growing capacity to know others and to find more awareness of how ideals from the cosmic realm of thoughts enter into the human soul and into our earthly interactions.

Seek ideals in ideas.

© iStockPhoto

JAN. 5: TWELFTH HOLY NIGHT,
Soul Perception—Eternal Self in Other

The first Holy Night guides us to touch our own "holy of holies," the pure spirit of our own individuality. On the twelfth Holy Night, seek to be aware of that spirit in another human being. Begin with imagining the disappearance of the physical body of the other. Then shut out any awareness of this person's energies, biology, and personal history. Move past their personal thoughts, feelings, and intentions. This is the letting go of all the measurable aspects of their being, the parts you may like or dislike, agree or disagree with. If you succeed in letting go of all those perceptions you will meet the sacred center of their being—unclothed, pure, and free.

Having achieved this meeting, you move back away, allowing the layers of karma and material existence to again clothe the kernel of the Divine you just met. But now an intimate feeling for the other's holy individuality illuminates your sense of him or her.

In coming to know the full humanity of the other and feeling both love and freedom fill your soul, the Holy Nights come full circle back to the beginning of your heart.

Find God in all others.

JAN. 6: EPIPHANY

Epiphany has two definitions:

1. The manifestation of a divine being.

2. A sudden intuitive leap of understanding.

Your attention to the Holy Nights may give you both experiences of epiphany.

The gifts of Epiphany are found in your heart, bringing goodwill to your thoughts, words, and deeds in the coming year.

May who you are in the deepest part of your being uniquely bless the world. ⚡

LOOK UP

© iStockPhoto

The Art of Timing
Moving to the rhythm of the moon

By Johanna Paungger and Thomas Poppe

For thousands of years knowledge of the influence of nature's rhythms has been a tool available to those willing to embrace it. People all over the world, including shamans, priests, healers, midwives, fishermen, and farmers, knew that body, mind, and spirit form a continuous whole with everything around and above us. The temples of the Egyptians and Mayans, and the stone circles of the Druids and other ancient peoples give testimony to the importance our ancestors placed on the rhythms of the sun, moon, and planets.

But as these temples have fallen into disuse and ruin, so has the knowledge upon which they were based. One of the nearly forgotten or largely ignored facets of that knowledge was the art of acting at the right moment in time—depending on the task at hand and in harmony with certain natural rhythms.

Our ancestors used intuition, direct perception, and experience to gain insight into the laws governing optimal timing. They discovered that numerous natural phenomena—the tides, birth, meteorological events, women's menstrual cycles, and many more—are related to the movements of the moon. They observed that the behaviour of many animals depends on the position of the moon; that birds, for example, gather their nest material at particular times. They found that the success of many routine and not-so-routine activities in daily life—sowing, planting, pruning, making hay, fertilizing, harvesting, cutting wood, cooking, the administration of healing medicines, and so on—are to a certain measure subject to natural rhythms. And they realized that the inherent "quality" of a certain time and date is to a great extent influenced by five phases and positions of the moon—full moon, new moon, waxing moon, waning moon, and the exact position of the moon in the zodiac.

From these observations our ancestors fashioned general rules, which we tend to dismiss today as folklore and superstition, for certain activities. They obeyed these rules and thus experienced directly their validity—without scientific proof. These rules comprise an entirely legitimate and experiential corpus of knowledge.

The monthly charts presented on pages 68-79 are based on wisdom handed down in a family of Tyrolean mountain farmers about when to carry out certain tasks. Consider them as guidelines rather than as hard and fast rules. They will only become truly useful to you if you try them out for yourself and trust your own experience.

Our hope is that the rediscovery of these laws of nature's rhythms will contribute to our becoming physically and mentally whole and healthy again (and therefore to the healing of this little planet). Many of our environmental problems—from dying forests, worldwide topsoil loss, and water pollution to the problem of nourishing an ever-increasing world population —will be alleviated by the re-appreciation and application of these very simple principles by which our ancestors lived. May it be so. ✷

Johanna Paungger and Thomas Poppe are Europe's most successful nonfiction writers. To date there are 13 million copies of their books, translated into 22 languages, in print. Their books Guided by the Moon (Marlowe & Co., New York) and Moon Time (Rider Books, London) are available in English-language editions. Personal inquiries about the monthly charts should be directed to: Paungger & Poppe, Post Box 107, A – 3400 Klosterneuburg, Austria. Email: vrz@aon.at Web site: www.paungger-poppe.com

JANUARY 2006

HEALTH

- Detoxify & Cleanse Body
- Hair Cutting
- Skin Care (facial mask)
- Skin Care (remove calluses)
- Dental Work (crowns, bridges)
- Nail Care (trim fingers & toes)
- Relaxing Massage
- Invigorating Massage
- Give Up a Bad Habit
- Fall In Love

GARDENING

- Plant Root Plants
- Plant Leaf Plants (not salads)
- Plant Flower Plants
- Plant Fruit Plants
- Plant Salad Greens
- Plant Trees & Bushes
- Fertilize Fruits & Vegetables
- Transplant & Repot
- Water Indoor Plants
- Combat Pests Naturally
- Pull Up Weeds
- Cut & Trim Trees & Bushes
- Prune Fruit Trees
- Harvest & Store

HOUSEHOLD

- Heavy Laundry
- House Cleaning
- Windows (inside & outside)
- Paint & Varnish
- Build, Renovate, DIY Projects
- Bake Sourdough Bread
- Make Jams & Preserves

▲ Very Favorable   X Favorable   – Unfavorable

Zodiac Constellations

Sym.	Latin	Element
♈	Aries	Fire
♉	Taurus	Earth
♊	Gemini	Air
♋	Cancer	Water
♌	Leo	Fire
♍	Virgo	Earth
♎	Libra	Air
♏	Scorpio	Water
♐	Sagittarius	Fire
♑	Capricorn	Earth
♒	Aquarius	Air
♓	Pisces	Water

FEBRUARY 2006

Legend: ◀ Very Favorable   X Favorable   — Unfavorable

	Day	1 W	2 T	3 F	4 S	5 S	6 M	7 T	8 W	9 T	10 F	11 S	12 S	13 M	14 T	15 W	16 T	17 F	18 S	19 S	20 M	21 T	22 W	23 T	24 F	25 S	26 S	27 M	28 T
HEALTH	Detoxify & Cleanse Body	—																											
	Hair Cutting	X	◀	—	◀	X	X	X	X	—	—	—	◀	◀	◀	◀					X	X						X	X
	Skin Care (facial mask)	—	—	—	—	X	X	—	—	—	X	X	—	—	X	X	X	X	X	X	X	X	X	◀	◀	X	X		—
	Skin Care (remove calluses)	—	—	—	—	—	—	—	—	—	—	—	I	—	X	X	X	I	◀	X	X	X	X	X	I	◀	X	—	—
	Dental Work (crowns, bridges)	—	—	◀	—					◀				—				X	—	X	X		X	◀	◀	I			X
	Nail Care (trim fingers & toes)		X	X		X	X			X	X	X	X	X	X			X	X	X	X	X	X	X		X	X		X
	Relaxing Massage	◀							◀	◀							◀								◀				◀
	Invigorating Massage	◀	◀	◀	◀	◀	◀	◀	◀	◀	◀	◀	◀			◀	◀	◀	◀	◀	◀	◀	◀	◀	◀	◀	◀	◀	◀
	Give Up a Bad Habit				◖								○								◗								●
	Fall In Love	◀																											

	Day	1	2	3	4	5	6	7	8	9	10	11	12	13	14	15	16	17	18	19	20	21	22	23	24	25	26	27	28
GARDENING	Plant Root Plants	—	—	X	—	X	—	—	—	◀	—	—	—	—	X	X	X	X	X	X	◀	X	X	◀	◀	X	X	—	—
	Plant Leaf Plants (not salads)	◀	—	X	X	—	—	—	—	—	X	X	—	—	X	—	I	—	I	X	—	—	I	X	◀	X	—	—	—
	Plant Flower Plants	X	X	X	X	—	—	—	—	—	X	X	X	I	X	I	◀	I	X	X	X	I	X	X	◀	X	—	I	—
	Plant Fruit Plants	X	X	X	—	—	—	—	—	—	X	X	◀	—	X	—	I	X	X	X	◀	X	X	◀	X	X	I	X	—
	Plant Salad Greens	X	X	X	X	—	—	—	—	—	X	X	X	—	X	I	◀	—	—	—	◀	—	X	◀	X	X	X	I	◀
	Plant Trees & Bushes	—	X	X	X	—	—	—	—	—	X	X	X	I	X	X	◀	X	X	X	◀	X	X	◀	X	X	X	—	—
	Fertilize Fruits & Vegetables	X	—	X	X	—	—	—	—	—	X	X	X	—	X	X	◀	I	X	X	◀	X	X	◀	X	—	X	I	◀
	Transplant & Repot	X	X	X	X	—	—	—	◀	—	X	X	X	—	X	◀	◀	X	—	◀	◀	◀	◀	◀	—	◀	X	—	—
	Water Indoor Plants	◀							◀				◀				◀				◀				◀				◀
	Combat Pests Naturally																												
	Pull Up Weeds	—	—	—	—	—	—	—	—	—	—	—	—	—	X	X	X	X	X	X	◀	◀	X	X	—	◀	X	—	—
	Cut & Trim Trees & Bushes	—	—	—	—	—	—	—	—	—	—	—	—	—	◀	◀	X	X	X	◀	◀	◀	X	X	—	X	X	—	—
	Prune Fruit Trees	—	—	—	—	—	—	—	—	—	—	—	—	—	◀	◀	X	X	X	◀	X	X	X	X	—	X	X	—	—
	Harvest & Store	—	—	—	—	—	—	—	—	—	—	—	—	—	X	X	X	X	X	X	◀	◀	◀	X	—	◀	X	—	◀

	Day	1	2	3	4	5	6	7	8	9	10	11	12	13	14	15	16	17	18	19	20	21	22	23	24	25	26	27	28
HOUSEHOLD	Heavy Laundry	—	—	—	—	—	—	—	—	—	—	—	—	—	X	X	X	X	X	◀	◀	X	X	X	X	X	X	X	X
	House Cleaning	—	—	—	—	—	—	—	—	—	—	—	—	—	X	X	X	X	X	◀	◀	X	X	X	X	X	X	X	X
	Windows (inside & outside)	—	—	—	—	—	—	—	—	—	—	—	—	—	X	X	X	X	X	◀	◀	X	X	X	X	X	X	X	X
	Paint & Varnish	—	—	—	—	—	—	—	—	—	—	—	—	—	X	X	X	X	X	◀	◀	X	X	X	X	X	X	X	X
	Build, Renovate, DIY Projects	—	—	—	—	◀	—	—	—	◀	—	—	◀	—	X	X	X	X	X	X	◀	X	X	X	◀	X	X	X	X
	Bake Sourdough Bread	X	X	◀	X	X	—	—	—	—	—	—	—	—	X	X	X	X	X	◀	◀	X	X	◀	X	◀	X	X	●
	Make Jams & Preserves	—	—	—	—	—	—	—	—	—	—	—	—	—	X	X	X	X	X	X	◀	X	X	X	◀	X	X	X	X

Zodiacal Constellations

Sym.	Latin	Element
Y	Aries	Fire
♉	Taurus	Earth
♊	Gemini	Air
♋	Cancer	Water
♌	Leo	Fire
♍	Virgo	Earth
♎	Libra	Air
♏	Scorpio	Water
♐	Sagittarius	Fire
♑	Capricorn	Earth
♒	Aquarius	Air
♓	Pisces	Water

MARCH 2006

	Th	F	Sa	Su	M	Tu	W	Th	F	Sa	Su	M	Tu	W	Th	F	Sa	Su	M	Tu	W	Th	F	Sa	Su	M	Tu	W	Th	F
	W	T	F	S	S	M	T	W	T	F	S	S	M	T	W	T	F	S	S	M	T	W	T	F	S	S	M	T	W	T	F
	1	2	3	4	5	6	7	8	9	10	11	12	13	14	15	16	17	18	19	20	21	22	23	24	25	26	27	28	29	30	31

HEALTH

- Detoxify & Cleanse Body
- Hair Cutting
- Skin Care (facial mask)
- Skin Care (remove calluses)
- Dental Work (crowns, bridges)
- Nail Care (trim fingers & toes)
- Relaxing Massage
- Invigorating Massage
- Give Up a Bad Habit
- Fall In Love

GARDENING

- Plant Root Plants
- Plant Leaf Plants (not salads)
- Plant Flower Plants
- Plant Fruit Plants
- Plant Salad Greens
- Plant Trees & Bushes
- Fertilize Fruits & Vegetables
- Transplant & Repot
- Water Indoor Plants
- Combat Pests Naturally
- Pull Up Weeds
- Cut & Trim Trees & Bushes
- Prune Fruit Trees
- Harvest & Store

HOUSEHOLD

- Heavy Laundry
- House Cleaning
- Windows (inside & outside)
- Paint & Varnish
- Build, Renovate, DIY Projects
- Bake Sourdough Bread
- Make Jams & Preserves

▲ Very Favorable   X Favorable   — Unfavorable

Zodiacal Constellations

Sym.	Latin	Element
♈	Aries	Fire
♉	Taurus	Earth
♊	Gemini	Air
♋	Cancer	Water
♌	Leo	Fire
♍	Virgo	Earth
♎	Libra	Air
♏	Scorpio	Water
♐	Sagittarius	Fire
♑	Capricorn	Earth
♒	Aquarius	Air
♓	Pisces	Water

APRIL 2006

Column headings (zodiac sign / weekday / day):

Sign	♉	♊	♊	♋	♋	♌	♌	♍	♍	♎	♎	♎	♏	♏	♐	♐	♑	♑	♒	♒	♓	♓	♈	♈	♈	♉	♉	♊	♊
Day	S/Su	M	T	W	T	F	S	Su	M	T	W	T	F	S	Su	M	T	W	T	F	S	Su	M	T	W	T	F	S	Su
Date	1/2	3	4	5	6	7	8	9	10	11	12	13	14	15 16 17	18	19	20	21	22	23	24	25	26	27	28	29	30

HEALTH
- Detoxify & Cleanse Body
- Hair Cutting
- Skin Care (facial mask)
- Skin Care (remove calluses)
- Dental Work (crowns, bridges)
- Nail Care (trim fingers & toes)
- Relaxing Massage
- Invigorating Massage
- Give Up a Bad Habit
- Fall In Love

GARDENING
- Plant Root Plants
- Plant Leaf Plants (not salads)
- Plant Flower Plants
- Plant Fruit Plants
- Plant Salad Greens
- Plant Trees & Bushes
- Fertilize Fruits & Vegetables
- Transplant & Repot
- Water Indoor Plants
- Combat Pests Naturally
- Pull Up Weeds
- Cut & Trim Trees & Bushes
- Prune Fruit Trees
- Harvest & Store

HOUSEHOLD
- Heavy Laundry
- House Cleaning
- Windows (inside & outside)
- Paint & Varnish
- Build, Renovate, DIY Projects
- Bake Sourdough Bread
- Make Jams & Preserves

▲ Very Favorable   ✕ Favorable   — Unfavorable

Zodiacal Constellations

Sym.	Latin	Element
♈	Aries	Fire
♉	Taurus	Earth
♊	Gemini	Air
♋	Cancer	Water
♌	Leo	Fire
♍	Virgo	Earth
♎	Libra	Air
♏	Scorpio	Water
♐	Sagittarius	Fire
♑	Capricorn	Earth
♒	Aquarius	Air
♓	Pisces	Water

MAY 2006

	1 M	2 T	3 W	4 T	5 F	6 S	7 S	8 M	9 T	10 W	11 T	12 F	13 S	14 S	15 M	16 T	17 W	18 T	19 F	20 S	21 S	22 M	23 T	24 W	25 T	26 F	27 S	28 S	29 M	30 T	31 W
HEALTH																															
Detoxify & Cleanse Body	X	X	X	X	X	X	X	X	X	X	X		X	X	X	X	X							X	X	X					
Hair Cutting			–	–	–	–	–	–	–	–	–	X		X	X	X	X	X	X	X					–	X	–	X	X	X	X
Skin Care (facial mask)	X	X	X	X	X	▲	▲	▲									▲	▲										–	–	–	–
Skin Care (remove calluses)	–	–	–	–	–	–	–	–	–	–	–	–	X	X	X	X	▲	▲	X	X	X	X	X	X				–	–	–	–
Dental Work (crowns, bridges)	–	–	–	–	▲	–			–			▲	–			▲	▲	▲							–						
Nail Care (trim fingers & toes)					▲		–	–		–			–																		
Relaxing Massage	X	X	X	X	X	X	X	X	X	X	X	X	X	X	X	X	X	X	X	X	X	X	X	X	X	X					X
Invigorating Massage	X	X											X	X	X	X	X	X	X	X	X	X	X	X	X	X	X				
Give Up a Bad Habit	▲	▲	▲	▲	▲	▲	▲	▲	▲	▲	▲			▲	▲	▲	▲	▲	▲	▲	▲	▲	▲	▲		●	▲	▲	▲	▲	▲
Fall In Love	▲												▲																		
GARDENING																															
Plant Root Plants	–	–	–	–	X	X	X	X	X	X	X	X	–	–	▲	▲	–	–	–	X	X	X	▲	▲	X	–			–	–	–
Plant Leaf Plants (not salads)	X	X	X	▲	X	X	X	X	▲	▲	X	X	–	–	–	–	–	–	–	–	–	–	–	–	X	X	–	▲	X	X	X
Plant Flower Plants	X	X	X	▲	▲	▲	▲	–	X	X	X	X	–	X	X	–	–	–	–	–	–	–	–	–	X	X	–	▲	X	X	X
Plant Fruit Plants	X	X	▲	–	–	–	–	–	–	–	X	X	–	X	X	–	–	–	–	–	–	–	–	X	X	X	–	X	X	X	X
Plant Salad Greens	X	X	X	X	X	X	X	X	X	X	X	X	–	▲	▲	X	X	–	X	X	X	X	X	X	X	X	–	X	X	X	X
Plant Trees & Bushes	X	X	X	X	X	X	X	X	X	X	X	X	–	–	–	–	–	–	–	–	–	–	–	X	X	X	–	–	–	–	–
Fertilize Fruits & Vegetables	X	X	▲	–	▲	X	X	X	–	X	X	X	–	X	X	–	–	–	–	–	–	–	–	X	X	X	–	X	X	X	X
Transplant & Repot	–	–											▲	▲	▲	▲	▲	▲	▲	▲	▲	▲	▲	▲		–	–	–	–	–	–
Water Indoor Plants																										–					
Combat Pests Naturally	–	–	–	–	–	–	–	–	–	–	–	–	–	X	X	X	X	X	X	X	X	X	X	X	X	–	–	–	–	–	–
Pull Up Weeds	–	–	–	–	–	–	–	–	–	–	–	–	–	X	X	▲	▲	▲	X	▲	▲	▲	▲	X	X	–	–	–	–	–	–
Cut & Trim Trees & Bushes	X	X	X	X	X	X	X	X	X	X	X	X	–	X	X	▲	▲	▲	X	X	X	X	▲	▲	X	X	–	–	–	–	X
Prune Fruit Trees	X	X	▲	–	–	–	–	–	–	–	X	X	▲	▲	▲	▲	▲	▲	X	▲	▲	X	X	X	X	X	–	–	X	X	X
Harvest & Store	▲	▲	▲	▲	▲	▲	▲	▲	▲	▲	▲	▲	▲	▲	▲	▲	▲	▲	▲	X	X	X	X	X	X	–	X	X	X	X	▲
HOUSEHOLD																															
Heavy Laundry	X	X	X	X	X	X	X	X	X	X	X	X	–	X	X	X	X	X	X	▲	▲	X	X	X	X	X	X	–	–	–	–
House Cleaning	–	–	–	–	▲	▲	X	X	X	X	X	X	–	X	X	X	X	X	X	▲	X	X	X	X	X	X	X	–	–	–	–
Windows (inside & outside)	–	–	–	–	–	–	–	–	–	–	–	–	–	X	X	▲	▲	X	X	▲	▲	X	X	X	X	X	–	–	–	–	–
Paint & Varnish	–	–	–	–	–	–	–	–	–	–	–	–	–	X	X	X	X	X	X	X	X	X	X	X	X	X	–	–	–	–	–
Build, Renovate, DIY Projects	–	–	–	–	▲	X	X	X	X	X	X	X	▲	X	X	▲	▲	▲	▲	▲	▲	▲	X	X	X	X	–	–	–	–	X
Bake Sourdough Bread	X	X	X	X	X	X	X	X	X	X	X	X	–	X	X	X	X	X	X	X	X	X	X	X	X	–	X	X	X	X	X
Make Jams & Preserves	–	–	–	–	▲	–	–	–	–	–	–	–	–	X	X	▲	▲	▲	▲	▲	▲	▲	▲	▲	X	–	–	–	–	–	–

▲ Very Favorable   X Favorable   – Unfavorable

Zodiacal Constellations

Sym.	Latin	Element
♈	Aries	Fire
♉	Taurus	Earth
♊	Gemini	Air
♋	Cancer	Water
♌	Leo	Fire
♍	Virgo	Earth
♎	Libra	Air
♏	Scorpio	Water
♐	Sagittarius	Fire
♑	Capricorn	Earth
♒	Aquarius	Air
♓	Pisces	Water

JUNE 2006

HEALTH

- Detoxify & Cleanse Body
- Hair Cutting
- Skin Care (facial mask)
- Skin Care (remove calluses)
- Dental Work (crowns, bridges)
- Nail Care (trim fingers & toes)
- Relaxing Massage
- Invigorating Massage
- Give Up a Bad Habit
- Fall In Love

GARDENING

- Plant Root Plants
- Plant Leaf Plants (not salads)
- Plant Flower Plants
- Plant Fruit Plants
- Plant Salad Greens
- Plant Trees & Bushes
- Fertilize Fruits & Vegetables
- Transplant & Repot
- Water Indoor Plants
- Combat Pests Naturally
- Pull Up Weeds
- Cut & Trim Trees & Bushes
- Prune Fruit Trees
- Harvest & Store

HOUSEHOLD

- Heavy Laundry
- House Cleaning
- Windows (inside & outside)
- Paint & Varnish
- Build, Renovate, DIY Projects
- Bake Sourdough Bread
- Make Jams & Preserves

▲ Very Favorable   X Favorable   — Unfavorable

Zodiacal Constellations

Sym.	Latin	Element
♈	Aries	Fire
♉	Taurus	Earth
♊	Gemini	Air
♋	Cancer	Water
♌	Leo	Fire
♍	Virgo	Earth
♎	Libra	Air
♏	Scorpio	Water
♐	Sagittarius	Fire
♑	Capricorn	Earth
♒	Aquarius	Air
♓	Pisces	Water

JULY 2006

HEALTH
- Detoxify & Cleanse Body
- Hair Cutting
- Skin Care (facial mask)
- Skin Care (remove calluses)
- Dental Work (crowns, bridges)
- Nail Care (trim fingers & toes)
- Relaxing Massage
- Invigorating Massage
- Give Up a Bad Habit
- Fall In Love

GARDENING
- Plant Root Plants
- Plant Leaf Plants (not salads)
- Plant Flower Plants
- Plant Fruit Plants
- Plant Salad Greens
- Plant Trees & Bushes
- Fertilize Fruits & Vegetables
- Transplant & Repot
- Water Indoor Plants
- Combat Pests Naturally
- Pull Up Weeds
- Cut & Trim Trees & Bushes
- Prune Fruit Trees
- Harvest & Store

HOUSEHOLD
- Heavy Laundry
- House Cleaning
- Windows (inside & outside)
- Paint & Varnish
- Build, Renovate, DIY Projects
- Bake Sourdough Bread
- Make Jams & Preserves

▲ Very Favorable   X Favorable   – Unfavorable

Zodiacal Constellations

Sym.	Latin	Element
♈	Aries	Fire
♉	Taurus	Earth
♊	Gemini	Air
♋	Cancer	Water
♌	Leo	Fire
♍	Virgo	Earth
♎	Libra	Air
♏	Scorpio	Water
♐	Sagittarius	Fire
♑	Capricorn	Earth
♒	Aquarius	Air
♓	Pisces	Water

AUGUST 2006

	♎ T 1	♏ W 2	♏ T 3	♏ F 4	♏ S 5	♐ S 6	♐ M 7	♑ T 8	♑ W 9	♒ T 10	♒ F 11	♓ S 12	♓ S 13	♈ M 14	♈ T 15	♉ W 16	♉ T 17	♊ F 18	♊ S 19	♋ S 20	♋ M 21	♌ T 22	♌ W 23	♍ T 24	♍ F 25	♍ S 26	♎ S 27	♎ M 28	♏ T 29	♏ W 30	♏ T 31
HEALTH																															
Detoxify & Cleanse Body		X	X	X	X	X	X	X		—	—	—	X	X	X	X	X	X	—	—	—	X	X	▲	▲	▲	▲	—	X	X	
Hair Cutting	▲	—	—	—	—	—	—	—	X	—	—	—	—	—	—	—	—	—	—	—	▲	▲	X	X	X	X	▲	▲	—	—	▲
Skin Care (facial mask)			X	X	X	X	X	X		X	X	X	X	X	X	X	X	X	X	X			X							X	X
Skin Care (remove calluses)	—	—			—	—	—	—	—	X	X	X	X	X	X	X	X	—	X	X	X	X	—	—	—	—	—	—	—	—	—
Dental Work (crowns, bridges)				▲	—		▲	▲		▲	X	—	—	—	—	—	▲	—	—	—	—		▲	▲	—						
Nail Care (trim fingers & toes)								▲		X	—	—	—	—	—	X	▲	—	X	—				▲	—						
Relaxing Massage	X	X			X	X	X	X		X	X	X	X	X	X	X	X	X	X	X	X		X	X						X	X
Invigorating Massage	X	X			X	X	X	X		X	—	—	—	—	—	X	—	—	X	—	X		X	X						X	X
Give Up a Bad Habit	▲	▲			—	—	▲	▲									▲	—	—	▲	▲	▲	—							X	X
Fall In Love	▲	▲			—	▲	▲	▲										▲	▲	▲	▲	▲	▲							▲	▲
GARDENING										●						☾					○		●								
Plant Root Plants	—	▲	X	X	X	—	—	—	—	X	—	X	▲	▲	X	X	—	—	X	▲	▲	—	—	X	X	X	X	▲	▲	X	X
Plant Leaf Plants (not salads)	X	▲	X	X	X	X	X	X	—	X	—	—	—	—	X	X	—	—	X	▲	▲	—	—	X	X	X	▲	X	X	X	X
Plant Flower Plants	X	▲	X	X	X	X	▲	▲	—	X	—	—	—	—	X	X	—	—	▲	▲	▲	—	—	▲	▲	X	X	X	X	X	X
Plant Fruit Plants	—	—	—	X	X	▲	▲	▲	—	X	—	—	—	X	X	X	—	—	X	X	X	X	—	X	X	X	X	X	X	—	—
Plant Salad Greens	X	▲	X	X	X	X	X	X	—	X	—	—	—	—	X	X	—	X	X	▲	X	—	—	X	X	X	▲	X	X	X	X
Plant Trees & Bushes	X	▲	X	X	X	—	—	—	—	X	—	—	—	—	X	X	—	—	X	▲	X	—	—	X	X	X	▲	▲	X	X	X
Fertilize Fruits & Vegetables	—	—	—	X	X	▲	▲	▲	—	X	—	—	—	X	X	X	—	—	X	X	X	X	—	X	X	X	X	X	X	—	—
Transplant & Repot	X	▲	X	X	X	X	X	X		X	X	X	X	X	X	X	X	X	X	X	X		X	X	X	X	X	X	X	X	X
Water Indoor Plants	—	▲	X	X	—	X	X	—		—	X	▲	▲	X	X	X	—	—	X	▲	▲		—	X	X	X	X	▲	▲	X	X
Combat Pests Naturally																						X	X	X	X	X	X	X	X	X	X
Pull Up Weeds						—	—	—		X	X	X	X	X	X	X	X	X	X	—	X	X	X	X	X	X	X	X	X	X	X
Cut & Trim Trees & Bushes	—	—	—	—	—	—	—	—		X	X	X	X	X	X	X	X	▲	X	▲	▲	X	—	—	—	—	—	—	—	—	—
Prune Fruit Trees	—	—	—	—	—	—	—	—		X	X	X	X	X	X	X	X	▲	X	▲	▲	X	—	—	—	—	—	—	—	—	—
Harvest & Store	—	—	—	—	—	—	—	—		X	X	X	X	X	X	X	X	X	X	▲	▲	X	—	X	—	—	—	—	—	X	X
HOUSEHOLD										●						☾					○		●								
Heavy Laundry	—	—	—	—	—	—	—	—		X	X	X	X	X	X	X	▲	X	X	▲	X	X	X	—	—	—	—	—	X	X	—
House Cleaning	—	—	—	—	—	—	—	—		X	X	X	X	X	X	X	▲	X	X	▲	X	X	X	—	—	—	—	—	X	X	—
Windows (inside & outside)	—	—	—	—	—	—	—	—		X	X	X	X	X	X	X	X	X	X	▲	▲	X	X	—	—	—	—	—	X	X	—
Paint & Varnish	—	—	—	—	—	—	—	—		X	X	X	X	X	X	X	X	X	X	X	X	X	X	—	—	—	—	—	—	—	—
Build, Renovate, DIY Projects	—	—	—	—	—	—	—	—		—	X	X	X	X	X	X	X	X	X	X	X	X	X	—	—	—	—	—	—	—	—
Bake Sourdough Bread	X	X	—	—	▲	▲	X	X		X	X	X	X	X	X	X	X	X	X	▲	X	X	X	▲	X	X	X	X	X	X	X
Make Jams & Preserves	—	—	—	—	—	—	—	—		X	X	X	X	X	X	X	X	X	X	X	X	X	—	X	X	X	X	X	X	—	—

▲ Very Favorable   X Favorable   — Unfavorable

Zodiacal Constellations

Sym.	Latin	Element
♈	Aries	Fire
♉	Taurus	Earth
♊	Gemini	Air
♋	Cancer	Water
♌	Leo	Fire
♍	Virgo	Earth
♎	Libra	Air
♏	Scorpio	Water
♐	Sagittarius	Fire
♑	Capricorn	Earth
♒	Aquarius	Air
♓	Pisces	Water

SEPTEMBER 2006

Day columns: 1 F, 2 S, 3 S, 4 M, 5 T, 6 W, 7 T, 8 F, 9 S, 10 S, 11 M, 12 T, 13 W, 14 T, 15 F, 16 S, 17 S, 18 M, 19 W, 20 T, 21 T, 22 F, 23 S, 24 S, 25 M, 26 T, 27 W, 28 T, 29 F, 30 S

HEALTH

- Detoxify & Cleanse Body
- Hair Cutting
- Skin Care (facial mask)
- Skin Care (remove calluses)
- Dental Work (crowns, bridges)
- Nail Care (trim fingers & toes)
- Relaxing Massage
- Invigorating Massage
- Give Up a Bad Habit
- Fall In Love

GARDENING

- Plant Root Plants
- Plant Leaf Plants (not salads)
- Plant Flower Plants
- Plant Fruit Plants
- Plant Salad Greens
- Plant Trees & Bushes
- Fertilize Fruits & Vegetables
- Transplant & Repot
- Water Indoor Plants
- Combat Pests Naturally
- Pull Up Weeds
- Cut & Trim Trees & Bushes
- Prune Fruit Trees
- Harvest & Store

HOUSEHOLD

- Heavy Laundry
- House Cleaning
- Windows (inside & outside)
- Paint & Varnish
- Build, Renovate, DIY Projects
- Bake Sourdough Bread
- Make Jams & Preserves

Zodiacal Constellations

Sym.	Latin	Element
♈	Aries	Fire
♉	Taurus	Earth
♊	Gemini	Air
♋	Cancer	Water
♌	Leo	Fire
♍	Virgo	Earth
♎	Libra	Air
♏	Scorpio	Water
♐	Sagittarius	Fire
♑	Capricorn	Earth
♒	Aquarius	Air
♓	Pisces	Water

▲ Very Favorable   X Favorable   — Unfavorable

OCTOBER 2006

Legend: ▲ Very Favorable   X Favorable   — Unfavorable

	S 1	M 2	T 3	W 4	T 5	F 6	S 7	S 8	M 9	T 10	W 11	T 12	F 13	S 14	S 15	M 16	T 17	W 18	T 19	F 20	S 21	S 22	M 23	T 24	W 25	T 26	F 27	S 28	S 29	M 30	T 31
HEALTH																															
Detoxify & Cleanse Body	X	—	X	X	—	—	X	X	X	X	X	X	X	X	X	X	X	X	X	X	X	X	X	X	X	X	X	X	X	X	X
Hair Cutting				—	—	—							—	—																	
Skin Care (facial mask)	X	—	X	X	X	X	X	X	X	X	X	X			X	X	X	X	X	X	X		X	X	X	X	X	X	X	X	X
Skin Care (remove calluses)	—	—	—	—	—	—	—	—	X	—	X	X	X	X	—	—	—	—	—	—	—		—	—	—	—	—	—	—	—	—
Dental Work (crowns, bridges)	—	—	—	X	—	—	—	—	—	—	—	—	—		—	▲	▲	▲	—	—	—		—	—	—	▲	—	—	▲	—	—
Nail Care (trim fingers & toes)	▲	▲	—	—	—	—	X		—	—	—	—			▲	▲	▲	—	—	—	X		X	—	X	—	—	X	X	X	—
Relaxing Massage	▲	▲	X	X	X	X	X	X	X	X	X	X	X	X	▲	▲	▲	X	X	X	X	X	X	X	X	X	X	X	X	X	X
Invigorating Massage			X	X		X	X	X	X	X	X	X	X	X				X	X	X	X				X	X	X	X	X	X	X
Give Up a Bad Habit	▲	▲	X	X	▲	X	X	X	▲	▲	X	X	X	X	X	X	X	▲	▲	▲	X		X	X	X	▲	▲	X	X	X	▲
Fall In Love	▲	▲		X	▲	▲	X	▲	▲																						
GARDENING																															
Plant Root Plants	—	—	X	X	X	—	—	X	X	X	X	X	X	X	X	X	X	X	X	X	X	—	—	X	—	—	—	—	—	X	—
Plant Leaf Plants (not salads)	X	X	X	X	X	—	—	X	X	X	X	X	X	X	—	—	—	—	—	—	—	—	X	X	X	X	X	X	X	X	X
Plant Flower Plants	X	X	X	—	▲	X	X	X	X	X	X	X	X	X	—	—	—	—	—	—	—	—	X	X	X	X	X	X	X	X	X
Plant Fruit Plants	X	X	X	X	▲	X	—	X	X	X	X	X	X	▲	▲	▲	▲	▲	—	—	—	—	X	X	X	X	X	X	X	X	X
Plant Salad Greens	X	X	X	X	X	X	▲	X	X	X	X	X	X	—	—	—	—	—	X	X	X	—	X	X	X	X	X	X	X	X	X
Plant Trees & Bushes	—	—	—	—	X	▲	▲	▲	X	X	X	X	—	▲	▲	▲	▲	▲	—	—	X	—	X	▲	X	—	▲	—	▲	—	—
Fertilize Fruits & Vegetables	X	X	X	X	X	X	—	—	—	—	—	—	—	—	—	—	—	—	—	X	X	—	X	X	X	X	X	X	X	X	X
Transplant & Repot	X	X	X	X	X	—	▲	—	X	X	X	X	X	▲	▲	▲	▲	—	—	X	X	—	X	X	X	X	▲	X	X	X	X
Water Indoor Plants	▲	▲	▲	—	▲	▲	X	▲	X	X	X	X	X	▲	X	X	X	X	X	X	X	—	—	▲	—	—	—	▲	—	X	▲
Combat Pests Naturally			—	—	X			X	X	X	X	X	▲	X	X	X	X	X	X	X	X			▲							
Pull Up Weeds								X	X	X	X	X	X	X	X	X	X	X	X	X	X										
Cut & Trim Trees & Bushes	—	—	—	—	—	—	—	X	X	X	X	X	X	X	X	X	X	X	X	X	X		—	—	—	—	—	—	—	X	—
Prune Fruit Trees	—	—	—	—	—	—	—	X	X	X	X	X	X	X	X	X	X	X	X	X	X		—	—	—	—	—	—	—	X	—
Harvest & Store	X	X	X	X	X	▲	X	X	X	X	X	X	X	X	X	X	X	X	X	X	X		—	—	—	—	—	—	X	X	—
HOUSEHOLD																															
Heavy Laundry	—	—	—	—	—	—	—	X	X	X	X	X	▲	▲	X	X	X	X	X	X	X		—	—	—	—	—	—	—	X	—
House Cleaning	—	—	—	—	—	—	—	X	X	X	X	X	X	X	X	X	X	X	X	▲	▲		▲	▲	—	—	—	—	—	X	—
Windows (inside & outside)	—	—	—	—	—	—	X	X	X	X	X	X	X	▲	X	X	X	X	X	▲	X		X	X	▲	—	—	—	X	X	—
Paint & Varnish	—	—	—	—	—	—	X	X	X	X	X	X	X	X	X	X	X	X	X	▲	▲		X	X	—	—	—	—	—	X	—
Build, Renovate, DIY Projects	—	—	—	—	—	—	X	X	X	X	X	X	▲	▲	X	X	X	X	X	X	X		—	—	—	—	—	—	—	X	—
Bake Sourdough Bread	X	X	X	X	X	▲	X	X	X	X	X	X	X	X	X	X	X	X	X	X	X		X	X	—	—	—	—	X	X	X
Make Jams & Preserves	X	X	—	X	X	X	X	X	▲	X	X	X	X	X	X	X	X	X	X	X	X		—	—	X	X	—	X	X	X	—

Zodiacal Constellations

Sym	Latin	Element
♈	Aries	Fire
♉	Taurus	Earth
♊	Gemini	Air
♋	Cancer	Water
♌	Leo	Fire
♍	Virgo	Earth
♎	Libra	Air
♏	Scorpio	Water
♐	Sagittarius	Fire
♑	Capricorn	Earth
♒	Aquarius	Air
♓	Pisces	Water

NOVEMBER 2006

HEALTH

- Detoxify & Cleanse Body
- Hair Cutting
- Skin Care (facial mask)
- Skin Care (remove calluses)
- Dental Work (crowns, bridges)
- Nail Care (trim fingers & toes)
- Relaxing Massage
- Invigorating Massage
- Give Up a Bad Habit
- Fall In Love

GARDENING

- Plant Root Plants
- Plant Leaf Plants (not salads)
- Plant Flower Plants
- Plant Fruit Plants
- Plant Salad Greens
- Plant Trees & Bushes
- Fertilize Fruits & Vegetables
- Transplant & Repot
- Water Indoor Plants
- Combat Pests Naturally
- Pull Up Weeds
- Cut & Trim Trees & Bushes
- Prune Fruit Trees
- Harvest & Store

HOUSEHOLD

- Heavy Laundry
- House Cleaning
- Windows (inside & outside)
- Paint & Varnish
- Build, Renovate, DIY Projects
- Bake Sourdough Bread
- Make Jams & Preserves

Legend: ▲ Very Favorable   X Favorable   — Unfavorable

Zodiacal Constellations

Sym.	Latin	Element
♈	Aries	Fire
♉	Taurus	Earth
♊	Gemini	Air
♋	Cancer	Water
♌	Leo	Fire
♍	Virgo	Earth
♎	Libra	Air
♏	Scorpio	Water
♐	Sagittarius	Fire
♑	Capricorn	Earth
♒	Aquarius	Air
♓	Pisces	Water

DECEMBER 2006

HEALTH
- Detoxify & Cleanse Body
- Hair Cutting
- Skin Care (facial mask)
- Skin Care (remove calluses)
- Dental Work (crowns, bridges)
- Nail Care (trim fingers & toes)
- Relaxing Massage
- Invigorating Massage
- Give Up a Bad Habit
- Fall In Love

GARDENING
- Plant Root Plants
- Plant Leaf Plants (not salads)
- Plant Flower Plants
- Plant Fruit Plants
- Plant Salad Greens
- Plant Trees & Bushes
- Fertilize Fruits & Vegetables
- Transplant & Repot
- Water Indoor Plants
- Combat Pests Naturally
- Pull Up Weeds
- Cut & Trim Trees & Bushes
- Prune Fruit Trees
- Harvest & Store

HOUSEHOLD
- Heavy Laundry
- House Cleaning
- Windows (inside & outside)
- Paint & Varnish
- Build, Renovate, DIY Projects
- Bake Sourdough Bread
- Make Jams & Preserves

▲ Very Favorable X Favorable — Unfavorable

Zodiacal Constellations

Sym.	Latin	Element
♈	Aries	Fire
♉	Taurus	Earth
♊	Gemini	Air
♋	Cancer	Water
♌	Leo	Fire
♍	Virgo	Earth
♎	Libra	Air
♏	Scorpio	Water
♐	Sagittarius	Fire
♑	Capricorn	Earth
♒	Aquarius	Air
♓	Pisces	Water

COSMO'S **URBAN ALMANAC**
2006
CALENDAR

I will return on the wings of the clouds

CALENDAR KEY

Symbol	**Zodiacal Constellations** Latin Name	English Name	Element		Sun, Moon, and Planets		The Course of the Moon
♈	Aries	Ram	Fire	☉	Sun	●	New Moon
♉	Taurus	Bull	Earth	☽	Moon	◑	First Quarter
♊	Gemini	Twins	Air	♁	Earth	○	Full Moon
♋	Cancer	Crab	Water	☿	Mercury	◐	Last Quarter
♌	Leo	Lion	Fire	♀	Venus		
♍	Virgo	Virgin	Earth	♂	Mars		
♎	Libra	Scales	Air	♃	Jupiter		
♏	Scorpio	Scorpion	Water	♄	Saturn		
♐	Sagittarius	Archer	Fire	♅	Uranus		
♑	Capricorn	Goat	Earth	♆	Neptune		
♒	Aquarius	Waterman	Air	♇	Pluto		
♓	Pisces	Fishes	Water				

Planetary events

☍ Opposition   ☌ Conjunction   △ Trine (120°)

A note about time

Central Standard (or Daylight) Time (-6 hours from Universal Time [UT]) is used throughout this calendar. Rising and setting times for the Sun and Moon are for Minneapolis, Minnesota (longitude W93.3, latitude N45.0). Adjustments for other locations can be found at www.usno.navy.mil. Dates given for Islamic and Jewish holidays are for the evening on which the holiday begins, at sunset.

2005

January
S	M	T	W	T	F	S
						1
2	3	4	5	6	7	8
9	10	11	12	13	14	15
16	17	18	19	20	21	22
23	24	25	26	27	28	29
30	31					

February
S	M	T	W	T	F	S
		1	2	3	4	5
6	7	8	9	10	11	12
13	14	15	16	17	18	19
20	21	22	23	24	25	26
27	28					

March
S	M	T	W	T	F	S
		1	2	3	4	5
6	7	8	9	10	11	12
13	14	15	16	17	18	19
20	21	22	23	24	25	26
27	28	29	30	31		

April
S	M	T	W	T	F	S
					1	2
3	4	5	6	7	8	9
10	11	12	13	14	15	16
17	18	19	20	21	22	23
24	25	26	27	28	29	30

May
S	M	T	W	T	F	S
1	2	3	4	5	6	7
8	9	10	11	12	13	14
15	16	17	18	19	20	21
22	23	24	25	26	27	28
29	30	31				

June
S	M	T	W	T	F	S
			1	2	3	4
5	6	7	8	9	10	11
12	13	14	15	16	17	18
19	20	21	22	23	24	25
26	27	28	29	30		

July
S	M	T	W	T	F	S
					1	2
3	4	5	6	7	8	9
10	11	12	13	14	15	16
17	18	19	20	21	22	23
24	25	26	27	28	29	30
31						

August
S	M	T	W	T	F	S
	1	2	3	4	5	6
7	8	9	10	11	12	13
14	15	16	17	18	19	20
21	22	23	24	25	26	27
28	29	30	31			

September
S	M	T	W	T	F	S
				1	2	3
4	5	6	7	8	9	10
11	12	13	14	15	16	17
18	19	20	21	22	23	24
25	26	27	28	29	30	

October
S	M	T	W	T	F	S
						1
2	3	4	5	6	7	8
9	10	11	12	13	14	15
16	17	18	19	20	21	22
23	24	25	26	27	28	29
30	31					

November
S	M	T	W	T	F	S
		1	2	3	4	5
6	7	8	9	10	11	12
13	14	15	16	17	18	19
20	21	22	23	24	25	26
27	28	29	30			

December
S	M	T	W	T	F	S
				1	2	3
4	5	6	7	8	9	10
11	12	13	14	15	16	17
18	19	20	21	22	23	24
25	26	27	28	29	30	31

2006

January
S	M	T	W	T	F	S
1	2	3	4	5	6	7
8	9	10	11	12	13	14
15	16	17	18	19	20	21
22	23	24	25	26	27	28
29	30	31				

February
S	M	T	W	T	F	S
			1	2	3	4
5	6	7	8	9	10	11
12	13	14	15	16	17	18
19	20	21	22	23	24	25
26	27	28				

March
S	M	T	W	T	F	S
			1	2	3	4
5	6	7	8	9	10	11
12	13	14	15	16	17	18
19	20	21	22	23	24	25
26	27	28	29	30	31	

April
S	M	T	W	T	F	S
						1
2	3	4	5	6	7	8
9	10	11	12	13	14	15
16	17	18	19	20	21	22
23	24	25	26	27	28	29
30						

May
S	M	T	W	T	F	S
	1	2	3	4	5	6
7	8	9	10	11	12	13
14	15	16	17	18	19	20
21	22	23	24	25	26	27
28	29	30	31			

June
S	M	T	W	T	F	S
				1	2	3
4	5	6	7	8	9	10
11	12	13	14	15	16	17
18	19	20	21	22	23	24
25	26	27	28	29	30	

July
S	M	T	W	T	F	S
						1
2	3	4	5	6	7	8
9	10	11	12	13	14	15
16	17	18	19	20	21	22
23	24	25	26	27	28	29
30	31					

August
S	M	T	W	T	F	S
		1	2	3	4	5
6	7	8	9	10	11	12
13	14	15	16	17	18	19
20	21	22	23	24	25	26
27	28	29	30	31		

September
S	M	T	W	T	F	S
					1	2
3	4	5	6	7	8	9
10	11	12	13	14	15	16
17	18	19	20	21	22	23
24	25	26	27	28	29	30

October
S	M	T	W	T	F	S
1	2	3	4	5	6	7
8	9	10	11	12	13	14
15	16	17	18	19	20	21
22	23	24	25	26	27	28
29	30	31				

November
S	M	T	W	T	F	S
			1	2	3	4
5	6	7	8	9	10	11
12	13	14	15	16	17	18
19	20	21	22	23	24	25
26	27	28	29	30		

December
S	M	T	W	T	F	S
					1	2
3	4	5	6	7	8	9
10	11	12	13	14	15	16
17	18	19	20	21	22	23
24	25	26	27	28	29	30
31						

2007

January
S	M	T	W	T	F	S
	1	2	3	4	5	6
7	8	9	10	11	12	13
14	15	16	17	18	19	20
21	22	23	24	25	26	27
28	29	30	31			

February
S	M	T	W	T	F	S
				1	2	3
4	5	6	7	8	9	10
11	12	13	14	15	16	17
18	19	20	21	22	23	24
25	26	27	28			

March
S	M	T	W	T	F	S
				1	2	3
4	5	6	7	8	9	10
11	12	13	14	15	16	17
18	19	20	21	22	23	24
25	26	27	28	29	30	31

April
S	M	T	W	T	F	S
1	2	3	4	5	6	7
8	9	10	11	12	13	14
15	16	17	18	19	20	21
22	23	24	25	26	27	28
29	30					

May
S	M	T	W	T	F	S
		1	2	3	4	5
6	7	8	9	10	11	12
13	14	15	16	17	18	19
20	21	22	23	24	25	26
27	28	29	30	31		

June
S	M	T	W	T	F	S
					1	2
3	4	5	6	7	8	9
10	11	12	13	14	15	16
17	18	19	20	21	22	23
24	25	26	27	28	29	30

July
S	M	T	W	T	F	S
1	2	3	4	5	6	7
8	9	10	11	12	13	14
15	16	17	18	19	20	21
22	23	24	25	26	27	28
29	30	31				

August
S	M	T	W	T	F	S
			1	2	3	4
5	6	7	8	9	10	11
12	13	14	15	16	17	18
19	20	21	22	23	24	25
26	27	28	29	30	31	

September
S	M	T	W	T	F	S
						1
2	3	4	5	6	7	8
9	10	11	12	13	14	15
16	17	18	19	20	21	22
23	24	25	26	27	28	29
30						

October
S	M	T	W	T	F	S
	1	2	3	4	5	6
7	8	9	10	11	12	13
14	15	16	17	18	19	20
21	22	23	24	25	26	27
28	29	30	31			

November
S	M	T	W	T	F	S
				1	2	3
4	5	6	7	8	9	10
11	12	13	14	15	16	17
18	19	20	21	22	23	24
25	26	27	28	29	30	

December
S	M	T	W	T	F	S
						1
2	3	4	5	6	7	8
9	10	11	12	13	14	15
16	17	18	19	20	21	22
23	24	25	26	27	28	29
30	31					

How to Use This Calendar

Cosmo Doogood's Urban Almanac is designed to be used daily. The book is specially bound to lay flat so you can write in it without harming the binding. Permanent slipcovers, made from durable recycled fibers, are available to protect your almanac for day-to-day use and can be used year after year (see page 288).

EACH MONTH

Each month begins with two pages crammed with astronomical, phenological, and contemplative information, (Look Up, Look Out, Look In) to set the tone for the month. What's going on in the night sky? What's sprouting or blooming or fruiting or dying in your neighborhood? Who's mating or birthing or hibernating now? What's worth celebrating? What's stirring in your soul?

EACH WEEK

Each week offers a weather aphorism, a love quote (from Perugina chocolate wrappers), a "homeopathic" interpretation of Rudolf Steiner's "Calendar of the Soul," and a seasonal poem that explores the "soul mood" of each particular week. Some weeks also include stories and photos of **Urban Sanctuaries** like the New York Public Library Reading Room, **Essential Places** like Old Cutler Road in Miami, and **Civilizing Ideas** like National Night Out and Walkabout International, all suggested by our readers (see page 274). Also included are stories on the origins and meaning of various holidays and historic events; profiles of famous people; seasonal nature notes and suggested activities and recipes—all presented to deepen your sense of the living year.

EACH DAY

Each day presents noteworthy historic events, holidays, festivals, and celebrations—something to celebrate or remember for every day of the year. We also include the birth and death dates of famous people, an ephemeris of astrological events, the rising and setting times for the Sun and Moon, plus the times of the full, quarter, and new Moon. There's also space for your thoughts and notes. Use your calendar as an appointment book, a weather log, an exercise diary (see page 37), a phenology notebook (see pages 46 and 47), a dream journal—whatever suits your fancy. And this year we've added an additional notes page for every month, so you can scribble and doodle to your heart's content. We sincerely hope you enjoy it.

JANUARY

DEC 22 - JAN 19

JAN 20 - FEB 18

Capricorn

JANUARY BIRTHSTONE
Garnet

Aquarius

JANUARY FLOWER
Carnation

COURAGE BECOMES THE POWER TO REDEEM
Challenges: envy, greed, timidity

Outside, it is cold, silvery, and suffused with a delicate milky haze. Gray hushed days follow each other, calling us to inner activity. Sitting by the fire or hurrying through the streets, our power of thinking grows. Filled with new ideas, we feel creative and courageous. Legend says "words spoken in winter go unheard until next summer." This is the message from Janus, the old Etruscan god of the doorway, after whom January was named. Janus stands between past and future, new and old. He has two faces. One looks back, the other forward. His third face is invisible. This is the face of eternity, the present moment: NOW. Warmth settles around our hearts. Summoned to great deeds of right action and selfless love, Janus bids us pass through his gate. – *Christopher Bamford*

WEST COAST / PACIFIC MARITIME

Huddled flocks of thousands of ducks, geese, and other waterbirds wait out the storms in San Francisco Bay and in the marshy regions around Sacramento and Portland. Large numbers of bald eagles gather around these concentrations waiting for an easy meal as ducks fall prey to sickness and cold. Along the coast, gray whales undertake their famous migration to Baja California where they will spend the winter and have their calves. Great horned owls begin nesting around cities and farms and can be easily viewed in leafless trees. Iced-over ponds display flower-like patterns in the ice.

MOUNTAIN REGION / BASIN & RANGE

Wherever the snow lies deepest, this is the season for finding animal tracks laying down their stories. You might find the signs where a coyote cautiously stalked a cottontail then made its final eager chase, or you might find the scuff marks of deer pawing down for old grass tufts. Around your house you're more likely to find evidence of the neighbor's cat on its nightly prowls, or the deep imprint of a great horned owl diving into the snow after a mouse. When visiting lakes and reservoirs, search barren treetops for wintering bald eagles; large numbers gather around Denver.

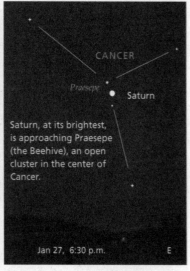

Saturn, at its brightest, is approaching Praesepe (the Beehive), an open cluster in the center of Cancer.

SW   Jan 2, 5:45 p.m.

Jan 27, 6:30 p.m.   E

LOOK UP:

3 Quadrantid meteor shower peaks, 1:00 PM

4 Earth closest to the sun

6 First quarter Moon, 12:57 PM

13 Venus at inferior conjunction (not visible)

14 Full Moon, 3:49 AM

22 Last quarter Moon, 9:15 PM

26 Mercury at superior conjunction (not visible)

27 Saturn at opposition and nearest to Earth

29 New Moon, 8:15 PM

31 Over the next week use binoculars to watch Saturn slip past the Beehive star cluster in Cancer

JANUARY

S	M	T	W	T	F	S
1	2	3	4	5	6	7
8	9	10	11	12	13	14
15	16	17	18	19	20	21
22	23	24	25	26	27	28
29	30	31				

JANUARY IS THE MONTH FOR:

HOBBIES · CREATIVITY · HOT SOUP · OATMEAL · RETAIL BAKERS · THANK-YOUS · VOLUNTEER BLOOD DONORS · MAIL-ORDER GARDENING · WALKING YOUR PET · EYE CARE · STAYING HEALTHY · BREAD MACHINE BAKING · GOURMET COFFEE · IMAGE IMPROVEMENT · CANCER PREVENTION · GLAUCOMA AWARENESS · FINANCIAL WELLNESS · RADON ACTION

MID-CONTINENT / CORN BELT & GULF

With temperatures dipping into negative numbers, northern birds like pine grosbeaks, redpolls, and crossbills may wander south in great numbers. Don't be surprised if they make an appearance at bird feeders in Minneapolis or Ann Arbor along with cardinals and chickadees. Look for white-headed bald eagles perching solemnly in trees around lakes. Now that the leaves have fallen, take a moment to appreciate the different textures of tree bark. Bull moose are dropping their antlers, while white-tailed deer tramp down the snow in areas where they gather.

EAST COAST / ATLANTIC SEABOARD

Frigid northern storms push snowy owls south, look for them within sight of New York City at Sandy Hook. If the going gets hard, deer may be reduced to nibbling on tree bark for nutrients. Grain fields can be filled with huge blackbird flocks looking for waste grain. Bald eagles huddle around icy feeding grounds at Chesapeake Bay, even as pairs in Florida are already starting to nest. Along the Atlantic coast, northern gannets can be observed in spectacular feeding dives. North of Tampa, manatees retreat to the warm waters of Crystal River. Near Jacksonville, shad move into shallow rivers to begin spawning. – *David Lukas*

© Dover Books

CELEBRATE: January 1

NEW YEAR'S DAY

Ring out the old, ring in the new,
Ring, happy bells, across the snow:
The year is going, let him go;
Ring out the false, ring in the true.

– Alfred, Lord Tennyson, 1850

© PhotoDisc

PRAYER / *His Holiness the Fourteenth Dalai Lama*
For as long as space endures
And for as long as living beings remain,
Until then may I too abide
To dispel the misery of the world.

Tiger Woods, *golfer, b.1975*	A single rose can be my garden ... a single friend, my world. — *Leo Buscaglia*	☾ R. 7:55 am S. 3:53 pm ☉ R. 7:51 am S. 4:42 pm	FRIDAY · DECEMBER 30 · 2005 **30**

Tracey Ullman, *actor, b.1959*

Sandy Koufax, *baseball pitcher, b.1935*

Rudyard Kipling, *author, b.1865*

Bo Diddley, *singer, b.1928*

New Moon
9:12 pm

☽ ☌ ☉ 9:12pm
☽ △ ♂ 11:24pm

First Night celebrations: U.S. & CAN

Orange Bowl parade

Henri Matisse, *artist, b.1869*

Anthony Hopkins, *actor, b.1937*

John Denver, *singer, b.1943*

As old sinners have all points Of the compass in their bones and joints Can by their pangs and aches find All turns and changes of the wind. — *Samuel Butler*

☾ R. 8:53 am   S. 5:09 pm
☉ R. 7:51 am   S. 4:42 pm

SATURDAY · DECEMBER 31 · 2005 **31**

☿ ☌ ♇ 5:18am

NEW YEAR'S EVE

1899: Cuba Liberation Day

Diet Resolution Week

1863: Emancipation Proclamation

Sandra Oh, *actor, b. 1971*

J.D. Salinger, *writer, b.1919*

E.M. Forster, *novelist, b.1879*

Paul Revere, *revolutionary, b.1735*

There is nothing new under the sun but there are lots of old things we don't know. — *Ambrose Bierce*

☾ R. 9:38 am   S. 6:33 pm
☉ R. 7:51 am   S. 4:42 pm

SUNDAY · JANUARY 1 · 2006 **1**

☽ ☌ ♀ 7:25am
☉ △ ♂ 3:21pm
☽ ☍ ♄ 11:04pm

NEW YEAR'S DAY   All times Central Time Zone, sun and moon rise and set Minneapolis, MN.

2 MONDAY · JANUARY 2 · 2006

☽ R. 10:12 am S. 7:58 pm
☉ R. 7:51 am S. 4:43 pm

☽ ☌ ♆ 9:02am

Kakizome:
First Writing/
Calligraphy Day,
Japan

*Christie
Turlington,
model, b.1969*

*Lynda Barry,
comedian, b.1956*

*Isaac Asimov,
writer, b.1920*

Love is an
exploding cigar
we willingly
smoke.
– Lynda Barry

---

3 TUESDAY · JANUARY 3 · 2006

☽ R. 10:38 am S. 9:21 pm
☉ R. 7:51 am S. 4:44 pm

☽ ☌ ♅ 8:35pm

Memento Mori
Day *(Latin:
Remember,
you die)*

*Jeanne Moreau,
actor, b.1928*

*Stephen Stills,
musician, b.1945*

*J.R.R. Tolkien,
writer, b.1892*

"It's a dangerous
business, Frodo,
going out of your
door," he used to
say. "You step
into the Road,
and if you don't
keep your feet,
there is no know-
ing where you
might be
swept off to."
– J.R.R. Tolkien

---

4 WEDNESDAY · JANUARY 4 · 2006

☽ R. 11:00 am S. 10:40 pm
☉ R. 7:51 am S. 4:45 pm

☽ △ ♃ 6:33am

1893:
Amnesty for
Polygamists

*Isaac Newton,
physicist, b.1643*

*Louis Braille,
inventor, b.1809*

*Jacob Grimm,
writer, b.1785*

There is a
wonder in
reading Braille
that the sighted
will never know:
to touch words
and have
them touch
you back.
– Jim Fiebig

EARTH AT PERIHELION
3PM

---

5 THURSDAY · JANUARY 5 · 2006

☽ R. 11:20 am S. 11:56 pm
☉ R. 7:51 am S. 4:46 pm

Organize Your
Home Day

*Diane Keaton,
actor, b.1946*

*Umberto Eco,
writer, b.1932*

*Alvin Ailey,
dancer, b.1931*

George Wash-
ington Carver,
agricultural
chemist, b.1864

To do nothing is
sometimes a
good remedy.
– Hippocrates

TWELFTH NIGHT
THE EVENING BEFORE EPIPHANY

Recipe: MAKE YOUR OWN YOGURT CHEESE

Put a colander or sieve over a bowl. Line with double thickness of
cheesecloth, letting it overhang generously. Pour in yogurt (try using
goat's milk yogurt). Let drain for a couple of hours. Tie ends of
cheesecloth together to make a bag; suspend it over the sink or a
bowl overnight. Eat with fruit; flavor with maple and lemon peel for
dessert; add herbs and spices for a spread or a dip. Yogurt cheese will
keep two weeks in the fridge. – *Martha Coventry*

© Jupiter Images

CHANGE / *Louis Jenkins*

All those things that have gone from your life, moon boots, TV trays
and the Soviet Union, that seem to have vanished, are really only
changed, dinosaurs did not disappear from the earth but evolved into
birds and crock pots became bread makers. Everything around you
changes. It seems at times (only for a moment) that your wife, the
woman you love, might actually be your first wife in another form.
It's a thought not to be pursued….

Carnivale Season
begins
Jan 6 – Feb 28

Poetry is a
packsack of
invisible
keepsakes.
— Carl Sandburg

Alan Watts,
writer, b.1916

Carl Sandburg,
poet, b.1878

Joan of Arc,
saint, b.1412

Kahlil Gibran,
poet, b.1883

☽ R. 11:39 am
☉ R. 7:51 am   S. 4:47 pm

FRIDAY · JANUARY 6 · 2006   6

First Quarter
12:56 pm

☽ ♂ ♄ 7:25am

THREE KINGS DAY

EPIPHANY or TWELFTH DAY

**Fasching
Carnival** begins,
Munich

Nanakusa: 7
medicinal plants
celebrated, *Japan*

Usokae:
Bullfinch
Exchange
Festival, *Japan*

Jann Wenner,
publisher, b.1946

Zora Neale
Hurston,
writer, b.1891

Love makes your
soul crawl out
from its
hiding place.
— Zora Neale
Hurston

☽ R. 11:59 am   S. 1:11 am
☉ R. 7:51 am   S. 4:48 pm

SATURDAY · JANUARY 7 · 2006   7

☽ △ ♆ 5:28am

**Women's or
Midwife's Day,**
Greece

1851: Earth's
rotation proved

Elvis Presley,
singer; b.1935

Yvette Mimieux,
actor, b.1942

Stephen Hawking,
physicist, b.1942

David Bowie,
musician, b.1947

We are just an
advanced breed
of monkeys on a
minor planet of
a very average
star. But we
can understand
the Universe.
That makes
us something
very special.
— Stephen
Hawking

☽ R. 12:21 pm   S. 2:26 am
☉ R. 7:51 am   S. 4:50 pm

SUNDAY · JANUARY 8 · 2006   8

☽ △ ☿ 2:16am
☽ ♂ ♂ 2:05pm
☽ ☍ ♃ 4:25pm

All times Central Time Zone, sun and moon rise and set Minneapolis, MN.

9   MONDAY · JANUARY 9 · 2006

☾ R. 12:49 pm   S. 3:40 am
☉ R. 7:50 am   S. 4:51 pm

☽△☉ 12:15am
☽△♀ 1:56pm

1793: Aviation in America

Martyrs' Day, *Panama*

Feast of the Black Nazarene, *Philippines*

Coming-of-Age Day, *Japan*

Joan Baez, folk singer, b.1941

Simone de Beauvoir, writer, b.1908

Dave Matthews, musician, b.1967

I tore myself away from the safe comfort of certainties through my love for the truth; and truth rewarded me.
— Simone de Beauvoir

---

10   TUESDAY · JANUARY 10 · 2006

☾ R. 1:23 pm   S.4:53 am
☉ R. 7:50 am   S. 4:52 pm

Eid-Al-Adha: Feast of the Sacrifice, *Islam*

1920: League of Nations founded

1878: Women's Suffrage Amendment introduced

Robinson Jeffers, poet, b.1887

Shawn Colvin, singer, b.1956

George Foreman, boxer, b.1949

The heads of strong old age are beautiful beyond all grace of youth.
— Robinson Jeffers

---

11   WEDNESDAY · JANUARY 11 · 2006

☾ R. 2:06 pm   S. 6:01 am
☉ R. 7:50 am   S. 4:53 pm

☽△♆ 3:42am
☽☌♆ 8:45pm

1973: Designated Hitter rule adopted

1964: Cigarettes declared hazardous

Eugenio Maria de Hostos, Puerto Rican leader, b.1839

Aldo Leopold, conservationist, b.1887

Alice Paul, women's advocate b.1885

William James, psychologist, b.1842

Alexander Hamilton, statesman, b.1755

---

12   THURSDAY · JANUARY 12 · 2006

☾ R.2:58 pm   S. 7:01 am
☉ R. 7:49 am   S. 4:54 pm

☽△♅ 9:42pm

1755: Tsarina Elizabeth established the first Russian university

1915: Women denied the vote in U.S.

Jack London, writer, b.1876

Edmund Burke, orator, b.1729

Charles Perrault, writer, b.1671

You can't wait for inspiration. You have to go after it with a club.
— Jack London

© Joan Baez.com

BIRTHDAY: *January 9, 1941*
JOAN BAEZ, Folk Singer

DIAMONDS AND RUST
*Words & Music
by Joan Baez*

…Well you burst on the scene
Already a legend
The unwashed phenomenon
The original vagabond
You strayed into my arms
And there you stayed
Temporarily lost at sea
The Madonna was yours
for free…
… Now you're telling me
You're not nostalgic
Then give me another
word for it
You who are so good with
words
And at keeping things vague
Because I need some of that
vagueness now
It's all come back too clearly
Yes I loved you dearly
And if you're offering me
diamonds and rust
I've already paid

Baez was the second of three daughters. Her Mexican father, a physicist who refused lucrative war industry jobs, and her mother, a drama professor, raised their children, who were subject to racial slurs and discrimination, in a Quaker family. At 18, Baez was introduced on stage at the 1959 Newport Folk Festival to sing in her pure, clear, and flexible soprano, resulting in her first record with Vanguard. She later became an advocate for—and lover of (see *Diamonds and Rust*)—fellow folk musician Bob Dylan and recorded an album entirely of his songs.

Baez regularly championed fellow artists and was not afraid to move beyond the acoustic guitar into rock and country genres. Her records have been highly successful, many of them going gold.

An activist artist in the 1960s—when it was neither safe nor fashionable—Baez withheld 60 percent of her income from the IRS to protest military spending. She sang at the Lincoln Memorial as part of Martin Luther King's march for civil rights and in the fields next to Cesar Chavez, paving the way for the Bonos and Springsteens of today.

– Kathleen Melin

© iStockPhoto

TO DO:
FULL MOON GIFTS

A full moon gift is an expression of love given on the day of the full moon. Why give a gift at the full moon? The lunar calendar provides a framework or timetable for pausing in the busyness of our lives to slow down and think about another person. Awareness of the moon's phases makes us more sensitive to the rhythms of nature. Thus by connecting two ancient concepts—gift giving and the lunar cycle—a lovely meaningful tradition evolves.

Gifts may be given in so many ways. You may ask a friend or a grandchild or a spouse to be your full moon partner. When two people are exchanging gifts, alternate each month. You may choose the deep delight of giving anonymously. Or give yourself a gift. Dream of a world in which everyone receives or gives a gift at the full moon! There are endless numbers of gifts that you may give. The following are but a few suggestions to spark your creativity:

From *As Long as the Moon Shall Rise: Reflections on the Full Moon,* edited by Ellen Moore Anderson, Holy Cow! Press, 2005

☽ Give a luxurious backrub

☽ Lie on your back and look at the stars

☽ Read aloud from a favorite author

☽ Arise at dawn to watch the sunrise

☽ Make homemade chocolate sauce ☽ Install a bird feeder

☽ Participate enthusiastically in another's hobby

☽ Take a cooking class

☽ Fix a leaky faucet ☽ Listen deeply

JANUARY, ANCHORAGE / *Linda McCarriston*

…Through window glass I look / out. In, I listen as the furnace turns /
over turns over in my house of old / toast, the spaces around outlets /
taped to blunt the scalpels of cold. / Underground, natural gas is streaming /
here to warm me in hidden lines I / hardly believe in. Earthquake country.

Tyvendedagen or St. Knut's Day, *Norway / Sweden*
Old New Year's Eve, *Russia*

Horatio Alger clergyman, b.1834

Alfred Fuller, salesman, b.1885

Tex Ritter, singer, b.1905

Winter lies too long in country towns; hangs on until it is stale and shabby, old and sullen.
— Willa Cather

☽ R. 3:59 pm S. 7:50 am
☼ R. 7:49 am S. 4:55 pm

☿△♂ 5:39am
☽☌♀☿ 11:11am
☽△♃ 11:21am
☉☌♀ 6:58pm

FRIDAY · JANUARY 13 · 2006 **13**

1784: End of the American Revolution

Julian Bond, US Rep (GA), b.1940

Albert Schweitzer, philosopher, b.1869

Benedict Arnold, traitor, b.1741

You must give some time to your fellow men. Even if it's a little thing, do something for others — something for which you get no pay but the privilege of doing it.
— Albert Schweitzer

☽ R. 5:05 pm S. 8:28 am
☼ R. 7:48 am S. 4:57 pm

Full Moon
1:48 am

☽☌♀ 3:32am
☽☌☉ 4:49am

SATURDAY · JANUARY 14 · 2006 **14**

1943: Pentagon completed

Martin Luther King, Jr. b.1929

Osip Mandelstam, poet, b.1891

Jean-Baptiste Moliere, writer, b.1622

The hope of a secure and livable world lies with disciplined nonconformists who are dedicated to justice, peace and brotherhood.
— Martin Luther King, Jr.

☽ R. 6:12 pm S. 8:59 am
☼ R. 7:48 am S. 4:58 pm

♂☌♃ 4:28am
☽☌♄ 10:11am

SUNDAY · JANUARY 15 · 2006 **15**

All times Central Time Zone, sun and moon rise and set Minneapolis, MN.

16 MONDAY · JANUARY 16 · 2006

☾ R. 7:18 pm S. 9:22 am
☉ R. 7:47 am S. 4:59 pm

☾☌♆ 1:31am
☾△♆ 7:35pm

Ditch Your New Year's Resolution Day

1883:
Civil Service created

1786: Religious Freedom Day

Robert Service, poet, b.1874

Ethel Merman, actor, b.1909

Ah! the clock is always slow;
It is later than you think.
— Robert Service

17 TUESDAY · JANUARY 17 · 2006

☾ R. 8:23 pm S. 9:42 am
☉ R. 7:46 am S. 5:00 pm

☿☌♀ 10:31am
☾☌♅ 9:59pm

Metric System Day

Muhammed Ali, "The Greatest," boxer, b.1942

James Earl Jones, actor, b.1931

William Stafford, poet, b.1914

Al Capone, entrepreneur, b.1899

Anton Chekov, playwright, b. 1860

Benjamin Franklin, b.1706

Hide not your talents. They for use were made. What's a sundial in the shade?
— Benjamin Franklin

18 WEDNESDAY · JANUARY 18 · 2006

☾ R. 9:27 pm S. 9:59 am
☉ R. 7:46 am S. 5:02 pm

☾△♂ 2:45pm
☾△♀ 10:43pm

Winnie the Pooh Day

Cary Grant, actor, b.1904

A.A. Milne, writer, b.1882

Daniel Webster, writer, b.1782

The world is governed more by appearances than realities, so that it is fully as necessary to seem to know something as to know it.
— Daniel Webster

19 THURSDAY · JANUARY 19 · 2006

☾ R. 10:30 pm S. 10:15 am
☉ R. 7:45 am S. 5:03 pm

☾△☿ 6:32am
☾△☉ 5:13pm

1870:
Tin Can patented

Janis Joplin, singer, b.1943

Paul Cezanne, painter, b.1839

Edgar Allan Poe, poet, b.1809

Dogen, poet, b.1200

It may well be doubted whether human ingenuity can construct an enigma ... which human ingenuity may not, by proper application, resolve.
— Edgar Allen Poe

Nature Note: RABBIT AND SQUIRREL TRACKS

Walking out your back door after a new snow, you'll most likely see a maze of animal tracks. You know you have rabbits and squirrels in your yard, but which tracks belong to whom? Squirrels have four toes on the front feet and five toes on the back, but when they run, the back feet come forward and between the front feet, making a kind of wobbly "W" pattern *(see figure at left)*. Rabbits are hoppers even when moving at a slow gait, and their back feet, too, lead the front to make the characteristic "Y" track *(see figure at right)* of all rabbits. —MC

EARLY DARKNESS / *D. Patrick Miller*

Think of it as ink: / an indigo dye descending / between the leaves of the trees / and down to the grasses. / There is no dying of the light— / just the washing of a bowl, / and overturning it for night. / When day arrives we must write with bottled darkness. / In the night we can dream free messages of light.

Cheese Day	The cable TV sex channels don't expand our horizons, don't make us better people, and don't come in clearly enough. — *Bill Maher*	☾ R. 11:34 pm S. 10:30 am ☉ R. 7:44 am S. 5:04 pm 	**FRIDAY · JANUARY 20 · 2006 20**
Bill Maher, satirist, b.1956 *Edwin "Buzz" Aldrin, astronaut, b.1930* *Frederico Fellini, cinéaste, b.1920*			

1915: Kiwanis Int'l. founded	*Roger Nash Baldwin, founder ACLU, b.1884*	☾ S. 10:47 am ☉ R. 7:44 am S. 5:06 pm	**SATURDAY · JANUARY 21 · 2006 21**
St. Agnes Day **Bald Eagle Appreciation Day**	*Ethan Allen, Revolutionary War hero, b.1738* *Christian Dior designer, b.1905*	☽ △ ♆ 3:20am	
Laughter is the sun that drives winter from the human face. — *Victor Hugo*	*Geena Davis, actor, b. 1957*		

1973: Roe v. Wade decision	*George Balanchine, choreographer, b.1904*	☾ R. 12:41 am S. 11:05 am ☉ R. 7:43 am S. 5:07 pm	**SUNDAY · JANUARY 22 · 2006 22**
Now hatred is by far the longest pleasure; Men love in haste, but they detest at leisure. — *Lord Byron*	*Lord Byron, poet, b.1788* *August Strindberg, composer, b.1849* *Francis Bacon, statesman, b.1561*	Last Quarter 9:14 am ☽ △ ♅ 10:09pm	

All times Central Time Zone, sun and moon rise and set Minneapolis, MN.

23 MONDAY · JANUARY 23 · 2006

☽ R. 1:50 am S. 11:28 am
☉ R. 7:42 am S. 5:08 pm

♀△♂ 5:20pm
☽♂♃ 12:49pm
☽♂♂♂ 4:54pm

Babin Den:
Midwife or
Grandmother's
Day, *Bulgaria*

1980: Carter
reinstates
Selective Service
registration

The country has
charms only for
those not obliged
to stay there.
– Édouard
Manet

*Edouard Manet,
painter, b.1832*

*Elizabeth
Blackwell, first
woman MD,
b.1849*

*John Hancock,
statesman,
b.1737*

24 TUESDAY · JANUARY 24 · 2006

☽ R. 3:04 am S. 11:57 am
☉ R. 7:41 am S. 5:10 pm

Alacitis:
honoring
Ekeko, god of
prosperity,
Bolivia

1935: First
canned beer

*John Belushi,
comic actor,
b.1949*

*Edith Wharton,
writer, b.1862*

There are
two ways
of spreading
light: to be the
candle or the
mirror that
reflects it.
– Edith Wharton

25 WEDNESDAY · JANUARY 25 · 2006

☽ R. 4:19 am S. 12:36 pm
☉ R. 7:40 am S. 5:11 pm

☽△♄ 4:00am

Burns' Nights,
*Scotland,
England,
Newfoundland*

Up Helly Aa,
Scotland

1984:
Macintosh
Computer
Debut

*Robert Burns,
poet, b.1759*

*Virginia Woolf,
writer, b.1882*

*W. Somerset
Maugham,
writer, b.1874*

Computers can
figure out all
kinds of prob-
lems, except the
things in the
world that just
don't add up.
– James Magary

26 THURSDAY · JANUARY 26 · 2006

☽ R. 5:32 am S. 1:29 pm
☉ R. 7:39 am S. 5:13 pm

☽♂♆ 10:25am
☉♂☿ 4:33pm

1788: Australia
Day: First
British
settlement

1950: Republic
Day, *India*

*Angela Davis,
activist, b.1944*

*Paul Newman,
actor, b.1925*

*Douglas
MacArthur,
general, b.1880*

*Jules Feiffer,
artist, b 1929*

Don't worry
about the world
coming to an
end today.
It's already
tomorrow
in Australia.
– Charles
M. Schulz

BIRTHDAY: January 25, 1759
ROBERT BURNS, Poet

Poet and songwriter Robert Burns, born to farming in the Scottish Lowlands and a farmer for much of his short life, is celebrated for his use of dialect, which infused English poetry with a new vitality. Beloved for his compassionate and playful descriptions of fellow rural Scots, his poetry echoes the universal themes and rising humanitarianism of his day. In addition to poetry, he wrote 286 songs, among them *Auld Lang Syne* and *Comin' thro' the Rye*. Burns died on July 21, 1796 at age 37.

A Red, Red Rose

O my Luve's like a red, red rose,
That's newly sprung in June:
O my Luve's like the melodie,
That's sweetly play'd in tune.

As fair art thou, my bonie lass,
So deep in luve am I;
And I will luve thee still, my dear,
Till a' the seas gang dry.

Till a' the seas gang dry, my dear,
And the rocks melt wi' the sun;
And I will luve thee still, my dear,
While the sands o' life shall run.

And fare-thee-weel, my only Luve!
And fare-thee-weel, a while!
And I will come again, my Luve,
Tho' 'twere ten thousand mile!

Gie me ae spark o' Nature's fire, That's a' the learning I desire.

BIRTHDAY: January 25, 1882
VIRGINIA WOOLF, Writer

Virginia Woolf once said that "fiction is like a spider's web, attached ever so lightly perhaps, but still attached to life at all four corners." One of the 20th century's great literary innovators, she and her sister Vanessa formed the core of the intellectual Bloomsbury group.

In 1917, Woolf and her husband Leonard Woolf, bought an old hand press and set two stories on it, one by each of them, which sold out almost immediately. Hogarth Press, as they called it, continued to publish, preferring young and unknown writers including Katherine Mansfield and T. S. Eliot.

As an experience, madness is terrific...and in its lava I still find most of the things I write about.

A woman must have money and a room of her own if she is to write fiction.

Woolf's hold on life was not attached at all four corners. Sexually abused by her stepbrothers, she had her first nervous breakdown at age 13. She ended her life on March 28, 1941, at age 59, when she filled her pockets with stones and walked into the River Ouse.

– *K.M.*

© Jupiter images

BIRTHDAY: *January 27, 1756*
WOFLGANG AMADEUS MOZART, Composer

Wolfgang Amadeus Mozart is among the most popular composers of all time. This year is the 250th anniversary of his birth and many festivals will be celebrating his music throughout the world. He was born in Salzburg, Austria. His father, Leopold, was one of Europe's leading music teachers, training Mozart in both piano and violin from the time he was a toddler. Mozart was already composing by the age of five.

Mozart toured extensively, being showcased by his father as a prodigy in the courts of Europe. He soon gained fame for playing the piano blindfolded with his hands behind his back, and also for his ability to improvise. He met many of the most influential composers of western classical music, including Johann Christian Bach, Joseph Haydn, and Ludwig van Beethoven. Beethoven said that he would never be able to compose a melody as great as one in the first movement of Mozart's *Piano Concerto No. 24*.

On August 4, 1782, he married Constanze Weber. They had six children, of whom only two survived infancy. Neither of these two married or had children.

Later in Mozart's short life he became a Freemason, like Benjamin Franklin, his contemporary, and Haydn who was in the same Masonic Lodge. Mozart even composed several pieces of music for Franklin's glass harmonica and his last opera, *The Magic Flute*, includes Masonic themes.

Mozart's life was fraught with financial difficulty and illness, both exacerbated by his extravagant lifestyle. Mozart died on December 5, 1791, while working on the *Requiem*, his final composition. The cause of Mozart's death is uncertain, but some speculate that a rival composer poisoned him.

© iStockPhoto

KINDNESS / *Naomi Shihab Nye*

…Before you know kindness as the deepest thing inside, / you must know sorrow as the other deepest thing. / You must wake up with sorrow. / You must speak to it till your voice / catches the thread of all sorrows / and you see the size of the cloth. / Then it is only kindness that makes sense anymore, / …only kindness that raises its head / from the crowd of the world to say, / "It is I you have been looking for," / and then goes with you everywhere / like a shadow or a friend.

1973: Vietnam Peace Agreement signed	*Wolfgang A. Mozart, composer, b.1756*	☾ R. 6:36 am S. 2:38 pm ☉ R. 7:38 am S. 5:14 pm **FRIDAY · JANUARY 27 · 2006 27**
St. Paul Winter Carnival begins, *Jan 27–Feb 5*	Sometimes I've believed as many as six impossible things before breakfast. — *Lewis Carroll*	☿ ☌ ♄ 8:03am ☉ ☌ ♄ 5:48am ☽ ☌ ♀ 9:06pm
Mikhail Baryshnikov, dancer, b.1948		
Lewis Carroll, writer, b.1832		
Thomas Crapper, inventor, b. 1910		
1986: Challenger Space Shuttle explosion	Man has to suffer. When he has no real afflictions, he invents some. — *José Martí*	☾ R. 7:28 am S. 3:59 pm ☉ R. 7:37 am S. 5:15 pm **SATURDAY · JANUARY 28 · 2006 28**
Blueberry Pancake Day		☽ △ ♂ 2:56am
José Martí, writer, b.1853		
Auguste & Jean-Felix Piccard, balloonists, b.1884		
Thomas Paine, revolutionary, b.1737	*Edward Abbey, playwright, b.1927*	☾ R. 8:07 am S. 5:27 pm ☉ R. 7:36 am S. 5:17 pm **SUNDAY · JANUARY 29 · 2006 29**
Emmanuel Swedenborg, inventor/ philosopher, b.1688	One man alone can be pretty dumb sometimes, but for real bona fide stupidity, there ain't nothin' can beat teamwork. — *Edward Abbey*	 New Moon 8:15 am ☽ ☌ ♄ 6:24am ☽ ☌ ☉ 9:14am ☽ ☌ ☿ 12:37pm ☽ ☌ ♅ 9:02pm
Anton Chekhov, writer, b.1860		
W.C. Fields, actor, b.1880		

Lᴜɴᴀʀ Nᴇᴡ Yᴇᴀʀ   All times Central Time Zone, sun and moon rise and set Minneapolis, MN.

30 MONDAY · JANUARY 30 · 2006

☾ R. 8:37 am S. 6:54 pm
☉ R. 7:35 am S. 5:18 pm

Holiday of the Three Hierarchs, *Greece*

1972: Bloody Sunday, *N. Ireland*

1948: Mahatma Gandhi assassinated

Saul Alinsky, activist, b.1909

Franklin D. Roosevelt, 32nd U.S. President, b.1882

A conservative is a man with two perfectly good legs who, however, has never learned to walk forward.
— *Franklin Delano Roosevelt*

---

31 TUESDAY · JANUARY 31 · 2006

☾ R. 9:02 am S. 8:18 pm
☉ R. 7:34 am S. 5:20 pm

☽ ☌ ♅ 8:00am
☽ △ ♃ 9:10pm

Hegira: Islamic New Year

1958: Explorer I Space Satellite launched

Alan Lomax, musicologist, b.1915

Thomas Merton, monk, b.1915

Franz Schubert, composer, b.1797

The least of learning is done in the classrooms.
— *Thomas Merton*

---

1 WEDNESDAY · FEBRUARY 1 · 2006

☾ R. 9:23 am S. 9:38 pm
☉ R. 7:33 am S. 5:21 pm

☿ ☌ ♆ 3:22pm

American Heart Month

Black History Month

St Brigid's Day, *Ireland*

S.J. Perelman, humorist, b. 1904

Langston Hughes, poet/ writer, b.1902

Clark Gable, actor, b.1901

Hold fast to dreams for if dreams die, life is a broken winged bird that cannot fly.
— *Langston Hughes*

---

2 THURSDAY · FEBRUARY 2 · 2006

☾ R. 9:42 am S. 10:57 pm
☉ R. 7:32 am S. 5:23 pm

☽ △ ♄ 6:02am

Imbolc: Wiccan Feast of Torches

Vasent Panchami, *Hindu*

Ayn Rand, writer, b.1905

James Joyce, writer, b 1882

Mistakes are the portals of discovery.
— *James Joyce*

CANDLEMAS
GROUNDHOG DAY

Nature Note: BIRDS IN WINTER

Many songbirds (chickadees, cardinals, gold finches, and more) remain in the north during the cold winter. Little living ovens, they maintain a constant body temperature of about 107° F (yes, 107°) although it may be well below freezing outside. Feathers provide excellent insulation, and a perching bird can increase the insulating effect both by puffing up its feathers and making its body as spherical as possible.

86°F   32°F   - 4°F

—*Craig Holdrege*

Drawing by Craig Holdrege

Notes

"I saw my shadow, it made me look fat."

FEBRUARY

JAN 20 - FEB 18

Aquarius

FEBRUARY BIRTHSTONE
Amethyst

FEB 19 - MAR 20

$)($

Pisces

FEBRUARY FLOWER
Violet

DISCRETION Becomes Meditative Strength
Challenges: indiscrimination

The days lengthen. The sun is still more red than gold. Yet the sky brightens when the clouds part and the rain (or snow) passes. The month opens with the Celtic festival of Imbolc, marking the lactation of the ewes, the flow of milk announcing the return of life: the joy of becoming. But spring is still far away. Patience and faith are called for. Perhaps this is why the month takes its name from Februa, the Roman festival of Purification. To purify is to separate the gold from the dross, the good from the bad. It requires memory and the practice of discernment. Discernment is often symbolized by a sword, but there is something feminine about February. It is a gentle month, filled with feasts celebrating female figures like St. Brigit, the Virgin Mary, and the Virgin Goddess Artemis. They ask us to practice keeping silent, pondering all things in our hearts. Great strength, you may be sure, will come from such discretion. – *CB*

WEST COAST / PACIFIC MARITIME

Tempted by a flush of warm false spring days, the first flowers make their appearance – red flowering currants along the coast, hazelnut and willow catkins in the forests, and odorous skunk cabbage in swamps of the north. Drawn forth by newly emerging flowers, Anna's hummingbirds in Los Angeles begin courting and nesting. Yellow-faced bumbles crawl forth to become the first conspicuous insect of the season as they buzz heavily from flower to flower in the Bay Area. Treefrogs fill the night with deafening choruses around Seattle. In bays along the coast, Pacific herring spawning runs attract thousands of predators like sea lions, gulls, and sea ducks.

MOUNTAIN REGION / BASIN & RANGE

Under ice-covered lakes, hibernating animals are using up the oxygen in the water, sometimes resulting in a fish die-off. Common ravens begin their acrobatic courtship flights over the open landscape. Down in the southlands the changing seasons make their first appearance as spring cautiously unfurls in some desert areas. Courageous lizards sun themselves on rocks around Phoenix. Butterflies and spiders make an appearance. In a good year, fields of lupines and poppies line roadsides west of Tucson. Meanwhile, around Salt Lake City the immense flocks of ducks on Great Salt Lake are starting to get a little restless in preparation for their long journey north next month.

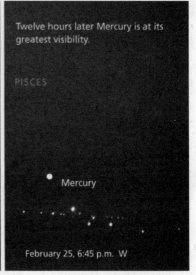

February 25 is a special day for sky observers. In the morning hours the waning sickle Moon is far beneath Venus.

Venus

Moon

February 25, 6:30 a.m   SE

Twelve hours later Mercury is at its greatest visibility.

PISCES

Mercury

February 25, 6:45 p.m. W

LOOK UP:

5 First quarter Moon, 12:29 AM

12 Full Moon, 10:45 PM

21 Last quarter Moon, 1:18 AM

24 Mercury at greatest eastern elongation (18° 08')

27 New Moon, 6:31 PM

FEBRUARY IS THE MONTH FOR:

INTERNATIONAL FRIENDSHIP · CHERRIES · WILD BIRD FEEDING · AMERICAN HISTORY · HEARTS · SNACK FOOD · SOUP · WEDDINGS · HOBBIES · EYE CARE · BLACK HISTORY · CHILDREN'S DENTAL HEALTH · EMBROIDERY · RESPONSIBLE PET OWNERS · BOOSTING SELF-ESTEEM · LIBRARY LOVERS · GRAPEFRUIT · SUCCESS · N.C. SWEET POTATOES

FEBRUARY						
S	M	T	W	T	F	S
				1	2	3	4
5	6	7	8	9	10	11
12	13	14	15	16	17	18
19	20	21	22	23	24	25
26	27	28				

MID-CONTINENT / CORN BELT & GULF

Brief spells of sunshine give the snow an icy crust, and may draw out hardy butterflies like mourning cloaks around Cincinnati. Warm days make the buds on maples swell. Large flocks of robins begin to return to northern areas, while the first songs of cardinals and chickadees may be heard. Spring peepers and frogs tentatively tune up their songs, which reach deafening peaks in March. American goldfinches molt in their first spring feathers. Woodcocks begin their nocturnal, aerial courtship flights. Tom turkeys gobble loudly in woodland patches around Little Rock. Sportfishing enthusiasts know this is the time when largemouth bass around Dallas move into shallow waters to spawn.

EAST COAST / ATLANTIC SEABOARD

A great season to find quiet and solitude on empty beaches, but an observant naturalist will note the growing signs of spring. Barred owls call whoo-cooks-for-you in the deep forest. Woodcocks are overhead at dusk sprinkling their twinkling courtship songs over the landscape. A few cautious spring peepers announce the approaching symphony of frog song. Mourning Doves speak of love in their soft mournful calls. In valley bottoms the maples turn red with the first flush of budding flowers. In Florida the wood storks are already on the nest even as deep snows still grip the countryside of Burlington. – *DL*

URBAN SURVIVAL STRATEGY:
HOW TO TELL YOUR PARENTS YOU'VE BEEN EXPELLED

Dear Mom & Dad

I've got something big I need to tell you. Your baby boy/girl is coming home! And not just for a visit this time—for good.

I've decided that college just isn't working out for me. And believe me, I've discussed this with the dean, my advisors, and several professors, so I'm very sure about it. In a while I'll probably be ready to try school again, at another college, one that is a better fit for my strengths and abilities. This just wasn't the right time and place.

Due to a whole tangle of academic rules and regulations—which were part of the problem, actually—you'll be getting a letter from the dean. Officially, of course, he has to come up with some important-sounding explanations and a lot of exaggerated descriptions of what I've done and not done, and reasons for not refunding the tuition.

But that's not important. What is important is that I miss you guys, and I think that it's best if I leave school now. After all, isn't college really about figuring out who you are and want to be?

I love you both very much. Please send a plane ticket and money to the local youth hostel, where I'm now staying. I look forward to seeing you soon.

Love,
Your son/daughter

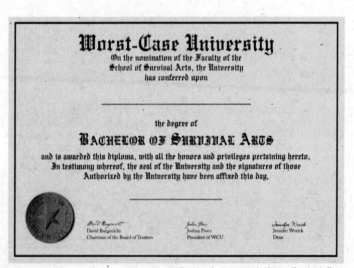

Worst-Case University
On the nomination of the Faculty of the
School of Survival Arts, the University
has conferred upon

the degree of

Bachelor of Survival Arts

and is awarded this diploma, with all the honors and privileges pertaining hereto. In testimony whereof, the seal of the University and the signatures of those Authorized by the University have been affixed this day.

David Borgenicht
Chairman of the Board of Trustees

Joshua Piven
President of WCU

Jennifer Worick
Dean

– From *The Worst Case Survival Handbook: College*

THE MODERN THINGS / *Bjork*

all the modern things, like cars and such, have always existed / they've
just been waiting in a mountain for the right moment / listening to
the irritating noises of dinosaurs and people / dabbling outside… /
…all the modern things have always existed, / they've just been
waiting / to come out, and multiply, and take over / it's their turn now.

Setsubun:
Bean-Throwing
Festival, *Japan*

Winterlude
begins, *Ottawa,
Canada
Feb. 3–19*

1947: Coldest
N. Amer. Temp
*-81°F Yukon
Territories,
Canada*

*Simone Weil,
mystic, b. 1909*

*Gertrude Stein,
writer, b.1874*

Silent gratitude
isn't very much
use to anyone.
— *Gertrude Stein*

☽ R. 10:03 am
☼ R. 7:30 am   S. 5:24 pm

♀ 4:18am
☽△♄ 1:32pm

FRIDAY · FEBRUARY 3 · 2006   **3**

1985: Torture
abolished by the
UN (signed but
still not ratified
by the U.S.)

1948:
Independence
Day, *Sri Lanka*

*Charles
Lindbergh,
aviator, b.1902*

*Betty Friedan,
feminist writer,
b.1921*

*Dietrich
Bonhoeffer,
theologian, b.1906*

I realized
that if I had to
choose, I would
rather have birds
than airplanes.
— *Charles
Lindbergh*

☽ R. 10:25 am   S. 12:14 am
☼ R. 7:29 am   S. 5:25 pm

SATURDAY · FEBRUARY 4 · 2006   **4**

**Four Chaplains
Sunday**

Superbowl XL
Detroit, MI

**Constitution
Day,** *Mexico*

Homstrom:
Burning of straw
men on poles:
winter's symbolic
departure,
Switzerland

1993: Family
Leave Bill passed

*Barbara Hershey,
actor, b.1948*

*Hank Aaron,
baseball player,
b.1934*

*John Jeffries,
physician/ mete-
orologist, b.1744*

Laughter is the
sun that drives
winter from the
human face.
— *Victor Hugo*

☽ R. 10:51 am   S. 1:30 am
☼ R. 7:28 am   S. 5:27 pm

First Quarter
12:29 am

☽△♀ 1:04am
☽☌♃ 4:01am
☽☌♂ 3:54pm

SUNDAY · FEBRUARY 5 · 2006   **5**

All times Central Time Zone, sun and moon rise and set Minneapolis, MN.

6 · MONDAY · FEBRUARY 6 · 2006

☽ R. 11:23 am S. 2:45 am
☉ R. 7:34 am S. 5:20 pm

☉☌♆ 12:33am

Pay a Compliment Day

Bob Marley, reggae musician, b.1945

Francois Truffaut, film director, b.1932

Zsa Zsa Gabor, celebrity, b.1919

Babe Ruth, baseball hero, b.1895

I have only one superstition. I touch all the bases when I hit a home run.
— Babe Ruth

7 · TUESDAY · FEBRUARY 7 · 2006

☽ R. 12:03 pm S. 3:55 am
☉ R. 7:25 am S. 5:30 pm

☽△♆ 11:11am
☽△☉ 2:07am

1974: Independence Day, Grenada

Chris Rock, comedian, b.1966

Laura Ingalls Wilder, writer, b.1867

Charles Dickens, writer, b.1812

Frederick Douglass, abolitionist, writer, b.1817

Train up a fig tree in the way it should go, and when you are old sit under the shade of it.
— Charles Dickens

8 · WEDNESDAY · FEBRUARY 8 · 2006

☽ R. 12:53 pm S. 4:57 am
☉ R. 7:24 am S. 5:31 pm

☽☌♆ 4:01am
☽△☿ 10:04am

1910: Boy Scouts of America est.

1999: Declared as the Warmest Year on Record

Nirvana Day, Buddhist

When love and skill work together, expect a masterpiece.
— John Ruskin

Paul Hawken, writer, b.1946

Lana Turner, actor, b.1921

Jules Verne, writer, b.1828

John Ruskin, critic, b.1819

9 · THURSDAY · FEBRUARY 9 · 2006

☽ R. 1:51 pm S. 5:49 am
☉ R. 7:23 am S. 5:33 pm

☽△♅ 6:17am
☽☌♀ 8:40pm
☽△♃ 11:01pm

Ashura, Islam

Alice Walker, writer, b.1944

Carole King, songwriter, b.1942

Gypsy Rose Lee, burlesque queen, b.1914

The animals of the planet are in desperate peril... Without free animal life I believe we will lose the spiritual equivalent of oxygen.
— Alice Walker

ESSENTIAL PLACE :: **OLD CUTLER ROAD, MIAMI, FLORIDA** :: To learn more, see pg. 274

© Photodisc

THE MINUTE I HEARD MY FIRST LOVE STORY
Rumi, translated by Coleman Barks

The minute I heard my first love story
I started looking for you,
not knowing how blind that was.

Lovers don't finally meet somewhere.
They are in each other all along.

Dr. Alex Comfort, writer, b.1920

Leontyne Price, singer, b.1927

Bertold Brecht, playwright, b.1898

Boris Pasternak, writer, b.1890

For the villainy of the world is great, and a man has to run his legs off to keep them from being stolen out fom underneath him.
— Berthold Brecht

☽ R. 2:55 pm   S. 6:30 am
☉ R. 7:21 am   S. 5:34 pm

FRIDAY · FEBRUARY 10 · 2006 10

St. Bernadette of Lourdes, *French*

1990: Nelson Mandela released from prison

Jennifer Aniston, actor, b.1969

Sheryl Crow, singer, b.1962

Thomas Edison, inventor, b.1847

Many of life's failures are people who did not realize how close they were to success when they gave up.
— Thomas Edison

☽ R. 4:02 pm   S. 7:02 am
☉ R. 7:20 am   S. 5:35 pm

☽ ☌ ♄ 12:07pm

SATURDAY · FEBRUARY 11 · 2006 11

Darwin Day

Lantern Festival, *China*

Triodion, *Orthodox Christian*

1909: NAACP founded

R. Buckminster Fuller, architect, engineer, b.1895

Charles Darwin, naturalist, b.1809

Abraham Lincoln, president, b.1809

We must... acknowledge as it seems to me, that a man with all his noble qualities... still bears in his bodily frame the indelible stamp of his lowly origin.
— Charles Darwin

☽ R. 5:09 pm   S. 7:27 am
☉ R. 7:18 am   S. 5:37 pm

Full Moon
10:44 pm

☽ ☌ ♅ 9:58am
☽ ☌ ☉ 11:45pm

SUNDAY · FEBRUARY 12 · 2006 12

All times Central Time Zone, sun and moon rise and set Minneapolis, MN.

13 MONDAY · FEBRUARY 13 · 2006

☽ R. 6:14 pm S. 7:48 am
☉ R. 7:17 am S. 5:38 am

☽ △ ♆ 3:54am

1945: Dresden fire bombing

1741: First magazine published in U.S.

Peter Gabriel, singer, b.1950

Grant Wood, painter, b.1892

Nothing takes the taste out of peanut butter quite like unrequited love.
— *Charles M. Schulz*

---

14 TUESDAY · FEBRUARY 14 · 2006

☽ R. 7:18 pm S. 8:05 am
☉ R. 7:15 am S. 5:40 pm

☽ ☌ ☿ 6:44am
☽ ☌ ♅ 7:16am
☿ ☌ ♅ 10:33am

1920: League of Women Voters founded

Ice T, rap artist, b.1960

Jack Benny, comedian, b.1894

Mary Ann Prout, activist, b.1801

Of all forms of caution, caution in love is perhaps the most fatal to true happiness.
— *Bertrand Russell*

St. Valentine's Day

---

15 WEDNESDAY · FEBRUARY 15 · 2006

☽ R. 8:21 pm S. 8:21 am
☉ R. 7:14 am S. 5:41 pm

☽ △ ♀ 1:05am
☽ △ ♂ 10:21pm

Kamakura: Snow Cave Festival, *Japan*

Matt Groening, cartoonist, 1954

Harold Arlen, songwriter, b.1905

Gallileo Gallilei, astronomer, b.1564

Susan B. Anthony, suffragist, b.1820

I've got the world on a string, / Sittin' on a rainbow, / Got the string around my finger, / What a world, what a life, / I'm in love!
— *Harold Arlen w/Ted Koehler*

Lupercalia: *Roman fertility festival*

---

16 THURSDAY · FEBRUARY 16 · 2006

☽ R. 9:25 pm S. 8:37 am
☉ R. 7:12 am S. 5:43 pm

1932: First patent issued for a tree: to James Markham for a peach tree

1918: Independence Day, *Lithuania*

John McEnroe, tennis player, b.1959

Edgar Bergen, ventiloquist, b.1903

Keeping your body healthy is an expression of gratitude to the whole cosmos — the trees, the clouds, everything.
— *Thich Nhat Hanh*

Three trees forming one crown

Nature Note: TREE FORMS IN WINTER

On a walk in the winter you can observe tree forms. Each species has its own characteristic shape. But you can also see how a group of two or more trees, perhaps of different species, have grown in concert to form one crown. Here you are observing a key element in life: when given a chance, nature forms unified wholes. – CH

L to R: White Ash *(Fraxinus americana)*, American Elm *(Ulmus americana)*, and Pignut Hickory *(Carya glabra)*

Drawing by Craig Holdrege

Notes

Corvus brachyrhyncos

Description: *Completely black*

Habitat: *Found everywhere in the United States*

Diet: *Omnivorous*

Size: *When fully grown, the American crow is 17 inches to 21 inches from tip of bill to tip of tail; wingspan is 26 inches.*

Age when independent: *Between 6 and 12 months*

Reproduction: *Usually crows lay four to six eggs and incubate them for about 18 days.*

Crows
Clever commuters, at home everywhere

To see them with their black bills, black eyes, and black feathers, it's easy to feel a vague frisson of fear from some primitive part of yourself. No wonder crows, and their cousin raven, have been seen as harbingers of disaster and death since the ancient Greeks. The goddess Athene was said to have turned the originally white birds black after one of them brought her bad news about her family. The crow is also the trickster in Native cultures—stealing food, upsetting village life, luring people into disaster—and thus encouraging the community to rally its forces and work together.

These highly intelligent and extremely sociable creatures would no doubt be surprised at the bad rap they've been getting all these years. True, they prey on songbirds and their nestlings, and get into garbage cans, pull up garden seedlings, and attack corn crops, but they also make 23 distinct vocalizations, keep down agricultural insect populations, and tend to solve problems in an eerily human way. It has recently been discovered that they know how to use tools.

Even though crows are widely distributed throughout the United States, we know strangely little about them. We think they're monogamous and mate for life, but we're not sure. The four to six young are tended in the nest until about one month old when they're ready to fledge. Then it appears that related birds flock together into the winter.

Crows have adapted well to city life, roosting in urban woodlots or parks by night and commuting to outlying agricultural areas during the day to feed. Their jet-black coloring makes it easy for them to recognize their own and it protects them at night.

If you've ever had a crow as a pet, you know how it can seem to look straight into your soul. It's another species, true, but a crow can fly over the boundary between human and animal like no other.

– Martha Coventry

With help from the Humane Society of the United States

© iStockPhoto

IS MY SOUL ASLEEP? / *Antonio Machado, translated by Robert Bly*
Is my soul asleep? / Have those beehives that labor / at night stopped? And the
water / wheel of thought, / is it dry, the cups empty, / wheeling, carrying only
shadows? / No my soul is not asleep. / It is awake, wide awake. / It neither
sleeps nor dreams but watches, / its clear eyes open, / far-off things, and
listens / at the shores of the great silence.

Bonten: Pole Festival, *Japan*

1974: *A Prairie Home Companion* nat'l premiere

Paris Hilton, heiress, b.1981

Michael Jordan, basketball player, b.1963

Jim Brown, football player, b.1936

I always turn to the sports pages first, which record people's accomplishments. The front page has nothing but man's failures.
— *Chief Justice Earl Warren*

☾ R. 10:30 pm   S. 8:52 am
☉ R. 7:11 am   S. 5:44 pm

☽△♆ 11:50am

FRIDAY · FEBRUARY 17 · 2006 **17**

Kuomboka: River Festival, *Zambia*

Satisfied Staying Single Day

1930: Planet Pluto discovered

Yoko Ono, artist, b.1933

Toni Morrison, writer, b.1931

Helen Gurley Brown, editor, b.1922

Ramakrishna, philosopher, b.1836

Unalloyed love of God is the essential thing. All else is unreal.
— *Ramakrishna*

☾ R. 11:38 pm   S. 9:09 am
☉ R. 7:09 am   S. 5:45 pm

☽△☉ 12:00pm

SATURDAY · FEBRUARY 18 · 2006 **18**

1942: Japanese internment began (lasted until 1945)

You see what power is — holding someone else's fear in your hand and showing it to them!
— Amy Tan

Amy Tan, writer, b.1952

Carson McCullers, writer, b.1917

Nicolaus Copernicus, astronomer, b.1473

☾   S. 9:30 am
☉ R. 7:08 am   S. 5:47 pm

☽△♅ 8:00am
☿△♃ 11:02pm

SUNDAY · FEBRUARY 19 · 2006 **19**

All times Central Time Zone, sun and moon rise and set Minneapolis, MN.

20 MONDAY · FEBRUARY 20 · 2006

☾ R. 12:48 am S. 9:55 am
☉ R. 7:06 am S. 5:48 pm

☽ ☌ ♃ 12:15am
☽ △ ☿ 12:23am

*Kurt Cobain,
singer / song-
writer, b.1967*

*Cindy Crawford,
model, b.1966*

*Ansel Adams,
photographer,
b.1902*

*Frederick
Douglass, d.1895*

Music has
charms to
soothe the
savage breast /
To soften rocks,
or bend a
knotted oak.
— *William
Congreve*

PRESIDENT'S DAY, U.S.

21 TUESDAY · FEBRUARY 21 · 2006

☾ R. 2:01 am S. 10:28 am
☉ R. 7:04 am S. 5:50 pm

Last Quarter
1:17 am

☽ ☌ ♂ 12:41am
☽ △ ♃ 8:37am

**1916: Battle of
Verdun:** Over
1 million men
killed, *France*

1925:
*New Yorker
Magazine*
debuts

*Charlotte
Church,
singer, b.1986*

*W.H. Auden,
poet/writer,
b.1907*

*Anais Nin, writer,
b.1903*

*Andres Segovia,
guitarist, b.1893*

Thousands have
lived without
love, not one
without water.
— *W.H. Auden*

22 WEDNESDAY · FEBRUARY 22 · 2006

☾ R. 3:13 am S. 11:13 am
☉ R. 7:03 am S. 5:51 pm

☽ ☌ ♆ 9:06pm

1956:
Montgomery,
Alabama, bus
boycott arrests

*Ishmael Reed,
writer, b.1938*

*Edna St.
Vincent Millay,
poet, b.1892*

*Arthur
Schopenauer,
philosopher,
b.1788*

*George
Washington, first
U.S. President,
b.1732*

All truth passes
through three
stages. First,
it is ridiculed.
Second, it is vio-
lently opposed.
Third, it is accep-
ted as being
self-evident.
— *Arthur
Schopenhauer*

23 THURSDAY · FEBRUARY 23 · 2006

☾ R. 4:19 am S. 12:13 pm
☉ R. 7:01 am S. 5:52 pm

1945:
Iwo Jima Day

*Veronica Webb,
model, b.1965*

*William Shirer,
writer, b.1904*

*W.E.B. DuBois,
educator, b.1868*

Believe in life!
Always human
beings will live
and progress to
greater, broader
and fuller life.
— *W.E.B. Du Bois*

© iStockPhoto

POSSIBILITY / *Charles Coe*

The new snow covers everything. / This morning the world was bathed / in that sharp-edged light / that comes in winter / after a storm blows through. / Outside my window, on the street below, / a small child, an electric blue bundle, / lets go of an adult's hand / to charge headfirst / into a towering snowdrift… / …People who pass each other without speaking / each morning on the way to work / are now laughing and shoveling together, / butts of Mother Nature's joke…

1855: U.S. Court of Claims established for cases against the government

1955: Pact of Baghdad between Iraq and Turkey signed

Steven Jobs, founder Apple Computer, b.1955

George Harrison, musician, b.1943

Be a yardstick of quality. Some people aren't used to an environment where excellence is expected.
— Steven Jobs

☽ R. 5:15 am S. 1:27 pm
☉ R. 7:00 am S. 5:54 pm

☽ ☌ ♀ 7:23pm

FRIDAY · FEBRUARY 24 · 2006 24

1964: Cassius Clay (Muhammad Ali) becomes heavyweight champ

Edward Gorey, artist, 1925

Adelle Davis, nutritionist, b. 1904

Enrico Caruso, singer, b.1873

Auguste Renoir, painter, b.1841

Painting: The art of protecting flat surfaces from the weather and exposing them to the critic.
— Ambrose Bierce

☽ R. 5:59 am S. 2:50 pm
☉ R. 6:58 am S. 5:55 pm

☽ △ ♂ 11:33am
☽ ☌ ♄ 2:24pm

SATURDAY · FEBRUARY 25 · 2006 25

Transfiguration, *Christian*

1848: Communist Manifesto published

1919: Grand Canyon Nat'l. Park established

Johnny Cash, singer, songwriter, b.1932

"Buffalo Bill" Cody, frontiersman, b.1846

Victor Hugo, writer, b.1802

Life's greatest happiness is to be convinced we are loved.
— Victor Hugo

☽ R. 6:33 am S. 4:18 pm
☉ R. 6:56 am S. 5:56 pm

☽ ☌ ♆ 10:04am

SUNDAY · FEBRUARY 26 · 2006 26

All times Central Time Zone, sun and moon rise and set Minneapolis, MN.

MARCH

FEB 19 - MAR 20

Pisces

MARCH BIRTHSTONE
Aquamarine

MAR 21 - APR 19

Aries

MARCH FLOWER
Tulip

INNER BALANCE BECOMES PROGRESS
Challenges: apathy, inertia, covetousness

The days and nights approach each other in duration, balancing perfectly at the vernal equinox. Anything could happen. Despite the persistent winds and omnipresent mud (if you live in the country), promise is in the air. "The wind blows where it wants and you can hear the sound of it but you cannot tell where it is coming from and where it is going. So it is with those who are born of the spirit." March is the Martian month. We feel braced. Our great warrior's heart opens to the world in love. There's a warmth in the air. Nature begins her journey outward into beauty. Our senses awaken. Cosmic being flows into us. Winter's inwardness, its contraction, begins to turn inside out. Responding, we begin to flow outward, to expand. "March is the month of expectation," wrote Emily Dickinson. – *CB*

WEST COAST / PACIFIC MARITIME

With spring just around the corner, migratory animals start moving in great numbers. Gray whales are northbound along the coast, males leading the way, followed by mothers with brand-new calves. Ducks and geese nervously bunch up then fly north in long V's stretching across the sky. Swallows make their long-awaited arrival at Mission San Juan Capistrano on March 19 (so the legend says). At every city park both native and introduced squirrels are making a ruckus with the wild chases that characterize their courtship. Rough-skinned newts are still breeding in some areas.

MOUNTAIN REGION / BASIN & RANGE

Wander into the wooded hills of Texas this month and you are likely to hear the insistent gobbling of male wild turkeys calling from their lofty perches. By the end of the month, spring truly arrives in the desert as the sweet cooing of white-winged doves fills neighborhoods around San Antonio. To the north, cottonwoods, poplars, and willows erupt in lacy displays of flowering catkins even before setting leaves. In colder areas, American robins scan for worms on freshly thawed soil. Winter often makes a final hard showing this month with lengthy icy storms.

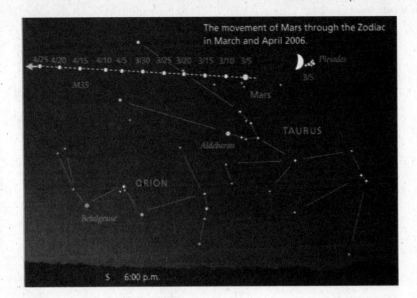

The movement of Mars through the Zodiac in March and April 2006.

4/25 4/20 4/15 4/10 4/5 3/30 3/25 3/20 3/15 3/10 3/5

Pleiades
3/5

M35

Mars

TAURUS

Aldebaran

ORION

Betelgeuse

S   6:00 p.m.

LOOK UP:

6 First quarter Moon, 2:16 PM

12 Mercury at inferior conjunction (not visible)

14 Full Moon, 5:36 PM
Penumbral lunar eclipse favoring Africa, Europe, and Asia; greatest eclipse occurs at 5:47 PM

20 Vernal equinox, 12:27 PM

22 Last quarter Moon, 1:11 PM

25 Venus at greatest western elongation (46° 32')

29 Total solar eclipse favoring Africa, Europe, and Asia; The path of totality crosses the eastern Mediterranean and the Black Sea; Greatest eclipse occurs at 4:11 PM New Moon, 4:16 PM

MARCH						
S	M	T	W	T	F	S
			1	2	3	4
5	6	7	8	9	10	11
12	13	14	15	16	17	18
19	20	21	22	23	24	25
26	27	28	29	30	31	

MARCH IS THE MONTH FOR:

AMERICAN RED CROSS · HELPING SOMEONE SEE · EYE DONORS · ETHICS · HONOR SOCIETIES · MIRTH · UMBRELLAS · IRISH-AMERICAN HERITAGE · LISTENING · MUSIC IN OUR SCHOOLS · KIDNEYS · WOMEN'S HISTORY · FROZEN FOODS · PLAYING THE RECORDER · TALKING WITH YOUR TEEN ABOUT SEX · OPTIMISM · YOUTH ART

MID-CONTINENT / CORN BELT & GULF

Toads join the nightly chorus of calling frogs. By day, the chorus is dominated by red-winged blackbirds that reside in every marshy patch. In the forests, there are a rash of early wildflowers like spring beauties and buttercups taking advantage of the abundant sunshine before the forest trees leaf out. Some trees also flower at this time; look for dogwoods and buckeyes around Dallas. Once the ground begins to warm up look for blue-bellied lizards courting with energetic bobs on fence posts. Overhead, broad-winged hawks undertake their migration back from South America. Snow-covered slopes near the Canadian border echo with the howls of wolves this month.

EAST COAST / ATLANTIC SEABOARD

Eastern screech owls begin courting in wooded Boston suburbs. Open ponds resound with the odd quacks of calling wood frogs and writhe with balls of mating spotted salamanders. Early spring violets and anemones bloom in Great Smoky Mountains National Park. Large flocks of American robins begin to wander north. A few courageous purple martins follow the line of melting snow north across the states. Groups of ducks and geese bunch up in restless preparation for migration. Armadillos in Florida are out with their new babies in tow, and the largemouth bass fishing season opens. – DL

27 MONDAY · FEBRUARY 27 · 2006

☾ R. 7:00 am S. 5:44 pm
☉ R. 6:54 am S. 5:58 pm

New Moon
6:31 pm

☾☌☉ 7:31pm
☾☌♅ 9:40pm

Elizabeth Taylor, actor, b.1932

Joanne Woodward, actor, b.1930

Marian Anderson, singer, b.1897

Rudolf Steiner, philosopher, educator, b.1861

Henry W. Longfellow, poet, b.1807

We judge ourselves by what we feel capable of doing, while others judge us by what we have already done.
— Henry Wadsworth Longfellow

28 TUESDAY · FEBRUARY 28 · 2006

☾ R. 7:23 am S. 7:08 pm
☉ R. 6:53 am S. 5:59 pm

☾△♃ 10:35am
☾☌♀ 11:03pm

Kalevala Day, Finland

Shrove Tuesday, Christian

1986: Olaf Palme, Prime Minister of Sweden, assassinated

Rae Dawn Chong, actor, 1961

Bernadette Peters, actor, b.1948

Michel de Montaigne, writer, b. 1553

No man is exempt from saying silly things; the mischief is to say them deliberately.
— Michel de Montaigne

1 WEDNESDAY · MARCH 1 · 2006

☾ R. 7:44 am S. 8:31 pm
☉ R. 6:51 am S. 6:01 pm

☉☌♅ 6:02am
☾△♄ 1:01pm

Ash Wednesday: Lent Begins, Christian

1872: Yellowstone Nat'l Park established

1999: U.N. Land Mine Ban

1961: Peace Corps established

Harry Belafonte, singer, b.1927

Robert Lowell, poet, b.1917

Ralph Ellison, writer, b.1914

When I discover who I am, I'll be free.
— Ralph Ellison

2 THURSDAY ·MARCH 2 · 2006

☾ R. 8:04 am S. 9:52 pm
☉ R. 6:49 am S. 6:02 pm

☿ 3:28pm
☾△♆ 11:36pm

1925: Highway numbers introduced

1899: Mount Ranier Nat'l Park established

Theodore Geisel "Dr. Seuss," writer, b.1904

Tom Wolfe, writer, b.1931

Mikhail Gorbachev, statesman, b.1931

Unless someone like you cares a whole awful lot, nothing is going to get better. It's not.
— Dr. Seuss

Health Notes:
FRENCH OLIVE OIL REMEDY FOR WINTER-DRY HAIR

According to the French, *L'almanach de la maison,*—an almanac of household, beauty, and health tips as well as recipes and gardening information—you can revitalize your winter-dry hair by rubbing it with olive oil and letting it rest for 30 minutes. Then wash it with a mild shampoo, rinse, and rinse a second time with lemon juice. If you nourish your hair this way every other week until spring, you'll have the hair of a French woman; as for her style and chic, you're on your own. — MC
— *For information on* L'almanach de la maison, *see page 276*

BIRTHDAY: *February 27, 1807*
HENRY WADSWORTH LONGFELLOW, Poet

Longfellow, the second of eight children, was born in Portland, Maine, and it is the wilderness and the sea that supplies his poetry, like *Song of Hiawatha, Evangeline,* and *The Courtship of Miles Standish*, with their images and meaning. He wrote poems as a young man during his years at Bowdoin College and then turned to academic writing and translation as a professor of modern languages at Harvard. His store of languages included French, Spanish, Italian, Dutch, Danish, Icelandic, Swedish, and some Finnish.

In 1854, at the age of 47, a skilled lecturer known for his courtesy to his students, he left academia and pursued his literary ambitions with remarkable publishing success.

In July 1861, his wife Fanny's dress caught fire while she was using sealing wax. She ran to Longfellow whose efforts to beat out the flames left him critically burned; Fanny died hours later. The scars on Longfellow's face made shaving impossible and from then on, he was the bearded man with the mane of white.

He finished his last poem, *The Bells of San Blas*, on March 15, 1882. "Out of the shadows of night / The world rolls into light; it is daybreak everywhere." He died nine days later on March 24, 1882. – *KM*

TO DO:

TAPPING YOUR BACK YARD MAPLE (or Box Elder) TREES

You don't have to have a sugarbush in the woods to get the sheer joy of taking the thin, watery sap of a maple tree and, as if by magic, transforming it into naturally thick, sweet, maple syrup. You just need one tree in your back yard and a lot of enthusiasm and energy. And there's no better way to be part of an ancient Native American springtime ritual.

The sugar maple will yield the most syrup—its sap has the highest sugar content—but other members of the Acer family, like red, silver, or even an ashed leaf maple, better known as the box elder, will also provide a perfectly wonderful syrup-making experience.

Before you start, you should know that you'll need about 30 parts sap to make one part syrup. Ideally, one backyard tree over the course of the sap-run should give you about 30 gallons, yielding one gallon of syrup. The sap begins running when the temperature is below freezing at night and at least 40 degrees during the day—sometime between late February and late March, depend-ing on where you live. It usually runs for four to six weeks.

Making syrup is a simple evaporation process, but it can be tricky business. The best thing to do before you start, both for the how-to of tapping and cooking and the advantage of collected wisdom, is to read Noel Perrin's *Making Maple Syrup* or Rink Mann's *Backyard Sugarin'.* They are terrific books for the beginning syrup maker and fun to read.

If you can't quite handle the syrup-making deal, tap your tree any way. A well-placed tap won't hurt the tree and it will fill in by itself in a few years. The fresh, cool sap is a spring tonic, perfect for chasing away the winter blues. Collect it each day, store it in your refrigerator, and drink each batch within about four days. The slightly sweet sap is delicious all by itself, or use it to make tea to sip as you watch spring come to your backyard.

– MC

For more information on the books mentioned, see page 276.

A VALLEY LIKE THIS / *William Stafford*

…What can a person do to help bring back the world? / We have to watch it, and then look at each other. / Together we hold it close and carefully / save it, like a bubble that can disappear / if we don't watch out. / Please think about this as you go on. Breathe on the world. / Hold out your hands to it. When mornings and evenings / roll along, watch how they open and close, how they / invite you to the long party that your life is.

World Day of Prayer, *Interfaith* Jean Harlow, actor, b.1911 Ring Lardner, Sr., writer, 1885 Alexander Graham Bell, inventor, b.1847	A good many young writers make the mistake of enclosing a stamped, self-addressed envelope, big enough for the manuscript to come back in. This is too much of a temptation to the editor. — *Ring Lardner*	☾ R. 8:26 am S. 11:12 pm ☉ R. 6:47 am S. 6:03 pm 	FRIDAY · MARCH 3 · 2006 **3**

1789: U.S. Constitution went into effect Miriam Makeba, singer, b. 1932 Casimir Pulaski, Polish hero of US revolutionary war, b. 1747 Antonio Vivaldi, composer, b. 1675	*Henry the Navigator, explorer, b.1394* Springtime is the land awakening. The March winds are the morning yawn. — *Lewis Grizzard*	☾ R. 8:51 am ☉ R. 6:46 am S. 6:05 pm ♃ 1:02pm ☽ ☌ ♃ 1:48pm	SATURDAY · MARCH 4 · 2006 **4**

78th Academy Awards **1770:** Boston Massacre Andy Gibb, singer, b.1958 William Blackstone, first Boston settler, b.1595 Gerhardus Mercator, cartographer, b.1512	A man should hear a little music, read a little poetry, and see a fine picture every day of his life, in order that worldly cares may not obliterate the sense of the beautiful which God has implanted in the human soul. — *J.W. Goethe*	☾ R. 9:22 am S. 12:30 am ☉ R. 6:44 am S. 6:06 pm	SUNDAY · MARCH 5 · 2006 **5**

All times Central Time Zone, sun and moon rise and set Minneapolis, MN.

6 MONDAY · MARCH 6 · 2006

☾ R. 10:00 am S. 1:44 am
☼ R. 6:42 am S. 6:07 pm

First Quarter
6:16 pm

☾♂♂ 12:55am
☾△♆ 7:27pm

1836: Fall of the Alamo

Shaquille O'Neal, basketball player, b.1972

Gabriel Garcia Marquez, writer, b.1928

Elizabeth Barrett Browning, poet, b.1806

Michelangelo, artist, b.1475

Measure not the work until the day's out and the labor done.
— *Elizabeth Barrett Browning*

7 TUESDAY · MARCH 7 · 2006

☾ R. 10:47 am S. 2:51 am
☼ R. 6:40 am S. 6:09 pm

☾♂ᵒ♆ 11:09am

1869: Suez Canal Opens

1876: Alexander Graham Bell receives a patent for the telephone

1933: Monopoly invented

Denyce Graves, singer, b.1965

Luther Burbank, naturalist, b.1849

I believe in God, only I spell it Nature.
— *Frank Lloyd Wright*

8 WEDNESDAY · MARCH 8 · 2006

☾ R. 11:43 am S. 3:46 am
☼ R. 6:39 am S. 6:10 pm

☾△♅ 3:17am

Int'l Working Women's Day

1913: U.S. income tax begins

1917: Russian Revolution begins

1983: President Reagan calls USSR an "evil empire"

Lyn Redgrave, actor, b.1943

Cyd Charisse, dancer, actor, b.1923

Kenneth Grahame, writer, b.1859

Oliver Wendell Holmes, Jr, jurist, abolitionist, b.1841

9 THURSDAY · MARCH 9 · 2006

☾ R. 12:46 pm S. 4:31 am
☼ R. 6:37 am S. 6:11 pm

☾△☉ 6:16am
☾△♃ 6:26am
☉△♃ 8:14am
☾△☿ 3:41

1841: U.S. Supreme Court rules Amistad slaves are free

1959: Barbie doll debuts

Bobby Fischer, chess master, b.1943

Yuri Gagarin, cosmonaut, b.1934

Irene Papas, actor, b.1926

Amerigo Vespucci, navigator, b.1451

Every artist dips his brush in his own soul, and paints his own nature into his pictures.
— *Henry Ward Beecher*

A surprising way to gently cook a chicken to retain all its inherent deliciousness.

Recipe: PERFECT POACHED CHICKEN

Fill a large soup kettle with water and bring to a boil. (An 8-quart pot, two thirds filled with water, works well for a 2 1/2- to 3-pound bird.) When the water boils, place a whole, cleaned chicken into it. The water will stop boiling. Bring it to a boil again, then cover the pot and turn off the heat. Leave the chicken in the pot and the pot on the stove. After 1 hour the chicken is done. The chicken is now ready to serve, or cool and use for salads, terrines, etc.

— *Adapted from* The Frugal Gourmet *by Jeff Smith, Ballantine Books, 1984*

© Dover Books

THE MAN IN THE MOON / *Billy Collins*

… tonight as I drive home over these hilly roads / I see him sinking behind
strands of winter trees / and rising again to show his familiar face. / And when
he comes into full view over open fields / he looks like a young man who has
fallen in love / with the dark earth, / a pale bachelor, well-groomed and full
of melancholy, / his round mouth open / as if he had just broken into song.

1862:
Paper Money
Issued in U.S.

Courage is the
ladder on which
all the other
virtues mount.
— *Clare Booth
Luce*

*Sharon Stone,
actor, b.1958*

*James Herriot,
veterinarian,
b.1916*

*Clare Booth Luce,
playwright, b.1903*

*Harriet Tubman,
abolitionist, d.1913*

☽ R. 1:52 pm   S. 5:05 am
☉ R. 6:35 am   S. 6:13 pm

FRIDAY · MARCH 10 · 2006 **10**

☽ ☌ ♀ 1:43pm
☽ ☌ ♄ 2:42pm

**Johnny
Appleseed Day**
1824: Bureau of
Indian Affairs
established

1918: Start of
Flu Pandemic

Tina Louise,
actor, b.1934

Ralph Abernathy,
activist, b.1926

*Lawrence Welk,
bandleader,
b.1903*

*Robert Paine,
jurist, b.1731*

In all things of
nature there is
something of
the marvelous.
— *Aristotle*

☽ R. 2:59 pm   S. 5:32 am
☉ R. 6:33 am   S. 6:14 pm

SATURDAY · MARCH 11 · 2006 **11**

♀ ☌ ♄ 2:31am
☽ ☌ ♆ 6:04pm
☉ ☌ ☿ 9:43pm

Canberra Day,
Australia

James Taylor,
singer, songwriter,
b.1948

Jack Kerouac,
writer, b.1922

Charlie "Bird"
Parker,
musician, d.1953

This is the story
of America.
Everybody's
doing what they
think they're
supposed to do.
— *Jack Kerouac*

☽ R. 4:05 pm   S. 5:54 am
☉ R. 6:31 am   S. 6:15 pm

SUNDAY · MARCH 12 · 2006 **12**

☽ △ ♆ 10:39am

All times Central Time Zone, sun and moon rise and set Minneapolis, MN.

13 MONDAY · MARCH 13 · 2006

☾ R. 5:10 pm S. 6:12 am
☉ R. 6:29 am S. 6:16 pm

☽ ☌ ♅ 4:37am

1781:
Planet Uranus
Discovered

1887:
Earmuffs
patented

Age is…wisdom,
if one has
lived one's
life properly.
— Miriam
Makeba

*Donella
Meadows,
writer, b.1941*

*Patricia W.
Amicone, mid-
wife, b.1938*

*L. Ron Hubbard,
scientologist,
b.1911*

*Susan B.
Anthony,
suffragist, d.1906*

14 TUESDAY · MARCH 14 · 2006

☾ R. 6:13 pm S. 6:29 am
☉ R. 6:27 am S. 6:18 pm

Full Moon
5:35 pm

☽ ☌ ☿ 8:02am
☿ △ ♃ 4:10pm
☽ ☌ ☉ 6:36pm

Purim, *Jewish*
**Fallas de
San Jose,** *Spain*
1743:
First Town
Meeting,
Fanueil Hall,
Boston

*Diane Arbus,
photographer,
b.1923*

*Albert Einstein,
physicist, b.1879*

*George Frederick
Handel, composer,
b.1681*

God may be
subtle, but He
isn't plain mean.
— Albert Einstein

PENUMBRAL LUNAR ECLIPSE
5:47PM

15 WEDNESDAY · MARCH 15 · 2006

☾ R. 7:17 pm S. 6:44 am
☉ R. 6:26 am S. 6:19 pm

Ides of March

1917: Czar
Nicolas II of
Russia abdicates
his throne

*Andrew Jackson,
7th U.S. president,
b.1767*

*Caroline Herschel,
astronomer,
b.1750*

*Julius Caesar,
d.44BC*

Friends, Romans,
countrymen, lend
me your ears;
I come to bury
Caesar, not to
praise him.
The evil that
men do lives
after them;
The good is
oft interred
with their bones.
— William
Shakespeare

16 THURSDAY · MARCH 16 · 2006

☾ R. 8:22 pm S. 6:59 am
☉ R. 6:24 am S. 6:20 pm

Quarter
x:xx UT

☽ △ ♀ 1:01am
☽ △ ♂ 10:17am
☽ △ ♆ 7:36pm

**Freedom of
Information
Day**

St. Urho's Day
**Return
of the Curlews,**
Umatilla, OR

*Isabelle Huppert,
actor, b. 1953*

*Ruth Bader-
Ginsberg,
jurist, b.1933*

*Joseph Campbell,
mythologist,
b.1904*

*James Madison,
4th president,
b.1751*

We must be
willing to get rid
of the life we've
planned, so as to
have the life that
is waiting for us.
— Joseph
Campbell

© California Board of Tourism

BIRTHDAY: March 14, 1879
ALBERT EINSTEIN, Physicist

Albert Einstein, an only child and a slow learner, was born in Ulm, Germany, to a featherbed salesman and his wife. He had little interest in formal schooling but eventually earned a doctorate in physics. Not interested in the demands of academia, he went to work as a clerk in the Bern, Switzerland, patent office where he could work on physics in the afternoons. During 1905, what is now called his "miracle year," he wrote a series of five seminal papers. One dealt with special relativity, and one introduced the world's most familiar equation: $E=mc^2$.

When Einstein moved to Berlin in 1914 to direct the Kaiser Wilhelm Institute for Physics, a campaign was begun to discredit him, but he survived it. Later, during Hitler's reign, Einstein's work was described as "Jewish physics" opposed to the preferred "Aryan physics." Seeing the damage Hitler was doing, Einstein renounced his German citizenship and revised his views on pacifism, believing Hitler could only be stopped by force. The FBI kept a record of Einstein's activities and recommended denying him immigration to the U.S., but Einstein moved to New Jersey, and Princeton University, and became a permanent U.S. citizen in 1940. In 1952, the government of Israel asked him to be its second president, an honor he declined.

As a personality, Einstein was noted for his kindness and amiability. Quirky and practical, he minimized his wardrobe—buying identical sets of clothing—so that he wouldn't have to think about what to wear. Though he had been an early advocate of nuclear energy, on April 5, 1955, he signed a letter to protest nuclear tests and bombs. Days later, on April 18, 1955, he died in his sleep. *– KM*

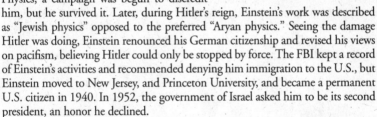

My religion consists of a humble admiration of the illimitable superior spirit who reveals himself in the slight details we are able to perceive with our frail and feeble mind.

I know not with what weapons World War III will be fought, but World War IV will be fought with sticks and stones.

It would be possible to describe everything scientifically, but it would make no sense; it would be without meaning, as if you described a Beethoven symphony as a variation of wave pressure.

Common sense is the collection of prejudices acquired by age 18.

URBAN SURVIVAL STRATEGY:
HOW TO SOUND INTELLIGENT: USEFUL NAMES

PHILOSOPHERS
Aristotle: AIR-is-tot-el
Confucius: Con-FYOO-shes
Descartes: Day-CART
Erasmus: Ir-ASS-muss
Kant: KAHNT
Kierkegaard: KEER-ki-guard
Machiavelli:
    Mock-ee-ah-VEL-lee
Nietzsche: NEE-cha
Plato: PLAY-toe
Sartre: SAR-tra
Schopenhauer:
    SHOW-pen-how-er
Socrates: SOCK-ra-tease
Sun Tzu: SOON ZOO

ARTISTS
Botticelli: Bot-i-CHEL-lee
Brueghel: BROY-gull
Cézanne: Say-ZON
Chagall: Sha-GALL
Dalí: DA-lee

Da Vinci: Da VIN-chee
Degas: Day-GA
Delacroix: Del-a-QUA
Duchamp: Doo-SHAN
Gauguin: Go-GAN
Gentileschi:
    Gen-tile-LESS-ski
Hokusai: HOE-koo-sigh
Klee: CLAY
Magritte: Ma-GREET
Manet: Ma-NAY
Matisse: Ma-TEESE
Miró: Mee-ROW
Monet: Moan-NAY
Munch: MOONK
Raphael: RA-fay-el
Renoir: REN-war
Rodin: ROW-dan
Seurat: Se-RA
Toulouse-Lautrec:
    Too-LOOSE Lo-TRECK
Van Dyck: Van DIKE
Van Gogh: Van GO

NOVELISTS, POETS,
    AND PLAYWRIGHTS
Aristophanes:
    Air-is-TOF-an-ees
Baudelaire: Bode-a-LARE
Brontë: BRON-tay
Camus: Cam-OO
Capote: Ca-PO-tee
Cervantes: Sir-VON-tease
Cocteau: Cock-TOE
Dante: DON-tay
Dostoyevsky:
    Dos-ta-YEF-ski
Dumas: Doo-MA
Flaubert: Flow-BEAR
García Márquez:
    Gar-SEE-ah MAR-kez
Goethe: GER-ta
Kafka: COUGH-ka
Kundera: Coon-DUH-ra
Maugham: MOM
Molière: Mole-YARE
Nabokov: Na-BOK-ov
Poe: PO
Pynchon: PIN-chin
Rabelais: RAB-a-lay
Rushdie: RUSH-dee
Shakespeare: SHAKE-spear
Solzhenitsyn:
    Soul-jen-EAT-zen
Yeats: YATES

– From *The Worst Case Survival Handbook: College*

THE MAN WATCHING / *Rainer Maria Rilke, translated by Robert Bly*
I can tell by the way the trees beat, after / so many dull days, on my worried /
windowpanes / that a storm is coming, / and I hear the far-off fields saying
things / I can't bear without a friend, / I can't love without a sister…/
…What we choose to fight is so tiny! / What fights with us is so great! /
If only we would let ourselves be dominated / as things do by some
immense storm, / we would become strong too, and not need names…

Cherry Blossom Festival begins, *U.S.*

Leslie Ann Down, actor, b.1954

Rudolf Nureyev, dancer, b.1938

Nat "King" Cole, singer, b.1919

You've got to do your own growing, no matter how tall your grandfather was.
— *Irish Proverb*

☾ R. 9:29 pm S. 7:16 am
☉ R. 6:22 am S. 6:22 pm

FRIDAY · MARCH 17 · 2006 **17**

St. Patrick's Day

Flag Day, *Aruba*

Natl. Quilting Day

1931: Electric razor debuted

Irene Cara, singer, b.1959

Wilson Pickett, singer, b.1941

John Updike, writer, b.1932

Edgar Cayce, clairvoyant, b.1877

Any activity becomes creative when the doer cares about doing it right, or better.
— *John Updike*

☾ R. 10:38 pm S. 7:35 am
☉ R. 6:20 am S. 6:23 pm

☽△♅ 4:48pm
☽△☿ 11:36pm

SATURDAY · MARCH 18 · 2006 **18**

Nat'l. Day of Oil, *Iran*

Swallows return to San Juan Capistrano, *Yearly since 1776*

Glenn Close, actor, b.1947

Ornette Coleman, saxophonist, b.1930

William Jennings Bryan, orator, politician, b.1860

Wyatt Earp, lawman, b.1848

I have come to the conclusion that politics are too serious a matter to be left to the politicians.
— *Charles De Gaulle*

☾ R. 11:50 pm S. 7:58 am
☉ R. 6:18 am S. 6:24 pm

☽☌♃ 5:56am

SUNDAY · MARCH 19 · 2006 **19**

All times Central Time Zone, sun and moon rise and set Minneapolis, MN.

20 MONDAY · MARCH 20 · 2006

☾ S. 8:28 am
☉ R. 6:16 am S. 6:26 pm

☽△☉ 2:54am
☽△♄ 12:21pm

1602: Dutch East India Company est.; lasted 196 years

1852: *Uncle Tom's Cabin* published

Holly Hunter, actor, b. 1958

Spike Lee, film-maker, b.1957

Henrik Ibsen, writer, b.1828

Ovid, writer, b.43 BC

Chance is always powerful. Let your hook be always cast; in the pool where you least expect it, there will be a fish.
— *Ovid*

SPRING EQUINOX
12:26PM

---

21 TUESDAY · MARCH 21 · 2006

☾ R. 1:01 am S. 9:08 am
☉ R. 6:14 am S. 6:27 pm

☽☍♂ 10:46am

Noruz: New Day, *Zoroastrian*

Nau-Roz: New Year, *Baha'i*

Ostara, *Wicca*

1965: Selma, Alabama civil rights march

Matthew Broderick, actor, b.1962

Rosie O'Donnell, actor, b.1962

Johann Sebastian Bach, composer, b.1685

Acting is a form of deception, and actors can mesmerize themselves almost as easily as an audience.
— *Leo Rosten*

---

22 WEDNESDAY · MARCH 22 · 2006

☾ R. 2:08 am S. 10:00 am
☉ R. 6:13 am S. 6:28 pm

Last Quarter
1:11 pm

☽☌Ψ 4:48am

1945: Arab League formed, *Cairo*

United Nations World Day for Water

George Benson, singer, b.1943

Billy Collins, poet, b.1941

Karl Malden, actor, b.1914

Let us be grateful to people who make us happy: They are the charming gar-deners who make our souls blossom.
— *Marcel Proust*

---

23 THURSDAY · MARCH 23 · 2006

☾ R. 3:07 am S. 11:06 am
☉ R. 6:11 am S. 6:29 pm

1775: Patrick Henry declares, "Give me liber-ty or give me death."

U.N. World Meteorological Day

Akira Kurosawa, director, b.1910

Joan Crawford, actor, b.1908

Erich Fromm, psychoanalyst and writer, b.1900

There is no meaning to life except the meaning man gives to his life by the unfolding of his powers.
— *Erich Fromm*

one year's growth

terminal budscars

Drawing by Craig Holdrege

Nature Note: TWIG AGE

The end twigs of tree branches can tell you their age. Twigs of many tree species have $1/8$" to $1/4$" bands that go around the twig—terminal bud scars. The space between two scars indicates a year's growth. If you count the number of spaces between scars you can discern the twig's age. The drawing shows the end twig of a beech tree branch. This little twig is seven years old, but only five inches long! – *CH*
Drawing of beech twig (American beech; *Fagus grandifolia*)

HORSES IN SPRING / *Connie Wanek*

Beware too much happiness! / The horses paused suspiciously before the open
door, / snorting and stamping, while sunlight poured / onto the cold cement.
They smelled snow / in the barn's shadow, mud along the south wall, /
matted grass in the thawing pasture. / Their nostrils flared and their ears /
lay back, then pricked forward, far forward, / and they stretched their
elegant necks / as if the world were offering them a slice of sweet apple, /
or something even more pure, on an open palm…

1989: Exxon Valdez oil spill

Lara Flynn Boyle, actor, b.1970

Wilhelm Reich, psychologist, b.1897

Harry Houdini, magician, b.1874

William Morris, poet, b.1834

In the state of nature…all men are born equal, but they cannot continue in this equality. Society makes them lose it, and they recover it only by the protection of the law.
— *Charles de Montesquieu*

☽ R. 3:54 am S. 12:24 pm
☉ R. 6:09 am S. 6:31 pm

FRIDAY · MARCH 24 · 2006 24

☽ ☌ ♂ ☌ ♄ 9:52am

Annunciation, *Christian*

Old New Year's Day, was on this date until 1751

Magha Puja Day, *Buddhist*

Danica Patrick, racecar driver, b.1982

Sarah Jessica Parker, actor, b.1965

Aretha Franklin, singer, b.1942

Elton John, singer/songwriter, b.1947

Béla Bartók, composer, b.1881

No opera plot can be sensible, for people do not sing when they are feeling sensible.
— *W. H. Auden*

☽ R. 4:30 am S. 1:47 pm
☉ R. 6:07 am S. 6:32 pm

SATURDAY · MARCH 25 · 2006 25

☉ △ ♄ 2:03am
☿ 8:42am
♂ △ ♅ 8:52am
☽ ☌ 9:22pm
☽ ☌ ♆ 9:38pm
☽ △ ♂ 10:08pm

1979: Anwar Sadat *(Egypt)* and Mencheim Begin *(Israel)* sign peace accord

Khordadsal, *Zoroastrian*

Keira Knightly, actor, b.1985

Diana Ross, singer, b.1944

Erica Jong, writer, b.1942

Victor Frankl, psychiatrist, b.1905

Robert Frost poet, b.1874

Beethoven, composer, d.1827

Happiness makes up in height for what it lacks in length.
— *Robert Frost*

☽ R. 4:59 am S. 3:11 pm
☉ R. 6:05 am S. 6:33 pm

SUNDAY · MARCH 26 · 2006 26

♀ ☌ ♆ 1:29am
♀ △ ♂ 9:40pm

All times Central Time Zone, sun and moon rise and set Minneapolis, MN.

27 MONDAY · MARCH 27 · 2006

☽ R. 5:23 am S. 4:35 pm
☉ R. 6:03 am S. 6:34 pm

☽ ☌ ♅ 11:05am
☽ ☌ ☿ 1:01pm
☽ △ ♃ 8:25pm

1866: President Andrew Johnson vetoes a civil rights bill which later passes as the 14th Amendment

Mariah Carey, singer, b.1970

Sarah Vaughan, singer, b.1924

Gloria Swanson, actor, b.1899

Wilhelm Roentgen, scientist, b.1845

True hope is swift, and flies with swallow's wings; Kings it makes gods, and meaner creatures kings.
— *William Shakespeare*

28 TUESDAY · MARCH 28 · 2006

☽ R. 5:44 am S. 5:58 pm
☉ R. 6:01 am S. 6:36 pm

☽ △ ♄ 10:35pm

Teacher's Day, *Czech Republic*

1979: Three Mile Island nuclear accident

Reba McEntire, singer, 1954

Dianne Wiest, actor, b.1948

Mario Vargas Llosa, writer, b.1936

Ours is a world of nuclear giants and ethical infants. If we continue to develop our technology without wisdom or prudence, our servant may prove to be our executioner.
— *Omar Bradley*

29 WEDNESDAY · MARCH 29 · 2006

☽ R. 6:05 am S. 7:20 pm
☉ R. 5:59 am S. 6:37 pm

New Moon
4:15 am

☽ ☌ ☉ 5:15am
♆ 7:39am

Youth Day, *Taiwan*

It is dangerous for a national candidate to say things that people might remember.
— *Eugene McCarthy*

Eric Idle, comic, actor, b.1943

Judith Guest, writer, b.1936

Pearl Bailey, singer, b.1918

Eugene McCarthy, politician, b.1916

TOTAL SOLAR ECLIPSE
4:11AM

30 THURSDAY · MARCH 30 · 2006

☽ R. 6:26 am S. 8:43 pm
☉ R. 5:58 am S. 6:38 pm

☽ △ ♆ 10:41am

Ramayan begins, *Hindu*

1858: Pencil patented

Eric Clapton, guitarist, b.1945

Sean O'Casey, playwright, b.1880

Vincent Van Gogh, painter, b.1853

Maimonides, physician, b.1135

Every action of our lives touches on some chord that will vibrate in eternity.
— *Sean O'Casey*

APRIL

MAR 21 - APR 19

Aries

APRIL BIRTHSTONE
Diamond

APR 20 - MAY 20

Taurus

APRIL FLOWER
Sweet Pea

© PhotoDisc

DEVOTION BECOMES THE FORCE OF SACRIFICE
Challenges: malice, defenselessness

April is the month of golden Aphrodite (Etruscan apru), modest, gentle goddess of love and beauty. She is the spirit of youth in everything. We find ourselves drawn outdoors again, into the breeze-filled air sitting warmly on our senses. We ray out into the light, the sun-illumined world. There are wider dawns and deeper twilights. As nature stirs, new life germinates within us. Outside, "wild puffing of emerald trees and flame-filled bushes" (D.H. Lawrence); within, an awakening sense of self in seeing. The intensity of nature's splendor all but overwhelms us. Light – liquid, yellow, and caressing, is poured over everything. Surrendering to its embrace with spontaneous devotion, our hearts are at peace. We, too, are reborn. We sense our freedom to do the good, to know the true, and to love the beautiful. We feel one with the world. – *CB*

WEST COAST / PACIFIC MARITIME

Everything unfolds at once in April! First there are countless blooming flowers carpeting nearly every hillside and valley. Lilies, monkeyflowers, violets, and more flamboyant blossoms can be found. By mid month, warblers, vireos, and flycatchers that have spent winter in Mexico and Central America are arriving in full force around Portland. Look overhead for another show of the season's exuberance – there you will see hawks circling, tumbling, and calling excitedly in the thrill of their beautiful aerial courtship dances. A few common loons in full breeding plumage can still be seen along the coast, but most have already flown north to nest. Pacific treefrog tadpoles gather at the shorelines of ponds.

MOUNTAIN REGION / BASIN & RANGE

Depending on the year and location, warming days equal spectacular runoff as snows melt on lower mountain slopes. Newly budding willow thickets along these waterways greet the first songbirds as they migrate north from Mexico and Central America. In the Reno area fantastic numbers of songbirds follow these moist slivers of green as they snake across the lonely desert. Around Albuquerque it's already getting warm enough that rattlesnakes start to emerge from their wintering dens to sun themselves on adjacent rocky slopes. Shorebirds move north in huge numbers, stopping to feed on mudflats around Great Salt Lake.

TAURUS

Mars

Moon

High in the sky
Mars and the Moon
have a rendezvous.

Aldebaran

Pleiades

W   April 2, after 9 p.m.

With binoculars, a clear morning sky,
and luck you can find Mercury standing
in line with Venus and the Moon just
before sunrise.

Venus

PISCES

Moon

Mercury

E   April 25, 6 a.m.

LOOK UP:

5   First quarter Moon,
    7:01 PM

8   Mercury at
    greatest western
    elongation (27° 46')

13 Full Moon, 11:41 AM

20 Last quarter Moon,
    10:29 PM

22 Lyrid meteor shower peaks;
    Moon interferes

27 New Moon, 1:45 PM

APRIL IS THE MONTH FOR:

ALCOHOL AWARENESS ·
ANIMAL CRUELTY
PREVENTION ·
COUPLE APPRECIATION ·
FLORIDA TOMATOES ·
HOLY HUMOR · PECANS ·
SELF-PUBLISHING ·
AMATEUR RADIO · POETRY ·
CUSTOMER LOYALTY ·
STRAW HATS · INT'L TWIT
AWARDS · WOODWORKING ·
AUTISM AWARENESS ·
CHILD ABUSE PREVENTION ·
GRILLED CHEESE

APRIL

S	M	T	W	T	F	S
						1
2	3	4	5	6	7	8
9	10	11	12	13	14	15
16	17	18	19	20	21	22
23/30	24	25	26	27	28	29

MID-CONTINENT / CORN BELT & GULF

Maple Sugar Making Month is the time
when syrupy sap and sweet love begins
to flow again. Flowers erupt into full splendor.
Mightiest of all may be the vast carpets of blue-
bonnets that turn the Texas landscape into a
piece of sky. The combination of warmth and rain
draws out spring mushrooms like morels. Box turtles in search of mates may be seen crossing
roads. Ruby-throated hummingbirds arrive like
jewels on fire. The coastline south of Houston
welcomes exhausted waves of songbirds that
have just crossed the Gulf of Mexico from Central
America. Northern regions start to see the break-
up of ice but late killing frosts are still possible.

EAST COAST / ATLANTIC SEABOARD

Spring's full splendor begins with shows of gor-
geous bluebells outside Washington, D.C. Along
the Blue Ridge Parkway, hillsides are splashed
with the colors of blooming shadbush, redbud,
and dogwood. Poke around under leaves to find
wild ginger flowers. Spring peepers and
American toads fill nights with their raucous
singing. Sunny days draw alligators out to
sun themselves in southern marshes. Purple
martins swoop back and forth in search of flying
insects. Bluebirds guard boxes where they are
building their nests. Great horned owls feed their
downy youngsters, maybe even in the same trees
where fox squirrels have their leafy nests. – DL

© iStockPhoto

CIVILIZING IDEA:

GREEN CITIES
The nation-state is dinosaur dead — long live the green world city.

Forget watered-down global treaties like the Kyoto Accords—green cities are the next environmental frontier. Last June, betting that "cities have more in common with each other than national governments," according to Randy Hayes, director of sustainability for Oakland under mayor Jerry Brown, some 50 mayors from São Paulo to Stockholm signed the San Francisco Urban Environmental Accords *(wed2005.org/3.0.php)*. The accords lay out 21 concrete steps to a greener city ranging from enacting strict new green construction guidelines to protecting critical habitat and urban wildlife corridors.

The global green cities movement has been quietly building for several decades as city officials have experimented with new approaches to issues like transportation, land use, urban food systems,

and alternative energy. The San Francisco accords are voluntary but include firm targets—like increasing renewable energy use to 10 percent within seven years, and reducing per capita water consumption by 10 percent by 2015.

There's no guarantee that these ideals will succeed where so many international treaties have failed, but mayors are more accountable to their constituents than presidents and parliaments. And if we're ever to address environmental decline and other crucial challenges of the 21st century, cities, not nations, may lead the way.

– Leif Utne

A longer version of this article appeared in *Utne* magazine (September/October 2005)

© PhotoDisc

WARMER / *Martha Collins*

In the store this morning, iris for sale.
Next door in the restaurant, fading poinsettias.

1959: Dalai Lama flees Tibet	Marge Piercy, writer, b.1936	☾ R. 6:50 am S. 10:04 pm ☉ R. 5:56 am S. 6:40 pm	**FRIDAY · MARCH 31 · 2006 31**

1889: Eiffel Tower Opens

Cesar Chavez, labor leader, b.1927

Charlotte Brontë, writer, d.1855

A ruffled mind makes a restless pillow.
— Charlotte Bronte

René Déscartes, philosopher, b.1596

☽ ♂ ♃ 9:39am

1970: TV Ads for Cigarettes banned	Debbie Reynolds, actor, 1932	☾ R. 7:18 am S. 11:23 pm ☉ R. 5:54 am S. 6:41 pm	**SATURDAY · APRIL 1 · 2006 1**

NCAA Basketball: Final Four, *April 1-3, Indianapolis*

Abraham Maslow, psychologist, b.1908

Alberta Hunter, singer, b.1895

All we know is still infinitely less than all that remains unknown.
— William Harvey

William Harvey, physician, b.1578

APRIL FOOL'S DAY

1513: Juan Ponce de Leon reaches Florida	Emile Zola, writer, b.1840	☾ R. 8:54 am ☉ R. 6:52 am S. 7:42 pm	**SUNDAY · APRIL 2 · 2006 2**

Emmylou Harris, singer, b.1947

Camille Paglia, writer, b.1947

Hans Christian Andersen, writer, b.1805

Casanova, philanderer, b.1725

Being born in a duck yard does not matter, if only you are hatched from a swan's egg.
— H.C. Andersen

DAYLIGHT SAVINGS TIME
BEGINS 2:00AM

All times Central Time Zone, sun and moon rise and set Minneapolis, MN.

---

3 · MONDAY · APRIL 3 · 2006

☾ R. 9:39 am S. 1:36 am
☉ R. 6:50 am S. 7:43 pm

☽△♆ 5:08am
☽♂♂ 2:18pm
☽♂♆ 7:09pm
☽△♀ 9:25pm

1860: Pony Express established

Sizdar-Bedah: Outdoor Day, *Iran*

NCAA Basketball Finals *Indianapolis*

Jane Goodall, conservationist, b.1934

Marlon Brando, actor, b.1924

Washington Irving, writer, b.1783

It is better for civilization to be going down the drain than to be coming up it.
— Henry Allen

---

4 · TUESDAY · APRIL 4 · 2006

☾ R. 10:33 am S. 2:38 am
☉ R. 6:48 am S. 7:45 pm

☿△♃ 10:24am

1968: Martin Luther King, Jr. assassinated

David Blaine, magician, b.1973

Muddy Waters, singer, b.1915

Maya Angelou, writer, b.1928

Dorothea Dix, social reformer, b.1802

One isn't necessarily born with courage, but one is born with potential. Without courage, we cannot practice any other virtue with consistency. We can't be kind, true, merciful, generous, or honest.
— Maya Angelou

---

5 · WEDNESDAY · APRIL 5 · 2006

☾ R. 11:35 am S. 3:28 am
☉ R. 6:46 am S. 7:46 pm

First Quarter
7:01 am

☽△♅ 1:21am
♄ 7:54am
☽△♃ 10:27am
☽△☿ 12:20pm

Tomb Sweeping Day, *Taiwan*

Gregory Peck, actor, b.1916

Bette Davis, actor, b.1908

Spencer Tracy, actor, b.1900

Booker T. Washington, educator, b.1856

Success is to be measured not so much by the position that one has reached in life as by the obstacles which he has overcome.
— Booker T. Washington

---

6 · THURSDAY · APRIL 6 · 2006

☾ R. 12:41 pm S. 4:07 am
☉ R. 6:45 am S. 7:47 pm

☽♂♄ 8:10pm

Ram Navami, *Hindu*

1830: Mormon Church founded

1896: First Modern Olympics, Athens, Greece

Merle Haggard, musician, b.1937

Ram Dass, writer, b.1931

Elizabeth Barrett Browning, poet, b.1806

Raphael, painter, b.1483

Earth's crammed with heaven.
— Elizabeth Barrett Browning

SKYLINE, CLEVELAND, OHIO

© iStockPhoto

ON COMMONWEALTH AVENUE AND BRATTLE STREET

Diana Der-Hovanessian

Last year the magnolias flared
like candelabra bursting into flame
quivering as if they had never bloomed
before, astonishing sight everywhere...

1994: Rwanda Massacres Remembrance Day

1948: W.H.O. founded

Jack Black, actor, b.1969

Jerry Brown, politician, b.1938

Billie Holiday, singer, b.1915

William Wordsworth, poet, b.1770

Poetry is the spontaneous overflow of powerful feelings.
— *William Wordsworth*

☾ R. 1:48 pm S. 4:36 am
☉ R. 6:43 am S. 7:48 pm

FRIDAY · APRIL 7 · 2006 **7**

WORLD HEALTH DAY

Hana Matsui: Flower Festival, *Japan*

Ryan White, AIDS vicitm, d.1990

Patricia Arquette, actor, b.1968

Betty Ford, 39th 1st Lady, b.1918

Barbara Kingsolver, writer, b.1955

Kofi Annan, UN Sect'y. Gen'l, b.1938

All that we are is the result of what we have thought.
— *Buddha*

☾ R. 2:55 pm S. 5:00 am
☉ R. 6:41 am S. 7:50 pm

☽△☉12:04am
☽☌♅ 2:13am
☽☌♆ 3:22am
☽△♆ 5:19pm

SATURDAY · APRIL 8 · 2006 **8**

BUDDHA'S BIRTHDAY
Siddhartha "the enlightened one"

Palm Sunday, *Christian*

1865: U.S. Civil War ends

1866: Civil Rights Bill passed

Paulina Porizkova, model, b.1965

Paul Robeson, singer, athlete, b.1898

J. William Fullbright, politician, b.1905

Dave van Ronk, singer, songwriter, b.1905

Charles Baudelaire, writer, b.1821

Beware of all enterprises that require new clothes.
— *H. D. Thoreau*

☾ R. 4:00 pm S. 5:19 am
☉ R. 6:39 am S. 7:51 pm

☽☌♀ 7:26am

· SUNDAY · APRIL 9 · 2006 **9**

All times Central Time Zone, sun and moon rise and set Minneapolis, MN.

10 MONDAY · APRIL 10 · 2006

☾ R. 5:03 pm S. 5:36 am
☼ R. 6:37 am S. 7:52 pm

☽☍♅ 2:11am
☽☍☿ 11:56pm

Siblings Day

1942: Bataan Death March

1849: Safety Pin patented

There are no hopeless situations; There are only people who have grown hopeless about them.
– Clare Boothe Luce

Steven Seagal, actor, b.1951

Paul Theroux, writer, b.1941

Clare Boothe Luce, journalist, b.1903

Samuel Hahnemann, physician, b.1755

Hugo Grotius, theologian, b.1583

11 TUESDAY · APRIL 11 · 2006

☾ R. 6:07 pm S. 5:51 am
☼ R. 6:36 am S. 7:53 pm

Mawlid an Nabi, Birth of the Prophet, *Islam*

1945: Liberation of Buchenwald

1968: Civil Rights Act signed into law

Barbershop Quartet Day

Ellen Goodman, columnist, b.1941

Louise Lasser, actor, 1939

Jane Matilda Bolin, 1st black female judge b.1908

Get up, stand up / Stand up for your rights / Get up, stand up / Never give up the fight.
– Bob Marley

12 WEDNESDAY · APRIL 12 · 2006

☾ R. 7:12 pm S. 6:06 am
☼ R. 6:34 am S. 7:55 pm

Passover begins, *Jewish*

Lord's Evening Meal, *Jehovah's Witness*

1934: "The Big Wind" 231mph *Mount Washington, NH*

1955: Polio vaccine

1961: 1st Man in Space, *Yuri Gagarin USSR*

David Letterman, comic, b.1947

Lionel Hampton, jazz artist, b.1908

Franklin D. Roosevelt, d.1945

If one does not know to which port one is sailing, no wind is favorable.
– Seneca

13 THURSDAY · APRIL 13 · 2006

☾ R. 8:19 pm S. 6:23 am
☼ R. 6:32 am S. 7:56 pm

Full Moon
11:40 am

☽△♆ 3:24am
☽☍☉ 11:40am

Maundy Thursday, *Christian*

1962: Silent Spring pub. by Rachel Carson

Al Green, singer, b.1946

Eudora Welty, writer, b.1909

Butch Cassidy, outlaw, b.1866

Thomas Jefferson, 3rd U.S. President, b.1743

I tried to resist his overtures, but he plied me with symphonies, quartettes, chamber music, and cantatas.
– S.J. Perelman

To Do: NATURALLY DYED EASTER EGGS

If you've only dyed Easter eggs with artificial colors, it's time to experience the subtle, sensual tones of natural dyes. Orange peel makes light yellow; grated beets, pink; grated red cabbage, blue; pear peels, yellow-green; onion skins, deep orange-brown; cranberries, purple-red. Put ingredients (the more you have, the richer the color) in a nonaluminum pan with the eggs, a teaspoon or two of vinegar, and enough water to completely cover the eggs. Boil for 15 minutes. When eggs are dry, rub with vegetable oil to make them shine. —*MC*

BIRTHDAY: April 13, 1743
THOMAS JEFFERSON,
President

A lawyer with a lisp and a dislike for court practice, Thomas Jefferson abandoned the law at the rise of the American Revolution. At only 33, he was chosen as a drafter of the Declaration of Independence and became its author. Six feet two and a half inches tall, sandy-haired, freckled, enigmatic, and versatile, he was a statesman, political philosopher, slave owner, architect; scientist, agriculturist, horticulturist, revolutionary, ambassador, archaeologist, and author. Jefferson was the first U.S. secretary of state and our third president, responsible for the Louisiana Purchase in 1803. He died, fittingly, on July 4, 1826. He wrote his epitaph and insisted that only his words and none other be inscribed:

> Here was buried
> Thomas Jefferson
> Author of the Declaration of Independence
> Of the State of Virginia for Religious Freedom
> & Father of the University of Virginia

– KM

Our liberty depends on the freedom of the press and that cannot be limited without being lost.

The two principles on which our conduct towards the Indians should be founded are justice and fear. After the injuries we have done them they cannot love us.

What country ever existed a century and a half without rebellion? And what country can preserve its liberties if its rulers are not warned from time to time that their people preserve the spirit of resistance?

I have often thought that nothing would do more extensive good at small expense than the establishment of a small circulating library in every county, to consist of a few well-chosen books, to be lent to the people of the county under regulations as would secure their safe return in due time.

If a nation expects to be ignorant and free, in a state of civilization, it expects what never was and never will be.

 *Notes*

© iStockPhoto

APRIL CHORES / *Jane Kenyon*

When I take the chilly tools / from the shed's darkness,
I come / out to a world made new / by heat and light. / The snake
basks and dozes / on a large flat stone. / It reared and scolded
me / from raking too close to its hole. / Like a mad red brain /
the involute rhubarb leaf / thinks its way up / through loam.

Baisakhi, *Sikh*

1865: Abraham Lincoln assassinated

1890: OAS formed

1828: First Webster's Dictionary

Loretta Lynn, singer, b.1935

GOOD FRIDAY
Christian

Sarah Michelle Gellar, actor, b.1977

Arnold Toynbee, historian, b.1889

Anne Sullivan, teacher, b.1866

The mind is the great lever of all things.
— Daniel Webster

☽ R. 9:28 pm   S. 6:41 am
☉ R. 6:30 am   S. 7:57 pm

☽△♂ 12:21am
☽△♀ 6:34pm

FRIDAY · APRIL 14 · 2006 **14**

1912: Sinking of the Titanic

1955: First McDonald's opens

Thomas Szasz, writer, b.1920

Bessie Smith, singer, b.1894

Thomas Hart Benton, artist, b.1889

INCOME TAX DAY

Henry James, writer, b.1843

Leonardo da Vinci, Renaissance man, b.1452

The hardest thing in the world to understand is the income tax.
— Albert Einstein

☽ R. 10:40 pm   S. 7:03 am
☉ R. 6:29 am   S. 7:58 pm

☽△♅ 1:26am
☽☌♃ 7:33am

SATURDAY · APRIL 15 · 2006 **15**

Ellen Barkin, actor, b.1954

Margarethe, Queen of Denmark, b.1940

Merce Cunningham, dancer, b.1919

Charlie Chaplin, actor, b.1889

EASTER SUNDAY
Christian

Spring makes its own statement, so loud and clear that the gardener seems to be only one of the instruments, not the composer.
— Geoffrey B. Charlesworth

☽ R. 11:52 pm   S. 6:31 am
☉ R. 6:27 am   S. 8:00 pm

☽△☿ 9:33am
☉△♆ 2:34pm
☽△♄ 5:42pm

SUNDAY · APRIL 16 · 2006 **16**

All times Central Time Zone, sun and moon rise and set Minneapolis, MN.

17 MONDAY · APRIL 17 · 2006

☽ S. 8:08 am
☉ R. 6:25 am S. 8:01 pm

1932: Haile Selassie ends slavery, *Ethiopia*

1961: Bay of Pigs invasion

1991: 1st time the Dow Jones tops 3,000

Thornton Wilder, author, b.1897

Isak Dinesen, writer, b.1885

J.P. Morgan, banker, b.1837

Money is better than poverty, if only for financial reasons.
— *Woody Allen*

18 TUESDAY · APRIL 18 · 2006

☽ R. 1:01 am S. 8:56 am
☉ R. 6:23 am S. 8:02 pm

♀☌♅ 4:43am
☽☌♆ 10:11am
☽△☉ 1:41pm
☽☍♂ 9:28pm

1775: Paul Revere's Midnight Ride

1906: San Francisco earthquake and fire kills over 500

Conan O'Brien, comedian b.1963

Susan Faludi, writer, b.1959

Albert Einstein, physicist, d.1955

Clarence Darrow, attorney, b.1857

Imagination is more important than knowledge.
— *Albert Einstein*

19 WEDNESDAY · APRIL 19 · 2006

☽ R. 2:02 am S. 9:57 am
☉ R. 6:22 am S. 8:04 pm

☿△♄ 4:08pm

1932: Herbert Hoover suggests 5-day work week

1993: Branch Davidian fire, *Waco, TX*

1775: Battle of Lexington & Concord: Start of American Revolution

Kate Hudson, actor, b.1979

Ashley Judd, actor, b.1968

Tim Curry, actor, b.1946

Roger Sherman, statesman, b.1721

I want all my senses engaged. Let me absorb the world's variety and uniqueness.
— *Maya Angelou*

20 THURSDAY · APRIL 20 · 2006

☽ R. 2:51 am S. 11:09 am
☉ R. 6:20 am S. 8:05 pm

Last Quarter
10:28 pm

♀△♃ 10:45am

Lima Bean Respect Day

1999: Columbine High School tragedy

Carmen Electra, actor, b.1972

Luther Vandross, singer, b.1951

Jessica Lange, actor, b.1949

Adolf Hitler, dictator, b.1889

The evil of the world is made possible by nothing but the sanction you give it.
— *Ayn Rand*

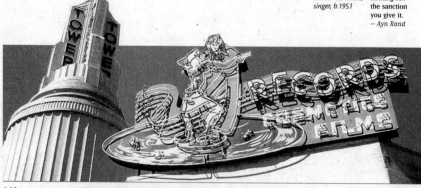

OUR MOTHER / *Susan Griffin*

At the center of the earth there is a mother… / Some of us have decided / this mother cannot hear all of us / in our desperate wishes. / Here, in this time, / our hearts have been cut into small chambers / like ration cards / and we can no longer imagine every / morsel nor each tiny / thought at once, / as she still can… / Do you think we are not all hearing and speaking / at the same time? / Our mother is somber. / She is thinking. / She puts her big ear / against the sky / to comfort herself. / Do *this*. She calls to us, / Do *this*.

Holy Friday, *Orthodox Christian*	*Rollo May, psychologist, b.1909*	☾ R. 3:30 am S. 12:29 pm ☉ R. 6:18 am S. 8:06 pm
Ridvan, *Baha'i*	*John Muir, naturalist, b.1838*	
Kartini Day, *Indonesia*	*Charlotte Brontë, writer, b.1816*	
1837: 1st kindergarten established	In health the flesh is graced, the holy enters the world.	☽ ☌ ♄ 4:51am
Friedrich Froebel, educator, b.1782	the world.	
Iggy Pop, singer, b.1947	— Wendell Berry	

FRIDAY · APRIL 21 · 2006 21

1955: Congress orders all U.S. coins to bear the motto *In God We Trust*	*Germaine de Stael, salonnaire, b.1766*	☾ R. 4:01 am S. 1:50 pm ☉ R. 6:17 am S. 8:07 pm
	Henry Fielding, novelist, b.1707	
John Waters, filmmaker, b.1946	A truly elegant taste is generally accompanied with excellency of heart.	☽ ☌ ♆ 6:16am
Jack Nicholson, actor, b.1937		
Charles Mingus, bassist, b.1922	— Henry Fielding	

SATURDAY · APRIL 22 · 2006 22

EARTH DAY
est. 1970

St. George's Day, *England*	*Bernadette Devlin, Irish civil rights leader, b.1947*	☾ R. 4:25 am S. 3:11 pm ☉ R. 6:15 am S. 8:09 pm
Easter Sunday, *Orthodox*	*Miguel Cervantes, writer, d.1616*	
William Shakespeare, b.1564 d.1616	If all the year were playing holidays; To sport would be as tedious as to work.	☽ △ ♂ 8:56am ☽ ☌ ⛢ 10:07pm
Valerie Bertinelli, actor, b.1960		
Michael Moore, filmmaker, 1954	— William Shakespeare	

SUNDAY · APRIL 23 · 2006 23

All times Central Time Zone, sun and moon rise and set Minneapolis, MN.

24 MONDAY · APRIL 24 · 2006

☾ R. 4:47 am S. 4:31 pm
☉ R. 6:13 am S. 8:10 pm

☽△♃ 1:03am
☽☌♀ 8:54am

1800: Library of Congress established

1898: Spain declares war on U.S.

Turn-Off Your TV Week

Barbra Streisand, singer, b.1942

Shirley MacLaine, actor, b.1934

Robert Penn Warren, 1st U.S. poet laureate, b.1905

Robert Bailey Thomas, Founder of "The Farmer's Almanac", b.1766

Income tax returns are the most imaginative fiction being written today.
— Herman Wouk

25 TUESDAY · APRIL 25 · 2006

☾ R. 4:07 am S. 5:52 pm
☉ R. 6:12 am S. 8:11 pm

☽△♄ 8:58am

Anzac Day, *Australia, New Zealand*

1915: Battle of Gallipoli

Holocaust Day, *Israel*

1901: First License Plates issued

Meadowlark Lemon, athlete, b.1932

Ella Fitzgerald, singer, b.1917

Oliver Cromwell, English statesman, revolutionary, b.1599

Better than a thousand hollow words, is one word that brings peace.
— Buddha

26 WEDNESDAY · APRIL 26 · 2006

☾ R. 5:27 am S. 7:13 pm
☉ R. 6:10 am S. 8:12 pm

☽☌☿ 12:20am
☽△♆ 8:44pm

1986: Chernobyl nuclear reactor disaster

1937: Massacre, Guernica *Spain*

I don't know why we are here, but I'm pretty sure that it is not in order to enjoy ourselves.
— Ludwig Wittgenstein

Ludwig Wittgenstein, philosopher, b.1889

Frederick Law Olmstead, landscaper, b.1822

John James Audubon, artist, b.1785

Charles Richter, scientist, b.1900

27 THURSDAY · APRIL 27 · 2006

☾ R. 5:49 am S. 8:34 pm
☉ R. 6.09 am S. 8:14 pm

New Moon 12:44 pm

☽☌☉ 2:44pm

1805: U.S. Marines attack Tripoli

August Wilson, playwright, b.1945

Anouk Aimee, actor, b.1932

Ulysses Grant, general, b.1822

Edward Gibbon, historian, b.1737

Ferdinand Magellan, explorer, b.1521

History is indeed little more than the register of the crimes, follies and misfortunes of mankind.
— Edward Gibbon

Nature Note: BIRD ALARM CALLS

Songbirds are everywhere in the urban environment. When you're listening to their songs, you may hear them suddenly shift to repeated chipping or shrieking. These calls show that something has come upon the scene that unsettles the birds. If you look on high you may see the cause—a hawk soaring close above the tree crowns in search of its next meal. —*David Lukas*

© Dover Books

Dandelion
A virtuous weed

Taraxacum officinale

Habitat: *Sunny or partly shaded areas*

Range: *Northern hemisphere world-wide, temperate zone.*

Plant Family: *Composite or Aster family, all of which have flower heads consisting of many individual flowers. Other members of the family include: daisies, thistles, asters, ragweed, chamomile, and calendula.*

Uses: *Young dandelion leaves are great for salads, the bitter tea of older leaves and roots makes a good digestive aid.*

Name: *The French "dent de lion" means lion's tooth, perhaps in reference to the jagged teeth of the leaves. "Taraxacum" derives from the Greek: "taraxos" means disorder and "akos" means remedy.*

Mythology: *The Greek Goddess Hecate fed Theseus dandelions for 30 days to give him strength to defeat the Minotaur.*

As Emerson said, "a weed is a plant whose virtues have not yet been discovered." The virtues of the dandelion are many. Prolific and hardy, its bursting yellow flower heads, rising above a rosette of sharply toothed leaves, can be found almost everywhere in the urban environment. The dandelion-sea of yellow in yet unmowed parks and lawns provides a feast for the winter weary eye. Thrusting its way up between cracks in the expanses of concrete and asphalt, a single dandelion can remind us of the power of life in a seemingly barren world. Dandelions won't be held back.

When you look closely at its flower, you'll discover many (one to two hundred) yellow ribbons. You might think that they are petals, like those of a rose or tulip. But no, each one is a complete tiny flower, so that the dandelion blossom as a whole is in fact a bouquet of tiny flowers! This development of a super-flower made of individual flowers represents the pinnacle of flower differentiation in the plant kingdom.

When the sun shines, dandelion flower heads open in the morning and close again in the afternoon. When clouds shield them from the sun they close up, as if they were saying: we are of the sun and for the sun. Dandelion flowers attract bees and nearly a hundred species of other insects that enjoy their nectar. This is a true gift of plant to animal, since—remarkably—their seeds can develop without fertilization. One day the flower head opens as a white feathery globe. The parachute-bearing seeds drift off to some new place just waiting for a dandelion to take root.

– Craig Holdrege

Springtime Rituals, Lore & Celebration

BELTANE

RAVEN GRIMASSI

Book cover: *Beltane* by Raven Grimassi (Llewellyn Books, ISBN 1567182836)

CELEBRATE: Sunday, April 30
BELTANE

Beltane—the ancient Celtic union of goddess and god, water and light. All fires are extinguished at sunset on Beltane Eve, the midpoint between the spring equinox and the summer solstice. In blackness of night, bonfires are struck from standing stone or drilled from sacred oak. Flames leap, youth jump over them...lovers melt into the night.

At dawn the sun dances! At the height of spring Beltane begins, celebrating all that is powerful and sensual in nature. The morning dew brings beauty to the face it bathes, the well's first water heals. Herbs make potent cures. Hawthorn flowers are everywhere. Atop the phallic Maypole, a womb-like inverted basket is hung with ribbons. Dancers of each sex grasp the ribbons, facing one another. The dancers weave, the ribbons intertwine: new being springs from sacred union. Lovers adorn each other with these ribbons, and tie them to sacred trees. Conception induces a liminal moment of chaos between old and new as the Lord and Lady of Misrule preside over all. At sunset the holy space is closed until next year, when springtime juices rise and the revelry begins once more.

Easter celebrations borrow from the pre-Christian, pagan Beltane. The ancient Celts saw joy and life as one with suffering, death, and rebirth. So it is in the Easter tradition that Mary, the mother, watches her son suffer and die. Then he is sealed in a cave, for the way of resurrection lies in deepest earth. Mary Magdalene is the first to find him risen, for Christ is also the lover, and only with the beloved can new life be sown.

– John Miller

We were there last night when
the dark drew down:
we set the bonfires leaping.
Then we vanished in the heather
and we couldn't be found until
the dawn came creeping.

– Celtic rock group Annwn

I THINK THAT I SHALL NEVER SEE... / *Jim Heynen*
... Any second now: exultant branches! / a choir of leaves! Oh!

1789: Mutiny on the Bounty

1945: Mussolini executed

Penelope Cruz, actor, b.1974

Jay Leno, comedian, b.1950

Alice Waters, restaurateur, b.1944

Mifflin Gibbs, judge, b.1828

James Monroe, 5th president, b.1758

Money is the opposite of the weather. Nobody talks about it, but everybody does something about it.
— *Rebecca Johnson*

☽ R. 6:15 am   S. 9:56 pm
☉ R. 6:07 am   S. 8:15 pm

☽ ☌ ♃ 3:05am

FRIDAY · APRIL 28 · 2006 28

Greenery Day, *Japan*

Uma Thurman, actor, b.1970

Dale Earnhardt, NASCAR driver, b.1951

Emperor Hirohito, b.1901

Duke Ellington, musician, b.1899

As the poet said, 'Only God can make a tree' — probably because it's so hard to figure out how to get the bark on.
— *Woody Allen*

☽ R. 6:48 am   S. 11:13 pm
☉ R. 6:06 am   S. 8:16 pm

SATURDAY · APRIL 29 · 2006 29

ARBOR DAY

Beltane, *Wicca*

Walpurgisnacht Witch's Night, *Europe*

St. James the Great Day, *Orthodox Christian*

Kirsten Dunst, actor, b.1982

Annie Dillard, writer, b.1945

William Lilly, almanac compiler, b.1602

Anyone who interprets or defines your rights controls your destiny.
— *Paul Walter*

☽ R. 7:29 am
☉ R. 6:04 am   S. 8:17 pm

☽ △ ♆ 3:34pm

SUNDAY · APRIL 30 · 2006 30

All times Central Time Zone, sun and moon rise and set Minneapolis, MN.

MAY

APR 20 - MAY 20

Taurus

MAY BIRTHSTONE
Emerald

© PhotoDisc

MAY 21 - JUN 20

Gemini

MAY FLOWER
Lily

EQUILIBRIUM Becomes Progress
Challenges: apathy, inertia, covetousness

The soul expands into the cosmos. The sun is fully released from the bondage of winter. The shackles of our lower self seem to drop away. This is "the charming month of May," named for the Earth goddess Maia. Children dance around the Maypole. The Green Man, decked in bright, tender leaves, runs wildly through the woods. May 1, Beltane, the Celtic festival of sacred fire, marks the opening of light and life. Thus spring turns toward summer. The Queen of the Fairies rides out on her white horse. Flowers everywhere reach for the heavens. Butterflies, hummingbirds return. In all this riot of life, growth, and color, we must strive for balance. With the equilibrium comes a certain dreaminess, but also increased intuitive powers. We feel prescient, no longer the captive of the brain. It is as if, in our soul-spiritual parts, we, too, can put forth shoots and leaves and flowers, returning to the heavens the life forces we have transformed through the winter. – CB

WEST COAST / PACIFIC MARITIME

At night, neighborhood skunks, opossums, and raccoons begin making regular rounds in San Diego, spurred by the need to find partners and breed. Many of them can be seen while crossing roads, so be extra careful while driving. Around woodlands and lawns, long-absent does reappear with their fragile spotted fawns in tow. Nearly every tree, shrub, or nest box is occupied by some form of nesting bird, from excitable chickadees to wispy swallows. Powerful spring winds off the ocean subside later in the month in the Bay Area, to be replaced by fog banks through the summer.

MOUNTAIN REGION / BASIN & RANGE

One of the year's favorite events around Tucson is the annual blooming of the mighty saguaro cacti. It's also a bonanza for pollinators, including large numbers of long-nosed bats that come out only at night. Migrating warblers are wrapping up their northbound migration and settling in to nest in northern areas like Missoula. Expect to see orange-crowned, yellow-rumped, and Wilson's warblers. Common raven eggs are already hatching. Red-winged blackbirds sing raucously around every marsh, and elk move upslope toward their summer feeding grounds.

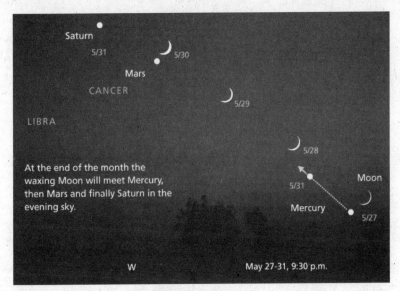

Saturn
5/31

Mars
5/30

CANCER
5/29

LIBRA
5/28

At the end of the month the waxing Moon will meet Mercury, then Mars and finally Saturn in the evening sky.

5/31

Moon

Mercury
5/27

W   May 27-31, 9:30 p.m.

LOOK UP:

4   Jupiter at opposition; It rises in the east at sunset and is visible all night long

5   First quarter Moon, 12:13 AM; Jupiter nearest to Earth; Eta Aquarid meteor shower peaks; Moon interferes

13   Full Moon, 1:51 AM

18   Mercury at superior conjunction (not visible)

20   Last quarter Moon, 4:21 AM

27   New Moon, 12:26 AM

MAY IS THE MONTH FOR:

BETTER HEARING & SPEECH · BREATHING EASY · MOVING · CLEAN AIR · CREATIVE BEGINNINGS · FAMILY SUPPORT · FIBROMYALGIA AWARENESS · READING · PHYSICAL FITNESS · EGGS · LAW ENFORCEMENT APPRECIATION · MENTAL HEALTH · BIKES · BOOKS · SALSA · HAMBURGERS · MELANOMA PREVENTION · WOMEN'S HEALTH CARE

MAY

S	M	T	W	T	F	S
	1	2	3	4	5	6
7	8	9	10	11	12	13
14	15	16	17	18	19	20
21	22	23	24	25	26	27
28	29	30	31			

MID-CONTINENT / CORN BELT & GULF

By now, deciduous forests are fully leafed out, creating a green-hued shade full of vibrant birdsong. Dozens of species of warblers, vireos, and tanagers defend territories and begin nesting this month. Moose and deer find secretive places to have their calves and fawns in northern Minnesota. The night air pulses with the strident songs of crickets and katydids under the occasional flashings of lightning bugs. Watch out, this is also the beginning of the chigger season. Wander the prairies in search of wildflowers with caution. Along the Gulf Coast the terns are nesting, six species in all.

EAST COAST / ATLANTIC SEABOARD

Breeding horseshoe crabs carpet the beaches of Delaware Bay with the spring tide. Close to a million gulls and shorebirds gather to feed on crab eggs. Early in the month, migrating birds reach their peak numbers, many species promptly nesting. Trilliums bloom in forests outside Pittsburgh. Great Smoky Mountains Nat'l Park hosts so many wildflowers that people sometimes call it "Wildflower National Park." Trees like beech and maple fully leaf out, closing the forest in deep green shade. At night, calls of nighthawks and whippoorwills ring out. Mosquitoes emerge in Florida emerge with a vengeance. – DL

1 · MONDAY · MAY 1 · 2006

☽ R. 8:20 am S. 12:22 am
☉ R. 6:03 am S. 8:19 pm

☽ ☌ ♅ ♆ 3:51am

Chocolate Parfait Day

Pierre Teilhard de Chardin, philosopher, b.1881

Mother Jones, labor leader, b.1830

Judy Collins, singer, b.1934

A man is not idle because he is absorbed in thought. There is a visible labor and there is an invisible labor.
— Victor Hugo

May Day

Labour Day
Worldwide Worker's Holiday

2 · TUESDAY · MAY 2 · 2006

☽ R. 9:20 am S. 1:19 am
☉ R. 6:01 am S. 8:20 pm

☽ ☌ ♂ 6:17am
☽ △ ♅ 12:08pm
☽ △ ♃ 12:53pm

Robert's Rules of Order Day

Sibling Appreciation Day

1611: King James Bible published

As a well-spent day brings happy sleep, so a life well used brings a happy death.
— Leonardo Da Vinci

Naomi Campbell, model, b.1970

Benjamin Spock, pediatrician, b.1903

Novalis (Friedrich Leopold von Hardenberg), poet, b.1772

Leonardo da Vinci, artist, d.1519

Henry M. Robert, general, b.1837

3 · WEDNESDAY · MAY 3 · 2006

☽ R. 10:27 am S. 2:03 am
☉ R. 6:00 am S. 8:21 pm

☿ △ ♆ 5:16am
☽ △ ♀ 8:43pm

Dia de la Cruz, *Mexico*

National Teacher's Day

1971: Nat'l Public Radio 1st News Broadcast

Those who don't know how to weep with their whole heart, don't know how to laugh either.
— Golda Meir

James Brown, singer, b.1928

Pete Seeger, musician, b.1919

Golda Meir, prime minister, b.1898

Niccolo Macchiavelli, statesman, b.1469

4 · THURSDAY · MAY 4 · 2006

☽ R. 11:35 am S. 2:37 am
☉ R. 5:58 am S. 8:22 pm

☽ ☌ ♄ 5:23am
☉ ☌ ♃ 9:36am
♃ △ ♅ 10:48pm

Nat'l Weather Observer's Day

1886: Haymarket Square riot

Keith Haring, artist, b.1958

Audrey Hepburn, actor, b.1929

Jane Jacobs, urbanist, b.1916

Horace Mann, educator, b.1796

Don't knock the weather. If it didn't change once in a while, nine out of ten people couldn't start a conversation.
— Kin Hubbard

Recipe: FRUIT FOOLS

"You old fool" can be said with a fond smile, and this simple recipe from 16th century England elicits the same affection. Fruit and cream—what could be nicer? Sweeten fresh raspberries, strawberries, or blackberries with powdered sugar to taste. Let stand for 10 minutes. Mix with an equal amount of whipped cream flavored with Madeira, Cointreau, Chambord, etc., if you wish. You can make the same dessert with cooked fruit—rhubarb, gooseberries, apricots—and add a little grated lemon rind to the mix. – MC

© iStockPhoto

CIVILIZING IDEA:
CREEK DAYLIGHTING

Few urban dwellers realize that water moves beneath their feet. Under parking lots and shopping malls, creeks and rivers flow in concrete pipes, buried deep as dreams. The waterways have been covered to make more land, or because they are difficult to cross or just too wet, spilling water where people want things dry.

Is there a way to let the waters flow free again?

The movement toward creek "daylighting" believes so, and it advocates removing pipes and opening covered waterways to air and light. The first North American project of this kind was in the city of Napa, California, in the 1970s. Northern California is still the country's daylighting leader, but there are at least 20 completed projects in this country and 20 more under way. Communities from DeKalb County, Georgia, to Kalamazoo, Michigan, have found opening streams can help with flood control, improve water quality, save money, and bring new life to neglected neighborhoods.

The symbolism of burying and unburying water is rich. At least two American poets have written on this topic, including Robert Frost, who in his elegiac *A Brook in the City*, tells of a childhood stream "thrown / Deep in a sewer dungeon under stone." Denise Levertov, inspired by plans to daylight Seattle's Ravenna Creek, wrote the poem *Salvation*, which begins, "They are going to / daylight a river here— / that's what they call it, noun to verb" and continues, in the spirit of urban compromise, "stars or at least street-lights / will gleam in it."

– Maria Dolan

For more information, see Richard Pinkham's *New Life for Buried Streams* on the Rocky Mountain Institute Web site, www.rmi.org

Notes

© iStockPhoto

LINGERING IN HAPPINESS / *Mary Oliver*

After rain after many days without rain, / it stays cool, private and cleansed, under the trees, / and the dampness there, married now to gravity, / falls branch to branch, leaf to leaf, down to the ground / where it will disappear— but not, of course, vanish / except to our eyes. The roots of the oaks will have their share / and the white threads of the grasses, and the cushion of moss; / a few drops, round as pearls, will enter the mole's tunnel; / and soon many small stones, buried for a thousand years, / will feel themselves being touched.

Children's Day, *Japan*	*Karl Marx, communist, b.1818*	☾ R. 12:42 pm S. 3:03 am ☉ R. 5:57 am S. 8:23 pm	**FRIDAY · MAY 5 · 2006** **5**
1904: Cy Young pitches a perfect game	*Soren Kierkegaard, philosopher, b.1813*	First Quarter 12:13 am	
Michael Palin, comic actor, b.1943	Reason has always existed, but not always in a reasonable form.	☽ ☌ ♇ 10:35am	
Tammy Wynette, singer, b.1942			
Nellie Bly, journalist, b.1864	— *Karl Marx*		

CINCO DE MAYO

Kentucky Derby, *Louisville, KY*	*Rabindranath Tagore, poet, b.1861*	☾ R. 1:48 pm S. 3:24 am ☉ R. 5:55 am S. 8:25 pm	**SATURDAY · MAY 6 · 2006** **6**
1955: West Germany joins NATO	*Sigmund Freud, founder of Psychoanalysis, b.1856*		
1527: Sack of Rome	Let your life lightly dance on the edges of Time like dew on the tip of a leaf.	☽ △ ♆ 12:02am ☽ △ ☿ 12:40pm	
George Clooney, actor, b.1961			
Orson Welles, actor/director, b.1915	— *Rabindranath Tagore*		

1824: Premiere of Beethoven's Ninth Symphony	Music is a discipline, and a mistress of order and good manners, she makes the people milder and gentler, more moral and more reasonable.	☾ R. 2:52 pm S. 3:41 am ☉ R. 5:54 am S. 8:26 pm	**SUNDAY · MAY 7 · 2006** **7**
Eva Peron, Argentina's "Evita," b.1919			
Gary Cooper, actor, b.1901		♂ △ ♃ 4:12am ☽ ☌ ♅ 11:49am ☽ △ ☉ 6:24pm ♂ △ ♅ 7:37pm ♀ △ ♄ 9:56pm	
Pyotr Tchaikovsky, composer, b.1840	— *Martin Luther*		

8 MONDAY · MAY 8 · 2006

☾ R. 3:55 pm S. 3:57 am
☼ R. 5:53 am S. 8:27 pm

1945: VE Day: Victory in Europe

Liberation Day, *Slovakia*

Victory Day, *France*

Helston Furry Dance, *England*

Beth Henley, playwright, b.1952

Rick Nelson, singer, b.1940

Gary Snyder, poet, b.1930

Robert Johnson, guitarist, b.1911

Antoine Lavoisier, chemist, b.1794

No race can prosper till it learns that there is as much dignity in tilling a field as in writing a poem.
— Booker T. Washington

9 TUESDAY · MAY 9 · 2006

☾ R. 4:59 pm S. 4:13 am
☼ R. 5:51 am S. 8:28 pm

☽☌♀
10:17am

1945: Victory Day, *Russia*

I'd rather laugh with the sinners than cry with the saints, sinners are much more fun.
— Billy Joel

Billy Joel, singer/ songwriter, b.1949

Candice Bergen, actor, b.1946

John Brown, abolitionist, b.1800

Pancho Gonzales, athlete, b.1928

10 WEDNESDAY · MAY 10 · 2006

☾ R. 6:05 pm S. 4:28 am
☼ R. 5:50 am S. 8:30 pm

☽△♆
11:31am

Trust Your Intuition Day

1994: Nelson Mandela inauguration

Linda Evangelista, model, b.1965

Paul "Bono" Hewson, singer, b.1960

T. Berry Brazleton, doctor, b.1918

Fred Astaire, dancer, b.1899

You can learn many things from children. How much patience you have, for instance.
— Franklin P. Jones

11 THURSDAY · MAY 11 · 2006

☾ R. 7:14 pm S. 4:46 am
☼ R. 5:49 am S. 8:31 pm

☿☌♃ 6:19am

1862: Merrimac destroyed

National Windmill Day, *Netherlands*

Dance is the hidden language of the soul.
— Martha Graham

Louis Farrakhan, Islamic leader, b.1933

Salvador Dali, artist, b.1904

Martha Graham, dancer, b.1894

Irving Berlin, lyricist, b.1888

© iStockPhoto

CONGRESS STREET BRIDGE, AUSTIN, TEXAS

A PATCH OF OLD SNOW / *Louis Jenkins*

Here's a patch of snow nestled in the roots of a spruce tree. A spot the sun never touches. Mid-May and there's still snow in the woods. It's startling to come upon this old snow on such a warm day. The record of another time. It's like coming across a forgotten photograph of yourself. The stylish clothes of the period look silly now. And your hair-cut! Awful. You were young, wasteful, selfish, completely mistaken and, probably, no less aware than today.

FRIDAY · MAY 12 · 2006 **12**

☾ R. 8:26 pm S. 4:07 am
☼ R. 5:48 am S. 8:32 pm

Limerick Day

Vesak: Buddha Day, *Buddhist*

Florence Nightingale, nurse, b.1820

Katharine Hepburn, actor, b.1907

Tony Hawk, skateboarder, b.1969

Edward Lear, limericist, b.1812

George Carlin, comedian, b.1937

There was a Young Lady whose eyes, / Were unique as to colour and size; / When she opened them wide, / People all turned aside, / And started away in surprise.
– Edward Lear

☽☌♃ 8:14am
☽△♅ 10:27am
☽☍☿ 11:06am
☽△♂ 3:34pm

SATURDAY · MAY 13 · 2006 **13**

☾ R. 9:39 pm S. 5:33 am
☼ R. 5:47 am S. 8:33 pm

Butterfly Day

Visakha Puja, *Buddhist*

Stevie Wonder, singer, b.1950

Mary Wells, singer, b.1943

I believe that there is a subtle magnetism in Nature, which, if we unconsciously yield to it, will direct us aright.
– Henry David Thoreau

Full Moon 1:51 am

☽☍☉ 1:51am

SUNDAY · MAY 14 · 2006 **14**

☾ R. 10:51 pm S. 6:07 am
☼ R. 5:45 am S. 8:34 pm

Int'l Migratory Bird Day

1607: Founding of Jamestown, VA

Midnight Sun, until July 30, *Norway*

Cate Blanchett, actor, b.1969

Robert Owen, scientist, b.1771

Thomas Gainsborough, artist, b.1727

Thou art thy mother's glass, and she in thee Calls back the lovely April of her prime.
– William Shakespeare

☽△♄ 2:22am
☽△♀ 3:40pm

MOTHER'S DAY

15 MONDAY · MAY 15 · 2006

☾ R. 11:56 pm S. 6:52 am
☼ R. 5:44 am S. 8:35 pm

☽ ☌ Ψ 3:16pm

Katharine Anne Porter, writer, b.1890

L. Frank Baum, writer, b.1856

Henry James, writer, b.1843

Live all you can — it's a mistake not to. It doesn't so much matter what you do in particular, so long as you have your life. If you haven't had that, what have you had?
— *Henry James*

---

16 TUESDAY · MAY 16 · 2006

☾ S. 7:50 am
☼ R. 5:43 am S. 8:36 pm

1763: Biographer's Day: Celebrates the meeting of Boswell & Johnson

St. Brendan's Day, *Ireland*

Studs Terkel, writer, b.1912

Elizabeth Palmer Peabody, writer, b.1804

Liberace, pianist, b.1919

Men are wise in proportion, not to their experience, but to their capacity for experience.
— *James Boswell*

---

17 WEDNESDAY · MAY 17 · 2006

☾ R. 12:49 am S. 9:00 am
☼ R. 5:42 am S. 8:38 pm

☽ ☌ ♂ 8:28am
☽ △ ☿ 7:19pm
☽ △ ☉ 9:11pm

1844: Rubber band patented

1954: School segregation banned, Brown vs. Board of Education

Constitution Day, *Norway*

Mia Hamm, soccer player, b.1972

Edward Jenner, doctor, b.1749

The human spirit needs places where nature has not been rearranged by the hand of man.
— *Author unknown*

---

18 THURSDAY · MAY 18 · 2006

☾ R. 1:31 am S. 10:18 am
☼ R. 5:41 am S. 8:39 pm

☽ ☌ ♄ 12:38pm
☉ ☌ ☿ 3:01pm

1980: Mt. St. Helen's eruption

Int'l Museum Day

Meredith Wilson, composer, b.1902

Pope John Paul II, b.1920

Frank Capra, filmmaker, b.1897

Bertrand Russell, philosopher, b.1872

The whole problem with the world is that fools and fanatics are always so certain of themselves, but wiser people so full of doubts.
— *Bertrand Russell*

Nature Note: HORSE CHESTNUT

The horse chestnut (*Aesculus hippocastanum*) is an ornamental tree planted widely in American parks. In spring its sticky buds swell to an enormous size (around two inches long). A cluster of leaves emerges rapidly out of each bud. Each leaf has five to seven leaflets that continue to droop listlessly from the long leaf stalks. Over the course of several days you can observe how the leaflets swell up and literally unfold, spreading out into the light—a sight to behold. —*CH*

Drawing by Craig Holdrege

© iStockPhoto

SO LIKE HER FATHER / *Connie Wanek*

My daughter sits cross-legged / on the tabletop and reads to me /
as I wash the floor on my hands and knees. / Through an open door
we smell the first lilacs. / In autumn she will leave this house… /
Still there exists a natural order / less compromising than our love, or hers, /
or the love I bear my parents. / I scrub with water mixed with tears /
and the footprints come away. / "I'm sorry," I say, "I wasn't listening." /
She takes a sip of tea and begins again.

National Bike to Work Day

1936: *Gone with the Wind* published

1780: Dark Day in New England

Ho Chi Minh, Vietnamese pres. b.1890

Malcom X, black civil rights leader, b.1925

The bicycle is just as good company as most husbands and, when it gets old and shabby, a woman can dispose of it and get a new one without shocking the entire community.
— *Ann Strong*

☾ R. 2:04 am   S. 11:38 am
☉ R. 5:40 am   S. 8:40 pm

☽ ☌ Ψ 12:19pm

FRIDAY · MAY 19 · 2006 19

Pick Strawberries Day

1927: First Trans-Atlantic flight, Charles Lindbergh

1932: Amelia Earhart Atlantic crossing

Henri Rousseau, painter, b.1844

Honoré de Balzac, writer, b.1799

All human power is a compound of time and patience.
— *Honoré de Balzac*

Last Quarter
4:21 am

☾ R. 2:30 am   S. 12:58 pm
☉ R. 5:39 am   S. 8:41 pm

SATURDAY · MAY 20 · 2006 20

Bay to Breakers Race: Largest footrace in the world, *San Francisco*

1955: 1st transcontinental solo flight

Int'l Jumping Frog Jubilee, *California*

Al Franken, comedian, b.1951

Alexander Pope, poet, b.1688

A man should never be ashamed to own he has been wrong, which is but saying, that he is wiser today than he was yesterday.
— *Alexander Pope*

☾ R. 2:51 am   S. 2:16 pm
☉ R. 5:38 am   S. 8:42 pm

☽ △ ♃ 1:53am
☽ ☌ ♅ 6:02am
☽ △ ♂ 7:29pm

SUNDAY · MAY 21 · 2006 21

---

22 MONDAY · MAY 22 · 2006

☾ R. 3:11 am S. 3:34 pm
☉ R. 5:37 am S. 8:43 pm

Ψ 8:05am
☽△♄ 7:02pm

Richard Wagner,
composer, b.1813

Sir Arthur Conan
Doyle, writer,
b.1859

Mary Cassatt,
painter, b.1844

How often
have I said
to you that
when you have
eliminated the
impossible, what-
ever remains,
however improb-
able, must be
the truth?
— *Sir Arthur*
Conan Doyle

23 TUESDAY · MAY 23 · 2006

☾ R. 3:30 am S. 4:52 pm
☉ R. 5:36 am S. 8:44 pm

World Turtle
Day

Declaration of
the Bab, Baha'i

1895:
NY Public
Library founded

Drew Carey,
actor, b.1961

Joan Collins,
actor, b.1933

Margaret Fuller,
author, b. 1810

I find television
very education-
al. The minute
somebody turns
it on, I go to the
library and read
a good book.
— *Groucho Marx*

24 WEDNESDAY · MAY 24 · 2006

☾ R. 3:51 am S. 6:11 pm
☉ R. 5:35 am S. 8:45 pm

☽♂♀ 12:36am
☽△Ψ 4:15am

Slavic Script
& Bulgarian
Culture Day

Buddha Day

1844:
First U.S. tele-
graph line opens

Patti LaBelle,
singer, b.1944

Bob Dylan,
singer, b.1941

When you feel
in your gut what
you are and then
dynamically
pursue it — don't
back down and
don't give up —
then you're going
to mystify a
lot of folks.
— *Bob Dylan*

25 THURSDAY · MAY 25 · 2006

☾ R. 4:15 am S. 7:31 pm
☉ R. 5:35 am S. 8:46 pm

☽♂♃ 6:28am
♀△Ψ 8:42pm

Ascension Day,
Christian

1963: African
Freedom Day,
Chad, Zambia

Raymond Carver,
writer, b.1938

Miles Davis,
musician, b.1926

Ralph Waldo
Emerson, writer,
b.1803

Bronson Alcott,
educator, b.1799

A foolish
consistency is
the hobgoblin
of little minds,
adored by little
statesmen and
philosophers
and divines.
— *Ralph Waldo*
Emerson

URBAN SANCTUARY :: **ALFRED CALDWELL LILY POND, CHICAGO, ILLINOIS** :: *To learn more, see pg. 274*

© iStockPhoto

LEAVES OF GRASS / *Walt Whitman, from the preface*

This is what you shall do: Love the earth and sun and the animals,
despise riches, / give alms to everyone that asks, stand up for the stupid
and crazy, / devote your income and labor to others, hate tyrants,
argue not / concerning God, have patience and indulgence toward
the people and your / very flesh shall be a great poem.

1805: Napoleon crowned king of Italy	To see the Summer Sky	☽ R. 4:44 am S. 8:50 pm ☉ R. 5:34 am S. 8:47 pm
	Is Poetry, though never in a Book it lie —	
1805: Lewis and Clark see the Rocky Mtns	True Poems flee. — *Emily Dickinson*	
John Wayne, actor, b.1907		
Sally Ride, astronaut, b.1951		

FRIDAY · MAY 26 · 2006 26

1930: Scotch Tape patented	*Isadora Duncan, dancer, b.1878*	☽ R. 5:21 am S. 10:03 pm ☉ R. 5:33 am S. 8:48 pm
1937: Golden Gate Bridge Opened, *San Francisco*	*Julia Ward Howe, social activist, poet, b.1819*	
Hubert H. Humphrey, politician, b.1911	A good traveler has no fixed plans, and is not intent on arriving. — *Lao Tzu*	
Rachel Carson, writer, b.1907		

SATURDAY · MAY 27 · 2006 27

New Moon
12:26 am

☽ ☌ ☉ 12:26am
☽ ☌ ☿ 9:21pm

St. Bernard of Montjoux, *France*	Forget not that the earth delights to feel your bare feet and the winds long to play with your hair. — *Kahlil Gibran*	☽ R. 6:07 am S. 11:06 pm ☉ R. 5:32 am S. 8:49 pm
1892: Sierra Club founded		
Rudolph Giuliani, NYC mayor, b.1944		
Ian Fleming, writer, b.1908		

SUNDAY · MAY 28 · 2006 28

☽ △ Ψ 1:11am
☽ ☌ ♇ 12:09am
☿ △ Ψ 10:33pm

---

29 MONDAY · MAY 29 · 2006

R. 7:05 am S. 11:56 pm
R. 5:32 am S. 8:50 pm

☽△♃ 3:48pm
☽△♅ 10:28pm

Ascension of Baha'u'llah, *Baha'i*

1453: Constantinople falls to the Turks

1953: Mt. Everest summit reached

John F. Kennedy, 35th president, b.1917

MEMORIAL DAY

Bob Hope, comedian, b.1903

G.K. Chesterton, writer, b.1874

Patrick Henry, patriot, b.1736

We need men who can dream of things that never were.
— John F. Kennedy

30 TUESDAY · MAY 30 · 2006

R. 8:10 am
R. 5:31 am S. 8:51 pm

☽☌♂ 11:42pm

1783: First U.S. newspaper published

1994: Pope forbids the ordination of women

Peter the Great, Russian tsar, b.1672

i thank you God for this most amazing day, for the leaping greenly spirits of trees, and for the blue dream of sky and for everything which is natural, which is infinite, which is yes.
— e.e. cummings

31 WEDNESDAY · MAY 31 · 2006

R. 9:18 am S. 12:34 am
R. 5:30 am S. 8:52 pm

☽☌♄ 5:37pm

World "No-Tobacco" Day

1889: Johnstown flood, *Pennsylvania*

1790: First U.S. copyright law passed

Walt Whitman, poet, b.1819

Now I see the secret of the making of the best persons. It is to grow in the open air and to eat and sleep with the earth.
— Walt Whitman

1 THURSDAY · JUNE 1 · 2006

R. 10:27 am S. 1:03 pm
R. 5:30 am S. 8:53 pm

☿☌♆ 12:14am
☽☌♃ 6:47pm

Ascension, *Orthodox Christian*

Procession des Bouteilles, *France*

1967: Sgt. Pepper's Lonely Hearts Club Band released

1980: CNN debuted

Alanis Morissette, singer, b.1974

Brigham Young, Mormon, b.1801

If a train station is where the train stops, what's a work station?
— Author unknown

© Jupiter Images

Health Note: **HOW TO TELL IF AN EGG IS FRESH**
Consulting the French *L'almanach de la maison,* we found that the best way to tell if an egg is fresh is to drop it gently into a bowl of cold water. If it sinks quickly to the bottom, it's fresh. If it sinks slowly, it's still good, but not ultra fresh. Best at this point to use it for baking or for something else where its less-than-perfect freshness is disguised. – MC

BIRTHDAY: May 27, 1907
RACHEL CARSON,
Writer

Rachel Carson is celebrated the world over as the catalyst of the ecology movement and savior of countless endangered species. She began her career writing pamphlets for the United States Fish and Wildlife Service. Educated as a marine biologist, Carson wrote her first book, *Under the Sea Wind*, from the viewpoint of the main character, the sea. She addressed the sea again in *The Sea Around Us*, which spent 81 weeks on the *New York Times* bestseller list and earned her the National Book Award in 1951 for best nonfiction book.

Her most famous work, *Silent Spring*, appeared in *The New Yorker* in three installments beginning June 1962. It presented the scientific evidence that everything is connected to everything else, and documented the demise of songbirds due to DDT poisoning. After reading it, President John F. Kennedy appointed a council to examine the use of pesticides. The chemical industry, unable to discredit her scientific work, attacked Carson personally as hysterical, a middle-aged kook, a faddist, and a threat to Americans who needed pesticides to have a quality life. Though weakened from cancer, she defended her ideas. The president's advisory report, issued finally on May 15, 1963, agreed with Carson. She died the following spring (April 14, 1964). *Time* magazine named her among the most 100 influential people of the 20th century.

– KM

For all at last returns to the sea—to Oceanus, the ocean river, like the ever-flowing stream of time, the beginning and the end.

Those who dwell, as scientists or laymen, among the beauties and mysteries of the earth are never alone or weary of life.

If a child is to keep alive his inborn sense of wonder, he needs the companionship of at least one adult who can share it, rediscovering with him the joy, excitement and mystery of the world we live in.

Only within the moment of time represented by the present century has one species—man—acquired significant power to alter the nature of his world.

JUNE

MAY 21 - JUN 20

JUN 21 - JUL 22

Gemini

JUNE BIRTHSTONE
Pearl

Cancer

JUNE FLOWER
Rose

PERSEVERANCE BECOMES FAITHFULNESS
Challenges: unfaithfulness, incapacitation

Juno, who gives this month its name, walks in golden sandals in the heavy early morning dew. Life thrusts heavenward, the vegetation thickens, stands of trees become dense blocks of solid green. Dragonflies sweep over lakes warm enough to swim in; by night, fireflies emulate the stars. On perfect days, the light is so sweet and unthreatening that we lose ourselves in it without fear. Trusting ourselves to its warmth, we know to lose ourselves will be to find ourselves. We sense why some traditions speak of June as the "door of the year," the gateway to the inner realms of nature. From the heights Cosmic Intelligence streams down, irradiating the clouds and surrounding the landscape in golden glory. Nature is transfigured. Matter is spiritualized; spirit materialized. – *CB*

WEST COAST / PACIFIC MARITIME

Suburban lawns may show an extra bit of activity this month as young broad-footed moles leave their parents' burrows and strike forth in search of new homes. Visitors to the redwood region will be delighted by the impressive show of sweet-blooming rhododendrons. Rocks along the coast are absolutely covered in nesting seabirds this month – white gulls, black cormorants, and delightfully clownish puffins. Pods of killer whales may be seen in Puget Sound.

MOUNTAIN REGION / BASIN & RANGE

Every evening at dusk a million Mexican free-tailed bats issue from the mouth of the cave at Carlsbad Caverns National Park creating an awe-inspiring nightly ritual. Find smaller bat flights at a cave in your own area. The high plains east of Denver are vibrant with birdsong this month, look for horned larks, several species of longspurs, mountain plovers, and many types of sparrows, along with burrowing owls, prairie dogs, and ferruginous hawks. Coyote pups may be seen around the mouths of their dens. Calliope hummingbirds begin nesting in mountain meadows, as glacier lilies bloom through the edges of melting snowbanks.

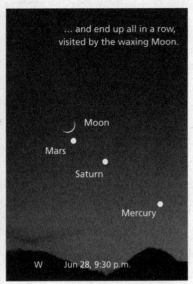

Saturn, Mars, and Mercury come together, then drift apart, like cosmic dancers ...

Saturn
6/1
6/1
Mars
6/18 (conjunction)
6/30
6/30
Mercury
6/1
6/30

W   9:30 p.m.

... and end up all in a row, visited by the waxing Moon.

Moon
Mars
Saturn
Mercury

W   Jun 28, 9:30 p.m.

LOOK UP:

3 First quarter Moon, 6:06 PM

11 Full Moon, 1:03 PM

17 Saturn and faint Mars gleam close together in the evening sky; Below them shines Mercury; Can you find the stellar twins, Castor and Pollux in Gemini, above and to the right of Mercury?

18 Last quarter Moon, 9:09 AM

20 Mercury at greatest eastern elongation (24° 56')

21 Summer solstice, 7:27 AM

25 New Moon, 11:06 AM

26 Mars farthest from the sun; Follow the waxing Moon: it's near Mercury on June 26, between Mercury and Saturn on the 27th, and above Mars on the 28th

JUNE

S	M	T	W	T	F	S
				1	2	3
4	5	6	7	8	9	10
11	12	13	14	15	16	17
18	19	20	21	22	23	24
25	26	27	28	29	30	

JUNE IS THE MONTH FOR:

FIREWORKS SAFETY · ADOPTING A SHELTER-CAT · GAY & LESBIAN PRIDE · PEOPLE SKILLS · PERENNIAL GARDENING · ACCORDIONS · REBUILDING YOUR LIFE · STUDENT SAFETY · ROSES · DAIRY · SKIN CANCER AWARENESS · TURKEY LOVERS · BLESSING-A-CHILD · CHILDREN'S SAFETY · VISION RESEARCH · ENTREPRENEURS

MID-CONTINENT / CORN BELT & GULF

With forests in deep shade, flowers continue to bloom along the sunny edges. Look for penstemons and daisies outside Chicago. Meanwhile, roadside milkweed flowers attract numerous butter-flies. Berries from strawberries to gooseberries are ripening; act quickly if you want to taste one because animals are eagerly waiting for the harvest. In the north, this is the peak season for black flies and mosquitoes. Turtles come ashore to lay their eggs. White-tailed deer are growing new sets of antlers. On the shimmering sandy beaches of the Gulf Coast, flocks of black skimmers can be readily seen.

EAST COAST / ATLANTIC SEABOARD

In New England songbirds are at their peak nesting activity, while spotted fawns venture forth from the thickets where they were born. Laurels and rhododendrons bloom with fervent splendor in Shenandoah National Park. Along creeks, it would be hard to miss the hatches of aquatic insects, clouds of mayflies may be especially prevalent. Barrier islands off the Carolina coast support colonies of nesting terns and skimmers. In the safety of trees nesting herons take up residence. Drawn by a mystery we can scarcely comprehend, loggerheads haul themselves onto beaches to lay their eggs by moonlight. – DL

© iStockPhoto

NATURE NOTE:

WHITE-FACED HORNET NESTS

The grey, papery orbs seen hanging from trees after the leaves have fallen, or under the house eaves, belong to the white-faced hornet and are the result of techniques perfected over perhaps 300 million years. A single female starts each nest in May. She scrapes dead wood from a branch, mixes it with her saliva, and uses the papier-mache-like slurry to make tissue-thin strips of paper by adding one load at a time on the bottom edge of the slowly growing nest. As her daughters come of age over the summer (the females are the nest builders), they will help in the continuing construction, adding layers of white, brown, and gray papers, differently hued depending on the wood. Despite its thinness, the paper does not dissolve in the rain, and a good soaking seldom wets anything beyond the first layer of the nest.

As the wasp family grows, the insects recycle paper from the inside walls to make new, larger ones outside. A nest starts out no bigger than a walnut and by late summer has dozens of layers of paper insulation surrounding almost as many horizontal combs containing pupae and larvae. Each air layer between successive sheets of paper acts as insulation, and the temperature inside the nest stays between 84° and 102° F even in weather down to 41° F. The wasps shiver to maintain their body temperature above 104° F and whatever heat is lost from their bodies heats the nest and young. Come really cold weather, they desert the nest and find shelter in cracks and crevices in tress and buildings until spring comes and a single female once more starts to build a home.

– MC

Adapted with permission from
Bernd Heinrich's *Winter World:
The Ingenuity of Animal Survival.*

THROW YOURSELF LIKE SEED /

Miguel De Unamuno, translated by Robert Bly

Shake off this sadness, and recover your spirit… / …Throw yourself like seed as / you walk, and into your / own field, / don't turn your face for that would be to turn it / to death, / and do not let the past weigh down your motion. / Leave what's alive in the furrow, what's dead / in yourself, / for life does not move in the same way as a group / of clouds; / from your work you will be able one day to / gather yourself.

Shavuot, *Jewish*

1692: Salem witch trials began

1953: Coronation of Queen Elizabeth, *UK*

A man's silence is wonderful to listen to.
— *Thomas Hardy*

Nikki Cox, actor, b.1978

Dana Carvey, comedian, b.1955

Thomas Hardy, writer, b.1840

Marquis de Sade, writer, b.1740

☾ R. 11:34 am S. 1:26 am
☉ R. 5:29 am S. 8:53 pm

☽ △ Ψ 6:49am

FRIDAY · JUNE 2 · 2006   **2**

1972: First U.S. woman Rabbi ordained

Curtis Mayfield, soul musician, b.1942

Allen Ginsberg, writer, b.1926

Lili St. Cyr, burlesque queen, b.1918

Josephine Baker, entertainer, b.1906

Jefferson Davis, confederate leader, b.1808

Never be haughty to the humble; never be humble to the haughty.
— *Jefferson Davis*

☾ R. 12:39pm S. 1:45am
☉ R. 5:29am S. 8:54pm

First Quarter 6:06 pm

☽ △ ♀ 2:37am
☽ ☌ ♅ 8:58pm

SATURDAY · JUNE 3 · 2006   **3**

Pentecost, *Christian*

Whitsunday, *Christian*

1989: Tiananmen Square Massacre, *China*

1942: Battle of Midway

Angelina Jolie, actor, b.1975

Dr. Ruth Westheimer, sex expert, b.1928

Socrates, philosopher, b.470 BC

Children today are tyrants. They contradict their parents, gobble their food, and tyrannize their teachers.
— *Socrates*

☾ R. 1:42pm S. 2:02am
☉ R. 5:28am S. 8:55pm

SUNDAY · JUNE 4 · 2006   **4**

All times Central Time Zone, sun and moon rise and set Minneapolis, MN.

5 · MONDAY · JUNE 5 · 2006

☾ R. 2:46pm S. 2:17am
☉ R. 5:28am S. 8:56pm

UN World Environment Day

1981: AIDS first noted

1968: Robt. F. Kennedy assassinated

Bill Moyers, journalist, b.1934

Frederico Garcia Lorca, writer, b.1898

John Maynard Keynes, economist, b.1883

Pancho Villa, revolutionary, b.1878

Adam Smith, economist, b.1723

Don't let it end like this. Tell them I said something.
— Pancho Villa

6 · TUESDAY · JUNE 6 · 2006

☾ R. 3:50pm S. 2:33am
☉ R. 5:28am S. 8:56pm

☽△☉ 11:55am
☽△♆ 7:39pm

1944: D-Day: Allied forces land at Normandy

1978: Prop. 13: taxpayers revolt, California

Sandra Bernhard, comic/actor, b.1955

Harvey Fierstein, playwright, b.1954

Alexander Pushkin, writer, b.1799

Nathan Hale, patriot, b.1755

I only regret that I have but one life to lose for my country.
— Nathan Hale

7 · WEDNESDAY · JUNE 7 · 2006

☾ R. 4:57pm S. 2:50am
☉ R. 5:27am S. 8:57pm

♀☍♃ 1:23am

Ice Cream Day

1975: VCR Introduced

Life being what it is, one dreams of revenge.
— Paul Gauguin

Prince R. Nelson, singer, b.1958

Louise Erdrich, writer, b.1954

Liam Neeson, actor, b.1952

Paul Gauguin, painter, b.1848

8 · THURSDAY · JUNE 8 · 2006

☾ R. 6:08pm S. 3:09am
☉ R. 5:27am S. 8:58pm

☽△☿ 8:10am
☽☌♃ 11:04am
☽☍♀ 2:45pm
☽△♅ 7:44pm

1783: Laki Volcano explosion, Iceland

Scott Adams, cartoonist, b.1957

Joan Rivers, comic, b.1933

Cochise, Apache leader, b.1874

Frank Lloyd Wright, architect, b.1867

TV is chewing gum for the eyes.
— Frank Lloyd Wright

This blade of grass starts...

...here!

Nature Note: A BLADE OF GRASS

Have you ever really looked at a blade of grass? Choose an unmowed spot where a grass stalk is growing upward. If you follow a blade from its tip down to where it meets the stem, you'll discover that the leaf doesn't stop. It wraps around the stem like a sheath for a number of inches until you come to a knobby node. Never fully unfolding, a grass blade gives strength to the inimitable vertical thrust so characteristic of grasses. — CH

Drawing of a grass plant (orchard grass; Dactylis glomerata)

Drawing by Craig Holdrege

TOUCH ME / *Stanley Kunitz*

Summer is late, my heart. / Words plucked out of the air / some forty years ago / when I was wild with love / and torn almost in two / scatter like leaves this night / of whistling wind and rain. / It is my heart that's late, / it is my song that's flown… / Darling, do you remember / the man you married? Touch me, / remind me who I am.

1898: Hong Kong lease signed from Britain

Johnny Depp, actor, b.1963

Letty Cottin Pogrebin, writer, b.1939

Donald Duck, cartoon, b.1934

Cole Porter, composer, b.1891

Teaching is the profession that teaches all the other professions.
— *Author unknown*

☾ R. 7:21pm S. 3:33am
☉ R. 5:27am S. 8:58pm

☿△♃ 6:45am

FRIDAY · JUNE 9 · 2006 9

1943: Ballpoint pen patented

1935: Alcoholics Anonymous founded

Elizabeth Hurley, actor, b.1965

F. Lee Bailey, lawyer, b.1939

Edward O. Wilson, sociobiologist, b.1929,

Maurice Sendak artist, b.1928

Judy Garland actor, b.1922

Saul Bellow, writer, b.1915

There must be more to life than having everything.
— *Maurice Sendak*

☾ R. 8:35pm S. 4:04am
☉ R. 5:26am S. 8:59pm

☽△♂ 7:29am
☉△♆ 1:02pm
☽△♄ 2:33pm

SATURDAY · JUNE 10 · 2006 10

Trinity, *Christian*

King Kamehameha Day, *Hawaii*

Ingrid Newkirk, PETA president, b.1949

William Styron, writer, b.1925

Richard Strauss, composer, b.1864

Jacques Cousteau, undersea explorer, b.1910

Ben Jonson, playwright, b.1572

He knows not his own strength that hath not met adversity.
— *Ben Jonson*

☾ R. 9:44pm S. 4:45am
☉ R. 5:26am S. 8:59pm

Full Moon
1:03 pm

☽☌☉ 1:03pm
☽☌♆ 9:34pm

SUNDAY · JUNE 11 · 2006 11

All times Central Time Zone, sun and moon rise and set Minneapolis, MN.

12 MONDAY · JUNE 12 · 2006

☾ R. 10:43pm S. 5:39am
☉ R. 5:26am S. 9:00pm

☿△♅ 11:43am

1939: Nat'l Baseball Hall of Fame opened

Baseball is 90% mental, the other half is physical.
— *Yogi Berra*

Anne Frank, writer, b.1929

George H.W. Bush, 41st US pres., b.1924

Djuna Barnes, writer, b.1892

Johanna Spyri, writer, b.1827

13 TUESDAY · JUNE 13 · 2006

☾ R. 11:30pm S. 6:47am
☉ R. 5:26am S. 9:01pm

☽♂☍☿ 8:36am
☽△♀ 11:51am

1963: Medgar Evars assassinated

1966: Miranda rights established

Eleanor Holmes Norton, politician, b.1937

William Butler Yeats, poet, b.1865

Fanny Burney, writer, b.1752

And say my glory was I had such friends.
— *William Butler Yeats*

14 WEDNESDAY · JUNE 14 · 2006

☾ S. 8:05am
☉ R. 5:26am S. 9:01pm

☽♂☍♂ 8:01pm
☽♂♄ 10:46pm

Royal Ascot horse races; *England*

1951: Univac Computer unveiled

Donald Trump, businessman, b.1946

Che Guevara, revolutionary, b.1928

Margaret Bourke White, photographer, b.1904

Harriet Beecher Stowe, writer, b.1811

As long as you are going to think anyway, think big.
— *Donald Trump*

FLAG DAY

15 THURSDAY · JUNE 15 · 2006

☾ R. 12:06am S. 9:26am
☉ R. 5:26am S. 9:01pm

☽♂Ψ 5:41pm

1215: Magna Carta chartered

Courteney Cox Arquette, actor, b.1964

Helen Hunt, actor, b.1963

Saul Steinberg, cartoonist, b.1914

Edvard Grieg, composer, b.1843

I think, therefore Descartes exists.
— *Saul Steinberg*

© Lagomarcino's Confectionery

Notes

© iStockPhoto

CONTEMPLATE:

BEWILDERMENT / Rumi, *translated by Coleman Barks*

There are many guises for intelligence.
One part of you is gliding in a high windstream,
while your more ordinary notions
take little steps and peck at the ground.

Conventional knowledge is death to our souls,
and it is not really ours.

It is laid on. Yet we keep saying
that we find "rest" in these "beliefs."

We must become ignorant of what we have been taught
and be instead bewildered.

Run from what is profitable
and comfortable.

If you drink those liqueurs,
you will spill the springwater of your real life.

Distrust anyone who praises you.
Give your investment money,
and the interest
on the capital, to those who are actually destitute.

Forget safety. Live where you fear to live.
Destroy your reputation.
Be notorious.

I have tried prudent planning long enough.
From now on, I'll be mad.

WHEN DEATH COMES / *Mary Oliver*

…When it's over, I want to say: all my life / I was a bride married to / amazement. / I was a bridegroom, taking the world into my arms. / When it's over, I don't want to wonder / if I have made of my life something particular, and real. / I don't want to find myself sighing and frightened / or full of argument. / I don't want to end up simply having visited this world.

1883: Ladies Day initiated in baseball

Tupac Shakur, rapper, b.1971

Joyce Carol Oates, writer, b.1938

John Howard Griffin, writer, b.1920

Katharine Graham, publisher, b.1917

Barbara McClintock, scientist, b.1902

Stan Laurel, comedian, b.1890

In love there are things — bodies and words.
— *Joyce Carol Oates*

☾ R. 12:34am S. 10:47am
☉ R. 5:26am S. 9:02pm

☽△☉ 2:44am
☉☌♆ 12:24pm

FRIDAY · JUNE 16 · 2006 **16**

1972: Watergate arrests, *Wash DC*

Venus Williams, tennis player, b.1980

M.C. Escher, artist, b.1898

Igor Stravinsky, composer, b.1882

John Wesley, founder of Methodism, b.1703

The word 'politics' is derived from the word 'poly', meaning 'many', and the word 'ticks', meaning 'blood sucking parasites'.
— *Larry Hardiman*

☾ R. 12:56am S. 12:06pm
☉ R. 5:26am S. 9:02pm

☽△♃ 3:09am
☽☌♅ 11:58am
☽△☿ 11:31pm

SATURDAY · JUNE 17 · 2006 **17**

Corpus Christi, *Roman Catholic*

All Saint's, *Orth. Christian*

1983: First U.S. woman in space, *Sally Ride*

War of 1812 declaration anniversary

Paul McCartney, singer, b.1942

Isabella Rossellini, actor, b.1952

Roger Ebert, critic, b.1942

Gail Godwin, writer, b.1937

Good teaching is one-fourth preparation and three-fourths theater.
— *Gail Godwin*

☾ R. 1:17am S. 1:23pm
☉ R. 5:26am S. 9:02pm

Last Quarter
9:08 am

♂☌♄ 1:03am

SUNDAY · JUNE 18 · 2006 **18**

All times Central Time Zone, sun and moon rise and set Minneapolis, MN.

19 MONDAY · JUNE 19 · 2006

☽ R. 1:36am S. 2:40pm
☉ R. 4:26am S. 9:03pm

♅ 2:39am
☽△♄ 5:04am
☽△♂ 6:07am

Juneteenth

Texas Emancipation Day

1932: Hailstones kill 200 in Hunan Province, *China*

Salmon Rushdie, writer, b.1947

Elbert Hubbard, writer, b.1856

Aung San Suu Kyi, peace activist, b.1945

Blaise Pascal, philosopher, b.1623

The heart has its reasons which reason knows nothing of.
— *Blaise Pascal*

FATHER'S DAY

20 TUESDAY · JUNE 20 · 2006

☽ R. 1:56am S. 3:57pm
☉ R. 4:26am S. 9:03pm

☽△Ψ 9:18am

1893: Lizzie Borden found not guilty

1948: Ed Sullivan Show premieres

Vegan World Day

Nicole Kidman, actor, b.1967

Ann Murray, singer/songwriter, b.1946

Chet Atkins, guitarist, b.1924

Errol Flynn, actor, b.1909

Lillian Hellman, writer, b.1905

Nothing, of course, begins at the time you think it did.
— *Lillian Hellman*

21 WEDNESDAY · JUNE 21 · 2006

☽ R. 2:18am S. 5:15pm
☉ R. 4:27am S. 9:03pm

☽♂°♃ 9:31am

First Nations Day, Canadian native people

Litha, *Wicca*

International Gnome Day

Maureen Stapleton, actor, b.1925

Mary McCarthy, writer, b.1912

Jean-Paul Sartre, existentialist, b.1905

Gottfried Wilhelm Liebniz, philosopher, b1646

We are the hero of our own story.
— *Mary McCarthy*

SUMMER SOLSTICE
8:26AM

22 THURSDAY · JUNE 22 · 2006

☽ R. 2:44am S. 6:33pm
☉ R. 4:27am S. 9:03pm

☽♂♀ 7:45pm

1870: U.S. Dept. of Justice created

Meryl Streep, actor, b.1949

Dianne Feinstein, politician, b.1933

Joseph Papp, producer, b.1921

Billy Wilder, director, b.1906

Anne Morrow Lindbergh, writer, aviatrix, b.1906

Hindsight is always twenty-twenty.
— *Billy Wilder*

Nature Note: EDIBLE FLOWERS

Before you eat a flower, be sure you are certain of its identity and that it has never been sprayed. As a general rule, you can eat any flowers from herbs and vegetables. You can candy them, toss them into salads, decorate cakes with them, stuff and fry them... Johnny jump-ups taste sweet, lilacs are perfume-y, nasturtiums taste sharp and peppery. Pansies, petunias, roses, squash blossoms, and dozens more have their own distinct flavors. See www.ext.colostate.edu/pubs/garden/07237.html. – MC

© Photodisc

AWAKENING GATHA / *Deena Metzger*

Waking in the morning
Time smiles in my hand.
This dawn
Lasts all day.

Sacred Heart of Jesus, *Roman Catholic*

1868: Typewriter patented

Frances McDormand, actor, b.1957

Wilma Rudolph, runner, b.1940

Richard Bach, writer, b.1936

Bob Fosse, choreographer, b.1927

Alfred Kinsey, sex researcher, b.1894

Learning is finding out what you already know.
— Richard Bach

☽ R. 3:17am S. 7:47pm
☉ R. 5:27am S. 9:04pm

FRIDAY · JUNE 23 · 2006 **23**

1497: Discovery of Newfoundland

St. John the Baptist Day

Bannockburn Day, *Scotland*

Robert Reich, writer/politician, b.1946

Jack Dempsey, boxer, b.1895

Ambrose Bierce, journalist, b.1842

Henry Ward Beecher, clergyman, b.1813

In Washington, it's dog eat dog. In academia, it's exactly the opposite.
— Robert Reich

☽ R. 3:59am S. 8:53pm
☉ R. 5:27am S. 9:04pm

☽△♆ 8:45am
☽☌♇ 7:03pm

SATURDAY · JUNE 24 · 2006 **24**

1950: Korean War begins

1962: Supreme Court bans school prayer

1990: Supreme Court upholds right to die

George Michael, singer, b.1963

Carly Simon, singer/songwriter, b.1945

George Orwell, writer, b.1903

To see what is in front of one's nose needs a constant struggle.
— George Orwell

☽ R. 4:52am S. 9:48pm
☉ R. 5:28am S. 9:04pm

New Moon 11:05 am

☽☌☉ 11:06am
☽△♃ 8:40pm

SUNDAY · JUNE 25 · 2006 **25**

All times Central Time Zone, sun and moon rise and set Minneapolis, MN.

26 MONDAY · JUNE 26 · 2006

☾ R. 5:54am S. 10:31pm
☉ R. 5:28am S. 9:04pm

☾△♅ 7:05am

Abner Doubleday invented base-ball, b.1819

Colin Wilson, writer, b.1931

Peter Lorre, actor, b.1904

Pearl S. Buck, writer, b.1892

Baseball is like church. Many attend, few understand.
— Leo Durocher

27 TUESDAY · JUNE 27 · 2006

☾ R. 7:02am S. 11:03pm
☉ R. 5:28am S. 9:04pm

☾☌☿ 11:03am

1859: "Happy Birthday to You" song composed

Anna Moffo, opera singer, b.1934

Helen Keller, writer, b.1880

Emma Goldman, anarchist, b.1869

Lafcadio Hearn, writer, b.1850

Joseph Smith Jr., Mormon Church founder, d.1844

The world is full of suffering, but it is also full of people overcoming it.
— Helen Keller

28 WEDNESDAY · JUNE 28 · 2006

☾ R. 8:12am S. 11:29pm
☉ R. 5:29am S. 9:04pm

☾☌♄ 7:22am
☾☌♂ 5:58pm

1969: Stonewall Riot, start of Gay Liberation movement

Gilda Radner, comic, b.1946

Mel Brooks, actor/director, b.1926

Ashley Montague, anthropologist, b.1905

Jean-Jacques Rousseau, philosopher, b.1712

Peter Paul Rubens, painter, b.1577

The person who has lived the most is not the one with the most years but the one with the richest experiences.
— Jean-Jacques Rousseau

29 THURSDAY · JUNE 29 · 2006

☾ R. 9:20am S. 11:49pm
☉ R. 5:29am S. 9:04pm

☾☌♆ 2:10am
☾△♆ 1:24pm

Sts. Peter and Paul Feast Day, *Christian*

1938: Olympic National Park established

Stokely Carmichael, civil rights activist, b.1941

Oriana Falacci, journalist, b.1930

Antoine de Saint-Exupéry, writer/adventurer, b.1900

William James Mayo, co-founder Mayo Clinic, b.1861

If someone wants a sheep, then that means that he exists.
— Antoine de Saint-Exupéry

© PhotoDisc

SKYLINE, BOSTON, MASSACHUSETTS

© Jupiter Images

Hypericum perforatum

Botany: *Each flower has five petals that hold a sunburst of over 50, pollen-rich stamens. The pistil bears multiple seeds and a plant can also propagate via runners at the base of the stem. It is a perennial.*

Name: *St. John the Baptist's birthday is June 24th; the plant was named after him. The second part of the Latin name—perforatum—refers to the perforated appearance of the leaves.*

Range: *Originally a Eurasian plant that has followed human culture around the globe; it can be found on all continents.*

Mythology: *In Germanic mythology, Saint-John's-Wort was associated with the Sun God Baldur.*

Saint-John's-Wort
Summer's blooming healer

As the sun's daily arc across the sky climbs higher and the days lengthen in the spring, Saint-John's-Wort sends up its sturdy, straight main stem from which many side stems branch upward. Around the summer solstice—the longest day of the year—it begins to bloom, bringing forth a multitude of brilliant, rich-yellow blossoms and it continues bringing forth new blossoms well into the summer. You'll happen upon this child of the light-filled time of year in sunny empty lots, roadsides, and fields.

Both its small oval leaves and yellow petals warrant a closer look. If you hold a leaf toward the light, you'll see many transluscent dots and, around the leaf edge, black dots. Both are oil-filled glands. The yellow petals also have many black dots and if you rub a few petals between your fingers, a reddish oil appears—a transformation of substances in the black dots stimulated by contact with the air and light. The same effect shows itself more slowly when you fill a jar with blossoms, pour oil over them, close the jar and let it stand outside in a sunny place for a week or two. The mixture turns brilliant scarlet red; this Saint-John's-Wort oil is great for treating minor burns and wounds.

Since ancient times Saint-John's-Wort has been prized for its various healing properties. Taken internally, extracts of the leaves and blossoms have long been known to help people suffering from mild depressions, lightening up the soul.   – *CH*

JULY

JUN 21 - JUL 22

Cancer

JULY BIRTHSTONE
Ruby

JUL23 - AUG 22

Leo

JULY FLOWER
Larkspur

© PhotoDisc

SELFLESSNESS BECOMES CATHARSIS (HEALING)
Challenges: overly willful, dependent

Now the senses are our guides and masters. Drawn out by the world's beauty, we awaken to the glory of the visible, touchable, smellable, hearable, tastable, feelable world. It draws us into selfless conversation. Everything is in motion. Purified, we flow with it. Leaves tremble, tall grass waves, a dreamy, swirling haze hallows the waters of lakes and ponds. Gardens team with life. Look into the intense bursts of color reaching to the heavens and think yourself clairvoyant! Everywhere beings are weaving – among the delphiniums and hollyhocks and in the chard and carrot tops. Somehow, we must carry the memory of this gift into winter. These are the dog days, when Sirius, the dog star is conjunct the sun. This is above all a brilliant, warm, dreamy, forceful, light-filled, and productive time. May we be so likewise. – *CB*

WEST COAST / PACIFIC MARITIME

Super low tides along the coast make this a favorite month for visiting tidepools. In the interior valleys, acorns begin forming on oak trees, though they are scarcely noticeable yet. In the mountains, however, this is the season of outrageous alpine wildflower displays. Lupines, sky pilots, columbines, and many others create a tapestry of solid color in the famous mountain meadows of Mt. Hood, Mt. Rainier, and other Cascade peaks.

MOUNTAIN REGION / BASIN & RANGE

On one of your sunset walks don't be surprised to run across a large hairy tarantula trotting alongside. In the dusk you may hear the plaintive nasal calls of common nighthawks looping back and forth in pursuit of flying insects. On a hot afternoon, the air may be filled with a veritable blizzard of fluffy white cottonwood seeds. Mountain meadows are at their peak flowering with gilias, penstemons, and asters brightening meadows in all colors of the rainbow. Bumbling young ground squirrels and chipmunks are abundant.

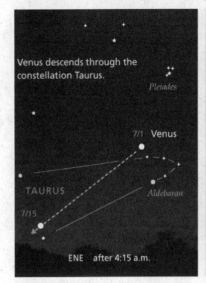

Venus descends through the constellation Taurus.

Pleiades

7/1 Venus

TAURUS

Aldebaran

7/15

ENE   after 4:15 a.m.

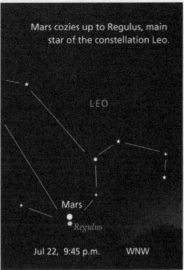

Mars cozies up to Regulus, main star of the constellation Leo.

LEO

Mars

Regulus

Jul 22, 9:45 p.m.   WNW

LOOK UP:

3 First quarter Moon, 11:37 AM; Earth farthest from the sun

10 Full Moon, 10:02 PM

17 Last quarter Moon, 2:13 PM

18 Mercury at inferior conjunction (not visible)

24 New Moon, 11:32 PM

28 Southern Delta Aquarid meteor shower peaks

JULY IS THE MONTH FOR:

ANTI-BOREDOM · CELL PHONE COURTESY · COPIOUS COMPLIMENTS · BAKED BEANS · BISON · HERBAL/PRESCRIPTION AWARENESS · CULINARY ARTS · DOGHOUSE REPAIRS · FOREIGN LANGUAGES · HOT DOGS · BLUEBERRIES · PARKS & RECREATION · PURPOSEFUL PARENTING

			JULY			
S	M	T	W	T	F	S
						1
2	3	4	5	6	7	8
9	10	11	12	13	14	15
16	17	18	19	20	21	22
23/30	24/31	25	26	27	28	29

MID-CONTINENT / CORN BELT & GULF

This month in midsummer can be a quiet drowsy time. Butterfly enthusiasts, however, do an annual 4th of July butterfly count because this is a great time to see fritillaries, skippers, and swallowtails. In marshy areas of the north, this is the season to harvest blueberries. Moose escape into deeper waters to avoid the torment of flies and mosquitoes. Songbirds are wrapping up their nesting efforts, and many species are feeding squabbling fledglings. Likewise, young prairie dogs are easily viewed this month as they wander forth from their burrows and scramble playfully among dry grasses outside Kansas City.

EAST COAST / ATLANTIC SEABOARD

Time to harvest blueberries in northern Pennsylvania, though the deer flies will be biting as well. Freshwater turtles hatch from their eggs and scramble to the nearest pond. Lightning bugs fill the night with light shows. Already wrapping up their nesting season, barn swallows gather in large flocks. New England's coastal marshes hum with mosquitoes and marsh flies so there's lots of food for the birds. Thunderstorms and lightning roll across Florida. Young alligators appear in the shallows of the same sloughs where the adults wait out the day's heat. The hot air drones with the shrill calling of cicadas. – *DL*

CIVILIZING IDEA:

COMMUNITY SUPPORTED AGRICULTURE

In the United States, grocery store produce travels an average of 1,300 miles. The possibility of mangos in Minnesota and pineapples in Pennsylvania is astonishing. But even more remarkable and more in keeping with the care and rhythm of the earth is the vision of Community Supported Agriculture (CSA).

Community Supported Agriculture brings consumers and farmers together in a harmonious relationship that provides locally grown food to consumers and offers support to farmers. CSA takes many forms, but in most, the consumer pays an annual fee, usually around $400, for fresh, local, seasonal produce throughout the growing season. The community shares the natural risks with the farmer, and the farm becomes, either legally or spiritually, the community's farm.

CSA originated in Japan in the 1960s when a group of women concerned about the chemicals used in food production, the importation of food, and consequent reduction in local farming organized *teikei*. Teikei means "partnership" or "cooperation." The first American CSA, an apple orchard, was founded in 1985 at Indian Line Farm in South Egremont, Massachusetts. Now, CSAs number over 1,100. Most offer vegetables, fruits, and herbs in season; some provide a full array of farm produce— eggs, milk, meat, baked goods, and even firewood.

Politically, CSA levels the playing field in a food market that favors large-scale industrialized agriculture over local food, and it keeps food dollars in local economies. Sensually and spiritually, it allows people to return to a deep connection with food and all its pleasures.

– KM

To learn more about CSA, see
www.nal.usda.gov/afsic

SECRET / *Dorothea Tanning*

…In summer the park, for an hour or so before night, / is at
its greenest, a whole implicit proposition / of green leaves,
a triumph of leaves enfolding me / that day in a green intimacy
so trustworthy I told / them my secret. "It's my birthday,"
I said out loud / before turning away to cross the avenue.

Burning of the Three Firs, *France*

1908: Meteor hits Siberia

1966: NOW founded

Everybody's got plans...until they get hit.
— Mike Tyson

Mike Tyson, boxer, b.1966

Susan Hayward, actor, b.1918

Lena Horne, singer, b.1917

Czeslaw Milosz, writer, b.1911

☾ R. 10:26am
☉ R. 5:30am S. 9:03pm

☉△♃ 6:21pm

FRIDAY · JUNE 30 · 2006 **30**

1867: Dominion Day, *Canada*

1862: First Income tax in U.S.

1963: Zip codes est.

1863: Battle of Gettysburg (>50,000 dead)

1941: 1st scheduled TV broadcast

Liv Tyler, actor, b.1977

Princess Diana of Wales, b.1961

Dan Aykroyd, actor, b.1952

Willie Dixon, musician, b.1915

Taxes grow without rain.
— Jewish Proverb

☾ R. 11:30am S. 12:06am
☉ R. 5:30am S. 9:03pm

☽♂♅ 4:55am

SATURDAY · JULY 1 · 2006 **1**

Palio Horse Race, *Italy*

Halfway Day, 182nd day of the year

1964: Civil Rights Act

1776: Declaration of Independence

Lindsay Lohan, actor, b.1986

Jerry Hall, model, b.1956

Thurgood Marshall, judge, b.1908

Hermann Hesse, writer, b.1887

Eternity is a mere moment, just long enough for a joke.
— Hermann Hesse

☾ R. 12:33pm S. 12:22am
☉ R. 5:31am S. 9:03pm

SUNDAY · JULY 2 · 2006 **2**

All times Central Time Zone, sun and moon rise and set Minneapolis, MN.

3 MONDAY · JULY 3 · 2006

☽ R. 1:36pm S. 12:37am
☉ R. 5:32am S. 9:03pm

First Quarter
11:37 am

☽△♀ 11:23am

Dog Days:
hottest days
of the year
Jul. 3 – Aug. 11

**Earth at
Aphelion:**
Furthest
from sun

1944: Belarus
Independence
Day

Tom Cruise,
actor, b.1962

Dave Barry,
writer, b.1947

Franz Kafka,
writer, b.1883

When the sea
boiled, wine
turned sour, dogs
grew mad, and
all creatures
became languid...
– Brady's Clavis
Calendarium

4 TUESDAY · JULY 4 · 2006

☽ R. 2:41pm S. 12:53am
☉ R. 5:32am S. 9:03pm

☽△♆ 3:09am

Joyce Brothers,
columnist, b.1949

Gina Lollabrigida,
actor, b.1928

Rube Goldberg,
artist, b.1883

Stephen Foster,
composer, b.1826

Nathaniel
Hawthorne,
writer, b.1804

John Adams, 2nd
US Pres, d.1826

Thomas Jefferson,
3rd US President,
d.1826

Mountains
are earth's
undecaying
monuments.
– Nathaniel
Hawthorne

INDEPENDENCE DAY, U.S.

5 WEDNESDAY · JULY 5 · 2006

☽ R. 3:49pm S. 1:11am
☉ R. 5:33am S. 9:02pm

♂☌♆ 7:46am
☽☌♃ 5:41pm

1946: First
bikini swimsuit

Tynwald Day:
Viking Mid-
summer Day,
Isle of Man

**Venezuela
Independence
Day**

Huey Lewis,
singer, b.1951

Robbie Robertson,
singer, b.1944

Jean Cocteau,
writer/filmmaker,
b.1889

P.T. Barnum,
circus promoter,
b.1810

We must believe
in luck. For
how else can we
explain the suc-
cess of those
we don't like?
– Jean Cocteau

6 THURSDAY · JULY 6 · 2006

☽ R. 5:01pm S. 1:33am
☉ R. 5:34am S. 9:02pm

♃ 2:18am
☽△☉ 3:36am
☽△♅ 4:28am
☉△♅ 2:58pm

1854:
Republican
Party formed

George W. Bush,
43rd president,
b.1946

Dalai Lama,
Tibetan leader,
b.1935

Janet Leigh,
actor, b.1927

Frida Kahlo,
painter, b.1907

Politics is
supposed to
be the second
oldest profession.
I have come
to realize that
it bears a
very close
resemblance
to the first.
– Ronald Reagan

Honey Bee
(Apis mellifera)

Yellow Jacket
(Vespula pennsylvanica)

Nature Note: HONEY BEE AND YELLOW JACKET

People often confuse the honey bee with wasps such as the yellow jacket.
Yellow jackets are attracted by soft drinks and food at picnics and are
often foraging at garbage cans. They have a striking black and bright yellow
striped body, which is not hairy. In contrast, the honey bee has a more
compact and hairy body that is yellowish tan in color. You will see it visiting
flowers, carrying golden packets of pollen on its rear pair of legs. —CH

Drawing by Craig Holdrege

CHILDREN NEAR THE WATER / *Connie Wanek*

…The children hardly notice as I join them. / They're so fresh, / like spruce buds in May. / Their feet are still round instead of long, / like smooth paws. How calm the water is today, / just the smallest ripples / wandering at the whim of the wind, / as many going out as there are / coming in.

Fiesta de San Fermin: Running of the Bulls, *Pamplona, Spain* **Tanabata:** Star Festival, *Japan* Ringo Starr, musician, b.1940 Margaret Walker, writer, b.1915 Robert A. Heinlein, writer, b.1907	Satchell Paige, baseball pitcher, b.1906 Marc Chagall, painter, b.1887 Gustav Mahler, composer, b.1860 A poet that reads his verse in public may have other nasty habits. – Robert A. Heinlein	☽ R. 6:14pm S. 2:00am ☉ R. 5:34am S. 9:01pm ☽△☿ 11:10am FRIDAY · JULY 7 · 2006 **7**

Festa dos Tabuleiros, *Portugal* Anna Quindlen, writer, b.1953 Anjelica Huston, actor, b.1951 Elisabeth Kubler-Ross, writer, b.1926 John D. Rockefeller, financier, b.1839	You cannot be really first-rate at your work if your work is all you are. – Anna Quindlen	☽ R. 7:25pm S. 2:36am ☉ R. 5:35am S. 9:01pm ☽△♃ 5:16am ☽☌♀ 5:09pm ☽△♂ 11:51pm SATURDAY · JULY 8 · 2006 **8**

Lobster Carnival, *Canada* **Martyrdom of the Bab,** *Baha'i* **1893:** 1st successful open-heart surgery Courtney Love, singer, b.1964 Tom Hanks, actor, b.1956	Otto Respighi, composer, b.1879 Nikola Tesla, inventor, b.1856 Our virtues and our failings are inseparable, like force and matter. When they separate, man is no more. – Nikola Tesla	☽ R. 8:30pm S. 3:24am ☉ R. 5:36am S. 9:00pm ☽☌♆ 5:32am ♀△♆ 10:35pm SUNDAY · JULY 9 · 2006 **9**

All times Central Time Zone, sun and moon rise and set Minneapolis, MN.

10 MONDAY · JULY 10 · 2006

☾ R. 9:23pm S. 4:27am
☿ R. 5:37am S. 9:00pm

Full Moon
10:02 pm

☾☌☉ 10:02pm

1985: Rainbow Warrior sunk, *Greenpeace*

Kim Deal, singer/songwriter, b.1961

Arthur Ashe, tennis player, b.1943

Marcel Proust, writer, b.1871

James M. Whistler, painter, b.1834

John Calvin, founder of Presbyterianism b.1509

From what we get, we can make a living; what we give, however, makes a life.
— *Arthur Ashe*

---

11 TUESDAY · JULY 11 · 2006

☾ R. 10:03pm S. 5:43am
☿ R. 5:37am S. 8:59pm

☾☌☿ 3:59pm

Asalha Puja Day, *Hindu*

St. Benedict Day, *Roman Catholic*

1804: Burr-Hamilton duel

Suzanne Vega, singer/songwriter, b.1959

E.B. White, writer, b.1899

John Constable, painter, b.1776

The bicycle, the bicycle surely, should always be the vehicle of novelists and poets.
— *Christopher Morley*

---

12 WEDNESDAY · JULY 12 · 2006

☾ R. 10:35pm S. 7:06am
☿ R. 5:38am S. 8:59pm

☾☌♄ 11:50am

1979: Kiribati Independence Day

Bill Cosby, comedian, b.1937

Pablo Neruda, poet, b.1904

Buckminster Fuller, inventor, b.1895

Henry David Thoreau, writer, b.1817

Nature is trying very hard to make us succeed, but nature does not depend on us. We are not the only experiment.
— *Buckminster Fuller*

---

13 THURSDAY · JULY 13 · 2006

☾ R. 11:00pm S. 8:30am
☿ R. 5:39am S. 8:58pm

☾☌♆ 12:15am
☾△♀ 6:56am
☾☌♂ 8:37am

1985: Live Aid concert

1930: 1st World Cup soccer championship

Obon: Feast of Lanterns, *Japan*

Cow Appreciation Day

Erno Rubik, inventor, b.1944

Harrison Ford, actor, b.1942

The best portion of a good man's life is his little, nameless, unremembered acts of kindness and of love.

© Photograph courtesy of Stefan D. Bruda

URBAN SANCTUARY :: MOUNT ROYALE PARK, MONTREAL, CANADA :: *To learn more, see pg. 274*

MOIST MOON PEOPLE / *Carl Sandburg*

… why did the moon command the valley, the green / mist and white river go a-roaming, and the moon by / itself take so high a stand in the sky? / If God and I alone saw it, the show was worth putting on, / Yet I remember others were there, Amos and Priscilla, / Axel and Hulda, Hank and Jo, Big Charley and / Little Morningstar, / They were all there; the clock ticks spoke with castanet / clicks.

Free Hot Dog Day, *Luverne, MN*

Bastille Day: *France*

Ingmar Bergman, director, b.1918

Woody Guthrie, singer, b.1912

Gerald Ford, 38th president, b.1913

Isaac Bashevis-Singer, writer, b.1904

I believe that truth is the glue that holds government together, not only our government but civilization itself.
— *Gerald Ford*

☾ R. 11:21pm S. 9:52am
☼ R. 5:40am S. 8:58pm

♂△♆ 2:07am
☽△♃ 8:55am
♀☌♇ 12:28pm
☽☌♅ 5:48pm

FRIDAY · JULY 14 · 2006 **14**

St. Swithin's Day, *England*

Kim Alexis, model, b.1960

Linda Ronstadt, singer, b.1946

Iris Murdoch, writer, b.1919

Clement Moore, writer, b.1779

Rembrandt, painter, b.1606

Love is the difficult realization that something other than oneself is real.
— *Iris Murdoch*

☾ R. 11:41pm S. 11:12am
☼ R. 5:41am S. 8:57pm

☽△☉ 7:48am
☽△☿ 2:57pm

SATURDAY · JULY 15 · 2006 **15**

1548: La Paz Day, *Bolivia*

1945: Atomic Bomb Tested

Will Ferrell, comic actor, b.1967

Ginger Rogers, dancer/actor, b.1911

Roald Amundsen, explorer, b.1872

Mary Baker Eddy, Christian Science founder, b.1821

Joshua Reynolds, painter, b.1723

The way to win an atomic war is to make certain it never starts.
— *Omar Bradley*

☾ S. 12:30pm
☼ R. 5:42am S. 8:56pm

☽△♄ 4:03pm

SUNDAY · JULY 16 · 2006 **16**

All times Central Time Zone, sun and moon rise and set Minneapolis, MN.

17 MONDAY · JULY 17 · 2006

☾ R. 12:01am S. 1:47pm
☉ R. 5:43am S. 8:55pm

Last Quarter
2:13 pm

☾△♆ 1:31pm
☾△♂ 5:31pm

1918: Czar Nicholas II and family executed

1955: Disneyland opened

It's kind of fun to do the impossible.
— Walt Disney

Phoebe Snow, singer, 1952

Donald Sutherland, actor, b.1934

Phyllis Diller, comic actor, b.1917

Erle Stanley Gardner, writer, b.1889

18 TUESDAY · JULY 18 · 2006

☾ R. 12:22am S. 3:05pm
☉ R. 5:44am S. 8:54pm

⊙☌☿ 2:07am
☾☌♃ 2:47pm

1936: Spanish Civil War begins

Hunter S. Thompson, writer, b.1939

Nelson Mandela, S. African leader, b.1918

Gilbert White, naturalist, b.1720

There is nothing like returning to a place that remains unchanged to find the ways in which yourself have altered.
— Nelson Mandela

19 WEDNESDAY · JULY 19 · 2006

☾ R. 12:47am S. 4:22pm
☉ R. 5:45am S. 8:54pm

1979: Nicaragua Liberation Day

1848: Women's Rights convention, Seneca Falls, NY

George McGovern, politician, b.1922

Eve Merriam, writer, b.1916

Charles Mayo, surgeon, b.1865

Edgar Degas, painter, b.1834

The direct use of force is such a poor solution to any problem, it is generally employed only by small children and large nations.
— Eve Merriam

20 THURSDAY · JULY 20 · 2006

☾ R. 1:17am S. 5:37pm
☉ R. 5:46am S. 8:53pm

Moon Day

1969: First human on the Moon

1874: Locust Plague

1968: Special Olympics founded

Carlos Santana, guitarist, b.1947

Natalie Wood, actor, b.1938

Sir Edmund Hillary, explorer, b.1919

It is not the mountain we conquer but ourselves.
— Sir Edmund Hillary

Nature Note: ANIMAL EYE COLOR

Some animals have a *tapetum lucidum,* a layer of mirror-like tissue at the back of their eyes to enhance the light. It makes the glow you see as your headlights catch animal eyes at night, reflecting the light back at you along with the color of the pigments in the animal's eyes. Crocodile eyes, for example, glow red, raccoon eyes look bright yellow, and opossum eyes are pale orange. Humans don't have a *tapetum lucidum.* The red-eye effect you get when taking a photo with a flash comes from light bouncing off the retinal blood vessels. —MC

Notes

CONTEMPLATE:

THE SUMMER DAY / Mary Oliver

Who made the world?
Who made the swan, and the black bear?
Who made the grasshopper?
This grasshopper I mean
the one who has flung herself out of the grass,
the one who is eating sugar out of my hand,
who is moving her jaws back and forth instead of up and down
who is gazing around with her enormous and complicated eyes.
Now she lifts her pale forearms and thoroughly washes her face.
Now she snaps her wings open, and floats away.
I don't know exactly what a prayer is.
I do know how to pay attention, how to fall down
into the grass, how to kneel down in the grass,
how to be idle and blessed, how to stroll through the fields,
which is what I have been doing all day.
Tell me, what else should I have done?
Doesn't everything die at last, and too soon?
Tell me, what is it you plan to do
with your one wild and precious life?

FROM BLOSSOMS / *Li-Young Lee*
From blossoms comes
this brown paper bag of peaches…
…O, to take what we love inside,
to carry within us an orchard…

Cheyenne Frontier Days
July 21-30, U.S.

1861: Battle of Bull Run

Robin Williams, comic/actor, b.1952

Yusuf Islam, (Cat Stevens) singer, b.1948

Isaac Stern, musician, b.1920

Marshall McLuhan, writer, b.1911

Ernest Hemingway, writer, b.1899

Courage is grace under pressure.
— Ernest Hemingway

☾ R. 1:56am S. 6:45pm
☉ R. 5:47am S. 8:52pm

FRIDAY · JULY 21 · 2006 **21**

☽△♆ 2:02pm

Rat Catcher's Day

Spooner's Day (celebrate slips of the tongue)

1376: Pied Piper of Hamelin, *Germany*

If little else, the brain is an educational toy.
— Tom Robbins

Tom Robbins, writer, b.1936

Alexander Calder, sculptor, b.1898

Karl Menninger, psychiatrist, b.1893

Edward Hopper, painter, b.1882

William Spooner, reverend, b.1844

☾ R. 2:44am S. 7:43pm
☉ R. 5:48am S. 8:51pm

SATURDAY · JULY 22 · 2006 **22**

☽☌♆ 12:22am
☽☌♀ 7:15pm

St. Appolinaris Day, *Christian*

Monica Lewinsky, intern, b.1973

Philip Hoffman, actor, b.1967

Woody Harrelson, actor, b.1961

Don Drysdale, baseball pitcher, b.1936

Raymond Chandler, writer, b.1888

When in doubt, have two guys come through the door with guns.
— Raymond Chandler

☾ R. 3:43am S. 8:29pm
☉ R. 5:49am S. 8:50pm

SUNDAY · JULY 23 · 2006 **23**

☽△♃ 4:06am
☽△♅ 1:17pm

All times Central Time Zone, sun and moon rise and set Minneapolis, MN.

24 MONDAY · JULY 24 · 2006

☾ R. 4:49am S. 9:04pm
☉ R. 5:50am S. 8:49pm

New Moon
11:31 pm

☽☌☉ 11:31pm

1847: Pioneer Day: Mormons enter Salt Lake City, *Utah*

Jennifer Lopez, singer/actor, b.1970

Zelda Fitzgerald, writer, b.1900

Amelia Earhart, aviatrix, b.1898

Alexandre Dumas, writer, b.1802

Simon Bolivar, South America liberator, b.1783

Courage is the price that life exacts for granting peace.
— Amelia Earhart

25 TUESDAY · JULY 25 · 2006

☾ R. 5:58am S. 9:31pm
☉ R. 5:51am S. 8:48pm

☽☌♄ 9:19pm

Pilgrimage of St. Anne d'Auray, *France*

St. James the Great Day, *Christian*

Matt LeBlanc, actor, b.1967

Iman, actor, model, b.1955

Walter Payton, football star, b.1954

Eric Hoffer, philosopher, b.1902

Rudeness is the weak man's imitation of strength.
— Eric Hoffer

26 WEDNESDAY · JULY 26 · 2006

☾ R. 7:07am S. 9:53pm
☉ R. 5:52am S. 8:47pm

☽☌♅ 8:20am
☽△♆ 7:33pm
♀△♃ 8:49pm

1953: Natl. Day of Cuba: 26th of July Movement

Sandra Bullock, actor, b.1965

Mick Jagger, musician, b.1943

Robert Graves, writer, b.1895

Aldous Huxley, writer, b.1894

Carl Jung, psychoanalyst, b.1875

Antonio Machado, poet, b.1875

George Bernard Shaw, writer, b.1856

Facts do not cease to exist because they are ignored.
— Aldous Huxley

27 THURSDAY · JULY 27 · 2006

☾ R. 8:14am S. 10:11pm
☉ R. 5:53am S. 8:46pm

☽☌♂ 12:49pm

Procession of the Penitents, *Belgium*

1866: Atlantic telegraph cable laid

Alex Rodriguez, baseball player, b.1975

Maya Rudolph, comic actor, b.1972

Peggy Fleming, skater, b.1948

José C. Barbosa, Puerto Rican patriot, b.1857

In summer, the song sings itself.
— William Carlos Williams

MOON OVER PORTLAND, OREGON

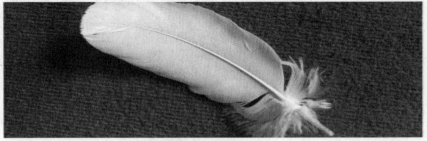

SO WHERE IS IT? / *James P. Lenfestey*

So where is it, your tree, / your bird? / So when you sit / cross-legged, / palms out, / they come. / When you sleep, / they brush all around / your bed. / When you wake, / there's a familiar feather, and a seed.

1914:
WWI Begins:
Archduke
Ferdinand killed

*Gerard Manley
Hopkins,
poet, b.1844*

☾ R. 9:18am S. 10:28pm
☉ R. 5:54am S. 8:44pm

FRIDAY · JULY 28 · 2006 28

*Jacqueline O.
Kennedy, first
lady, b.1929*

*Marcel
Duchamp,
surrealist, b.1887*

*Beatrix Potter,
writer, b.1866*

*If you bungle
raising your
children, I don't
think whatever
else you do
well matters
very much.
— Jacqueline
O. Kennedy*

☽ ♂ ♅ 11:10am
☿ 7:39pm

Olsok:
Commemorates
Viking King
Olaf, *Norway*

1958: NASA
Established

*Ken Burns, film-
maker, b.1953*

*Peter Jennings,
TV journalist,
b.1938*

*Paul Taylor,
choreographer,
b.1930*

*Booth
Tarkington,
writer, b.1869*

☾ R. 10:21am S. 10:43pm
☉ R. 5:55am S. 8:43pm

SATURDAY · JULY 29 · 2006 29

*Cherish all your
happy moments;
they make a
fine cushion
for old age.
— Booth
Tarkington*

1980:
Vancouver
Independence
Day

1935:
Paperback books
introduced

*Arnold
Schwarzenegger,
actor, b.1947*

*Henry Ford,
industrialist,
b.1863*

*Thorstein Veblen,
economist, b.1857*

☾ R. 11:24am S. 10:58pm
☉ R. 5:56am S. 8:42pm

SUNDAY · JULY 30 · 2006 30

*You can't build
a reputation on
what you are
going to do.
— Henry Ford*

*Henry Moore,
sculptor, b.1848*

*Emily Bronte,
writer, b.1818*

♀ △ ♅ 1:19pm

All times Central Time Zone, sun and moon rise and set Minneapolis, MN.

AUGUST

JUL 23 - AUG 22

♌
Leo

AUGUST BIRTHSTONE
Peridot

AUG 23 - SEPT 22

♍
Virgo

AUGUST FLOWER
Gladiolus

© PhotoDisc

DISCRETION Becomes Meditative Strength
Challenges: indiscrimination

The days seem to shorten. The nights, deep and warm, grow longer. Tree frogs and crickets echo in the darkness. Summer is short. Apples are on the trees. The first fruits are gathered. It's the Celtic feast of Lugh, the God of Light, Christian Lammastide or Loaf Mass, when the first grains are ground and baked and placed upon the alter. For the Celts, Lugh ordained the feast be held in honor of his mother Tailltiu, the Earth Mother. Christians, too, celebrate Mary, Mother of Compassion, who carried all things in her heart and gave birth to the light. What gifts! What freedom! This is the time to put on the garments of the spirit, to hold memories in our hearts. Something is germinating secretly, silently within us. Tread softly and take care of yourself and the world so that what you are carrying might come to birth. – *CB*

WEST COAST / PACIFIC MARITIME

With grasslands brown and crackling dry, birds begin preparing for their migration south, starting with the gathering of massive swallow flocks in Willamette Valley and shorebirds arriving from the north to feed at the edges of lakes and ponds. Ripening in the lush warmth, this is the season to pick blackberries for the tastiest cobblers and pies, if you can find a way to penetrate the prickly thickets. Around Seattle look for colorful, ripe madrone, Oregon grape, and kinnickinnick berries. Along the coast, sea lions disperse north and south from their breeding colonies, showing up in areas where they have been absent for months.

MOUNTAIN REGION / BASIN & RANGE

Along with the summer monsoon season in the desert Southwest come torrential daily downpours and new life for spadefoot toads that come out at night to breed around ephemeral pools. In the mountains outside Albuquerque the rains also nourish a late summer wildflower bloom that seems totally out of character with the otherwise scorching hot days. At one time this was also the month when the prairies would have rumbled with highly agitated male buffalos launching into full battle and stirring up great clouds of dust in preparation for mating. Tasty berries like huckleberries, raspberries, and currants are ripening.

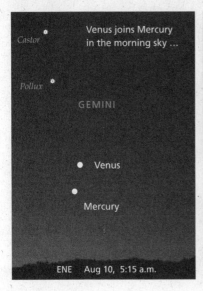

Venus joins Mercury in the morning sky ...

Castor

Pollux

GEMINI

Venus

Mercury

ENE   Aug 10, 5:15 a.m.

... and 17 days later comes into close conjunction with Saturn.

Saturn

Venus

ENE   Aug 27, 6 a.m.

LOOK UP:

2 First quarter Moon, 3:46 AM

3 As Venus descends slowly into twilight early August mornings, Mercury jumps up to meet it; On August 3, Venus far outshines the stars Castor and Pollux to its left, but has dropped below them by August 10, when Mercury is closest

7 Mercury at greatest western elongation (19° 11') Saturn in conjunction with the sun (not visible)

9 Full Moon, 5:55 AM

10 Venus and Mercury closest this morning

12 Perseid meteor shower peaks; Moon interferes

15 Last quarter Moon, 8:52 PM

23 New Moon, 2:10 PM

27 Venus and Saturn gleam together low in the east-northeast this morning in the hour before dawn; Binoculars help

31 First quarter Moon, 5:57 PM

AUGUST

S	M	T	W	T	F	S
		1	2	3	4	5
6	7	8	9	10	11	12
13	14	15	16	17	18	19
20	21	22	23	24	25	26
27	28	29	30	31		

AUGUST IS THE MONTH FOR:
FAMILY FUN · BACK TO SCHOOL · CIVILITY · VACATIONS · NEW ZEALAND KIWIFRUIT · THE GRATEFUL DEAD · NAT'L INVENTOR'S MONTH · VISION & LEARNING · CATARACT AWARENESS

MID-CONTINENT / CORN BELT & GULF

Male ducks are nervous and dull-colored because they are undergoing a molt that leaves them temporarily flightless. Most retreat to the centers of ponds and shy away from your approach. The changing season is signaled by shorebirds arriving from their boreal breeding grounds. Migrating ruby-throated hummingbirds start to show up in places like St. Louis. Colorful warblers take on their drab fall plumage and feed earnestly in preparation for their journey south. In the woods outside Indianapolis look for signs that deer have begun rubbing the velvet off their antlers.

EAST COAST / ATLANTIC SEABOARD

Shorebirds from the Arctic arrive on beaches and mudflats. Forest greens transform into the yellows of late summer. Wild cherries and huckleberries ripen in Great Smoky Mountains National Park. Young opossums are on the prowl and may find your garbage can. In the scorching heat, vultures take advantage of rising thermals. Spiders throw out silken balloons and ride updrafts to new homes; look for their silvery strands floating past high lookouts. The first cool northwest winds trigger the beginning of hawk migration in the northern Appalachians. Along the Florida coastline, coral begin spawning. – DL

31 MONDAY · JULY 31 · 2006

☾ R. 12:28pm S. 11:15pm
☉ R. 5:57am S. 8:41pm

☽△♆ 9:28am

St. Ignatius Loyola, *Roman Catholic*

1790: U.S. Patent Office opens

J.K. Rowling, writer, b.1965

Evonne Goolagong, tennis player, b.1951

Milton Friedman, economist, b.1912

Jean Dubuffet, painter, b.1901

Governments never learn. Only people learn.
– Milton Friedman

---

1 TUESDAY · AUGUST 1 · 2006

☾ R. 1:34pm S. 11:34pm
☉ R. 5:59am S. 8:40pm

Lammas: 1st harvest, *Wicca*

Homou'o: hooting at hunger, *Ghana*

1789: U.S. Customs est.

1990: World Wide Web established

Life's a voyage that's homeward bound.
—Herman Melville

Jerry Garcia, guitarist/singer, b.1942

Yves St. Laurent, designer, b.1936

Herman Melville, writer, b.1819

Maria Mitchell, astronomer, b.1818

---

2 WEDNESDAY · AUGUST 2 · 2006

☾ R. 2:43pm S. 11:58pm
☉ R. 6:00am S. 8:38pm

First Quarter
3:46 am

☽♂♃ 4:00am
☽△♅ 11:41pm
☽△♀ 7:30pm

Nuestra Señora de los Angeles, *Costa Rica*

1990: Iraq invades Kuwait

My doctor gave me two weeks to live. I hope they're in August.
– Ronnie Shakes

James Fallows, journalist, b.1949

James Baldwin, writer, b.1924

Carroll O'Connor actor, b.1924

Myrna Loy, actor, b.1905

---

3 THURSDAY · AUGUST 3 · 2006

☾ R. 3:54pm S.
☉ R. 6:01am S. 8:37pm

☽△☿ 4:08am

Niger Independence Day

Tisha B'av, *Jewish*

I catnap now and then, but I think while I nap, so it's not a waste of time.
– Martha Stewart

Martha Stewart, lifestyle maven, b.1941

Maggie Kuhn, founded Gray Panthers, b.1905

John T. Scopes, teacher, b.1900

Ernie Pyle, journalist, b.1900

Nature Note: **HOW TO READ A SUNDIAL**

The *gnomon* (shadow caster) on the sundial's face shows local solar time, but it's possible to estimate clock time from a sundial. **First,** if you live west of the center of your time zone, add four minutes to the sundial reading for every degree of longitude; if you live east, subtract four minutes for each degree. **Second,** add one hour for Daylight Savings Time (if applicable). **Third,** apply the Equation of Time—impossible to explain here—which can add as much as 15 minutes. **Lastly,** throw away all timekeepers and just follow your own rhythms.

– *Danielle Maestretti*

© Jupiter Images

© iStockPhoto

IN THE GROVE: THE POET AT TEN / *Jane Kenyon*

She lay on her back in the timothy / and gazed past the
doddering / auburn heads of sumac. / A cloud—huge, calm, / and
dignified—covered the sun / but did not, could not, put it out. / The light
surged back again. / Nothing could rouse her then / from that joy
so violent / it was hard to distinguish from pain.

Raksha Bandhan, *Hindu*

1790: Coast Guard Day

1962: Nelson Mandela arrested

Billy Bob Thornton, actor, b.1955

It is the nature of all greatness not to be exact.
— Edmund Burke

Jeff Gordon, race-car driver, b.1971

Wm. Schumann, composer, b.1910

Louis Armstrong, musician, b.1900

Knut Hamsun, writer, b.1859

Percy Bysshe Shelley, poet, b.1792

☾ R. 5:05pm S. 12:29am
☉ R. 6:02am S. 8:36pm

☽△☉ 5:04pm
☽△♄ 8:57pm

FRIDAY · AUGUST 4 · 2006   4

Picnic Day, *Australia*

Jamaica Independence Day

Eisteddfod Genedlaethol: Bard of the Year, *Wales (through Aug. 12th)*

Wendell Berry, poet, b.1934

Neil Armstrong, astronaut, b.1930

Raoul Wallenberg, humanitarian, b.1912

Mary Beard, historian, b.1876

To cherish what remains of the Earth and to foster its renewal is our only legitimate hope of survival.
— Wendell Berry

☾ R. 6:12pm S. 1:11am
☉ R. 6:03am S. 8:34pm

☽☌♆ 2:22pm

SATURDAY · AUGUST 5 · 2006   5

Transfiguratio of the Lord, *Orthodox Christian*

Hiroshima Day

1945: Atomic Bomb dropped on Hiroshima

Andy Warhol, artist, b.1928

Lucille Ball, comic actor, b.1911

Clara Bow, actor, b.1905

Scott Nearing, writer, b.1883

Alfred Lord Tennyson, poet, b.1809

In the future everyone will be famous for fifteen minutes.
— Andy Warhol

☾ R. 7:10pm S. 2:06am
☉ R. 6:04am S. 8:33pm

☽△♂ 4:34pm

SUNDAY · AUGUST 6 · 2006   6

All times Central Time Zone, sun and moon rise and set Minneapolis, MN.

7 MONDAY · AUGUST 7 · 2006

☾ R. 7:57pm S. 3:16am
☉ R. 6:05am S. 8:31pm

☉☌♄ 6:54am
☽☍♀ 4:54pm
☽☌☿ 8:44pm

1990: U.S. Desert Shield ops began

1882: Hatfield - McCoy feud erupts

1964: Gulf of Tonkin resolution

1959: First photo of Earth from space

Charlize Theron, actor, b.1975

Garrison Keillor, writer, b.1942

Dr. Ralph Bunche, diplomat, b.1904

Mata Hari, Dutch spy, b.1876

Sometime they'll give a war and nobody will come.
— Carl Sandburg

8 TUESDAY · AUGUST 8 · 2006

☾ R. 8:33pm S. 4:37am
☉ R. 6:07am S. 8:30pm

Sneak Some Zucchini onto Your Neighbor's Porch night

Roger Federer, tennis player, b.1981

The Edge, musician, b.1961

Randy Shilts, journalist, b.1951

Dustin Hoffman, actor, b.1937

Esther Williams, swimmer, b.1921

Marjorie Kinnan Rawlings, writer, b.1896

Anyone who has got a book collection and a garden wants for nothing.
— Cicero

9 WEDNESDAY · AUGUST 9 · 2006

☾ R. 9:01pm S. 6:02am
☉ R. 6:08am S. 8:29pm

Full Moon
5:54 am

☽☍♃ 3:15am
☽☍☉ 5:53am
☽☌♅ 8:41am

Moment of Silence, *Japan*

1945: Atomic bomb dropped on Nagasaki

1974: Nixon resigns

Gillian Anderson, actor, b.1968

Whitney Houston, singer, b.1963

Melanie Griffith, actor, b.1957

Coco Chanel, designer, b.1883

Izaak Walton, writer/compleat angler, b.1593

If you go on with this nuclear arms race, all you are going to do is make the rubble bounce.
— Sir Winston Churchill

10 THURSDAY · AUGUST 10 · 2006

☾ R. 9:24pm S. 7:27am
☉ R. 6:09am S. 8:27pm

☽△♃ 8:29pm
☽☍♂ 10:34pm

1945: Japan surrenders

1846: Smithsonian Institution est.

About the time we think we can make ends meet, somebody moves the ends.
— Herbert Hoover

Herbert Hoover, 31st president, b.1874

Angie Harmon, actor, b.1972

Tove Janssen, writer, b.1900

Antonio Banderas, actor, b.1960

© New York Recreational Park System

BIRTHDAY: August 7, 1942
GARRISON KEILLOR,
Writer

Garry Edward Keillor was the third child of six in a family where the religious doctrine of the Plymouth Brethren held sway. Born in Anoka, Minnesota, he grew up in a home that eschewed entertainment. How fitting that he became the creator and host of the widely popular weekly radio show, "A Prairie Home Companion," with its warm and extemporaneous celebration of that mythic everytown, Lake Wobegon.

Besides hosting and writing his weekly radio show, Keillor, who adopted the name Garrison, has a daily radio spot ("The Writer's Almanac"), a regular newspaper column, and a few novels under his belt, and he recently wrote the screenplay for the new Robert Altman film, *A Prairie Home Companion*.

– KM

A lovely thing about Christmas is that it's compulsory, like a thunderstorm, and we all go through it together.

Even in a time of elephantine vanity and greed, one never has to look far to see the campfires of gentle people.

I think the most un-American thing you can say is, "You can't say that."

Librarians . . . possess a vast store of politeness. These are people who get asked regularly the dumbest questions on God's green earth. These people tolerate every kind of crank and eccentric and mouth-breather there is.

Thank you, God, for this good life and forgive us if we do not love it enough.

Going to church no more makes you a Christian than standing in a garage makes you a car.

Republicans might be heathens and out to destroy all we hold most dear, but that doesn't mean we need to take them seriously. Or be bitter or vituperative just because they are swine. I think one can still have friends who are Republicans.

© iStockPhoto

CIVILIZING IDEA:
NATIONAL NIGHT OUT

Since 1984, communities from New Bedford, Massachusetts to Waxahachie, Texas, to Battleground, Washington, have been turning on the lights and gathering in the streets for National Night Out (NNO), an annual nationwide event promoting safe neighborhoods.

The concept grew out of the neighborhood watch programs that originated in the 1970s when crime was up and progressive police departments began recognizing the value of community-police partnerships. A guy in Philly, Matt Peskin, who'd been a volunteer in a local crime watch area and written the neighborhood newsletter, felt discouraged that only 2 to 5 percent of people participated in the neighborhood programs. He wanted a way to expand participation at no cost, and a bright idea was born. "When the lights are on, criminals won't do anything," says Peskin.

The annual event on the first Tuesday of August still includes turning on the lights in your house and holding porch vigils—along with tasty cookouts, festive block parties, musical extravangazas, exhibits, parades, a ride in a squad car, flashlight walks, three-on-three basketball, and, well, a night that fits each hosting community.

Peskin is now the executive director of the National Association of Town Watch (NATW), the umbrella organization for crime watch and NNO. He estimates that more than 10,000 communities and 34.2 million people participated in 2004. Says Peskin, "NNO represents the kind of spirit, energy, and determination that is helping to make many neighborhoods safer places throughout the year."

While the focus for NNO continues to be anticrime, the benefits glow all around as communities forge good relationships with their police departments, neighbors get to know each other, and everyone celebrates being together.

– K.M.

For more on National Night Out, see *www.nationalnightout.org.*

© iStockPhoto

TELESCOPE / *Ted Kooser*

This is the pipe that pierces the dam / that holds back the universe, /
that takes off some of the pressure, / keeping the weight of the
unknown / from breaking through / and washing us all down the valley. //
Because of this small tube, / through which cold light rushes / from
the bottom of time, / the depth of the stars stays always constant / and we
are able to sleep, at least for now, / beneath the straining wall of darkness.

1965: Watts Riot, *Los Angeles*

Carl Rowan, journalist, b.1925

Alex Haley writer, b.1921

Gifford Pinchot, environmentalist, b.1865

Only Robinson Crusoe had everything done by Friday.
— *Anonymous*

☾ R. 9:45pm S. 8:51pm
☉ R. 6:10am S. 8:26pm

☉☌♆ 12:13am
☽☌♅ 1:06am

FRIDAY · AUGUST 11 · 2006 **11**

1676: King Philip assassinated

1851: Sewing machine invented

Night of the Shooting Stars, Perseid meteor shower peaks

UN World Youth Day

William Goldman, writer, b.1931

George Soros, financier, b.1930

Cecil B. DeMille, director, b.1881

Mme. Blavatsky, occultist, b.1831

Creativity is a drug I cannot live without.
— *Cecil B. DeMille*

☾ R. 10:05pm S. 10:12am
☉ R. 6:11am S. 8:24pm

☽△♀ 2:17am
☽△☿ 6:17am

SATURDAY · AUGUST 12 · 2006 **12**

Women's Day, *Tunisia*

1961: Berlin Wall erected

Fidel Castro, Cuban president, b.1926

Cantinflas, comedian, b.1911

Alfred Hitchcock, director, b.1899

William Caxton, painter, b.1422

Television has done much for psychiatry by spreading information about it, as well as contributing to the need for it.
— *Alfred Hitchcock*

☾ R. 10:26pm S. 11:32am
☉ R. 6:12am S. 8:23pm

☽△♄ 4:55am
♂☌♅ 7:51am
☽△☉ 1:40pm
☽△♆ 7:14pm

SUNDAY · AUGUST 13 · 2006 **13**

All times Central Time Zone, sun and moon rise and set Minneapolis, MN.

14 MONDAY · AUGUST 14 · 2006

☾ R. 10:50pm S. 12:52pm
☉ R. 6:14am S. 8:21pm

1945: V-J Day
La Torta dei Fieschi, *Italy*

1935: Social Security Act established

Halle Berry, actor, b.1968

Earvin "Magic" Johnson, basketball star, b.1959

Gary Larson, cartoonist, b.1950

Steve Martin, comedian, b.1945

There's no trick to being a humorist when you have the whole government working for you.
— Will Rogers

15 TUESDAY · AUGUST 15 · 2006

☾ R. 11:19pm S. 2:11pm
☉ R. 6:15am S. 8:19pm

Last Quarter
8:51 pm

☽☌♃ 12:14am
☽△♂ 6:28am

Assumption of the Blessed Virgin, *Roman Catholic*

Dormition of Theotokos, *Orthodox Christian*

Julia Child, chef, b.1912

T.E. Lawrence, writer, b.1888

Sir Walter Scott, poet, b.1771

Napoleon Bonaparte, French emperor, b.1769

Never interrupt your enemy when he is making a mistake.
— Napoleon Bonaparte

16 WEDNESDAY · AUGUST 16 · 2006

☾ R. 11:55pm S. 3:28pm
☉ R. 6:16am S. 8:18pm

Krisham Jayanti, *Hindu*

Palio of the Contrade, *Siena, Italy*

1987: Harmonic Convergence

Madonna, singer, b.1958

Elvis Presley, singer, d.1977

George Meany, US labor leader, b.1894

Charles Bukowski, writer, b.1920

Babe Ruth, baseball player, d.1948

I don't know anything about music. In my line you don't have to.
— Elvis Presley

17 THURSDAY · AUGUST 17 · 2006

☾ S. 4:39pm
☉ R. 6:17am S. 8:16pm

☉△♆ 12:01am
☽△♆ 6:11pm

1863: Fort Sumter siege begun

You only live once, but if you do it right, once is enough.
— Mae West

Sean Penn, actor, b.1960

Robert de Niro, actor, b.1943

Mae West, actor, b.1898

Davy Crockett, frontiersman, b.1786

© PhotoDisc

Recipe: **SUN-DRYING TOMATOES (okay, oven-drying tomatoes)**
Cut a thin slice from each end of cleaned tomaotoes. Cut into half-inch slices. Arrange slices on cake racks and put racks in the oven. Place a sheet of aluminum foil on the bottom of the oven. Turn oven to 200° F and leave the tomatoes in for 30 minutes. Then turn the oven down to 140° F, leaving the door slightly open. Leave the tomatoes in the oven until they are leathery, about six to eight hours. Quickly dip slices in vinegar and pack them in clean pint jars, covering completely with olive oil. They'll keep in a cool, dry place for up to a year. —MC

SOUR, DOUGHY, NUMB AND RAW / *Rumi, translated by Coleman Barks*

If we're not together in the heart, / what's the point? When body and soul / aren't dancing, there's no pleasure / in colorful clothing. Why have / cooking pans when there's no food in / the house? In this world full of / fresh bread, amber, and musk, so many / different fragrances, what are they / to someone with no sense of smell? / If you stay away from fire, you'll / be sour, doughy, numb, and raw. You / may have lovely, just baked loaves / around you, but those friends cannot / help. You have to feel oven fire.

1960: First birth control pills sold	*Edward Norton, actor, b.1969*	☾ R. 12:40am S. 5:40pm ☉ R. 6:18am S. 8:15pm	**FRIDAY · AUGUST 18 · 2006 18**
1872: First mail-order catalog published	*Martin Mull, comic actor, b.1943*		
1920: Women's right to vote: 19th Amendment ratified	*Robert Redford, actor, b.1937* *Rosalynn Carter, 1st lady, b.1927*	☽ ☌ ♆ 5:09am	
Vote early and vote often. — Al Capone	*Meriwether Lewis, explorer, b.1774*		

National Aviation Day	A family is a unit composed not only of children but of men, women, an occasional animal, and the common cold. — Ogden Nash	☾ R. 1:36am S. 6:29pm ☉ R. 6:20am S. 8:13pm	**SATURDAY · AUGUST 19 · 2006 19**
Tipper Gore, public citizen, b.1948			
Bill Clinton, 42nd president, b.1946		☽ △ ♃ 2:22pm ☽ △ ♅ 5:26pm	
Ogden Nash, poet, b.1902			
Orville Wright, aviator, b.1871			

St. Stephen's Day, *Hungary*	*John Hiatt, singer/songwriter, b.1952*	☾ R. 2:39am S. 7:06pm ☉ R. 6:21am S. 8:11pm	**SUNDAY · AUGUST 20 · 2006 20**
1942: Plutonium first weighed	*Jacqueline Susann, writer, b.1921*		
The most merciful thing in the world . . . is the inability of the human mind to correlate all its contents. — H.P. Lovecraft	*H.P. Lovecraft, writer, b.1890* *Eliel Saarinen, architect, b.1873*	☿ ☌ ♄ 7:42pm	

All times Central Time Zone, sun and moon rise and set Minneapolis, MN.

21 MONDAY · AUGUST 21 · 2006

☾ R. 3:47am S. 7:36pm
☼ R. 6:22am S. 8:10pm

☿☍♆ 2:53pm

1983: Benigno Aquino assassinated

Carrie-Anne Moss, actor, b.1967

Peter Weir, director, b.1944

Wilt Chamberlain, basketball player, b.1936

Count Basie, bandleader, b.1904

Aubrey Beardsley, artist, b.1872

Until he extends his circle of compassion to include all living things, man will not himself find peace.
– Albert Schweitzer

22 TUESDAY · AUGUST 22 · 2006

☾ R. 4:56am S. 7:59pm
☼ R. 6:23am S. 8:08pm

☽☌♀ 12:07am
☽☌♄ 10:41am
☽☍♆ 1:18pm
☽☌☿ 5:44pm

Lailat al Miraj, *Islam*

1942: Battle of Stalingrad

Tori Amos, singer, b.1963

John Lee Hooker, blues singer, b.1915

Henri Cartier-Bresson, photographer, b.1908

Dorothy Parker, writer, b.1893

Claude Debussy, composer, b.1862

The cure for boredom is curiosity. There is no cure for curiosity.
– Dorothy Parker

23 WEDNESDAY · AUGUST 23 · 2006

☾ R. 6:03am S. 8:18pm
☼ R. 6:24am S. 8:06pm

New Moon
2:10 pm

☽△♆ 1:20am
☽☌☉ 2:10pm

1977: First human-powered flight

1927: Sacco and Vanzetti executed

Shelley Long, actor, b.1950

Keith Moon, drummer, b.1946

Barbara Eden, actor, b.1934

Gene Kelly, dancer, b.1912

Oliver H. Perry, naval hero, b.1785

Aerodynamically, the bumblebee shouldn't be able to fly, but the bumblebee doesn't know it so it goes on flying anyway.
– Mary Kay Ash

24 THURSDAY · AUGUST 24 · 2006

☾ R. 7:08am S. 8:34pm
☼ R. 6:26am S. 8:04pm

☿△♆ 3:34pm
☽☍♅ 3:50pm

Schäferlauf: Shepherd's Race, *Germany*

79AD: Mt. Vesuvius erupts, Pompeii destroyed

Rupert Grint, actor, b.1988

Marlee Matlin, actor, b.1965

Yassir Arafat, Palestinian pres., b.1929

Jorge Luis Borges, writer, b.1899

I have always imagined that Paradise will be a kind of library.
– Jorge Luis Borges

PARK, ATLANTA, GEORGIA

Notes

BIRTHDAY: *August 25, 1913*
WALT KELLY, Cartoonist

A 1971 Earth Day poster, written and illustrated by Walt Kelly, featured his well-known characters Pogo and Porkypine, as well as the first ever occurrence of the phrase, "We have met the enemy and he is us."

– KM

UNTITLED / *Emily Dickinson*

To make a prairie it takes / A clover and one bee, /
One clover, and a bee, / And revery. / The revery alone
will do, / If bees are few.

1939: "The Wizard of Oz" released

Kiss-&-Make-up Day

Now is the time for all good men to come to.
— *Walt Kelly "Pogo"*

Claudia Schiffer, model, b.1970

Elvis Costello, singer, b.1954

Sean Connery, actor, b.1930

Walt Kelly, cartoonist, b.1913

☾ R. 8:12am S. 8:50pm
☉ R. 6:27am S. 8:03pm

☽ ☌ ♂ 8:13am

FRIDAY · AUGUST 25 · 2006 **25**

1920: Women's Equality Day established

1883: Krakatoa erupts: 36,000 killed

Geraldine Ferraro, politician, b.1935

Ben Bradlee, journalist, editor, b.1921

Christopher Isherwood, writer, b.1904

Christopher Columbus, explorer, b.1451

Feminism is the radical concept that women are people.
— *Cheris Kramarae & Paula Treichler*

☾ R. 9:15am S. 9:05pm
☉ R. 6:28am S. 8:01pm

♀ ☌ ♄ 6:38pm

SATURDAY · AUGUST 26 · 2006 **26**

Ganesh Chaturthi, *Hindu*

1979: Lord Mountbatten assassinated

If you judge people, you have no time to love them.
— *Mother Teresa*

Peewee Herman, actor, b.1952

Mother Teresa, saint, b.1910

Theodore Dreiser, writer, b.1871

Georg W.F. Hegel, philosopher, b.1770

☾ R. 10:18am S. 9:21pm
☉ R. 6:29am S. 7:59pm

♀ ☍ ♅ 7:18am
☽ △ ♆ 2:38pm

SUNDAY · AUGUST 27 · 2006 **27**

All times Central Time Zone, sun and moon rise and set Minneapolis, MN.

28 MONDAY · AUGUST 28 · 2006

☽ R. 11:23am S. 9:39pm
☉ R. 6:30am S. 7:57pm

Feast of St. Augustine

1963: March on Washington: M.L. King, Jr. *"I have a dream"*

In the end, we will remember not the words of our enemies, but the silence of our friends.
— *Martin Luther King, Jr.*

LeAnn Rimes, singer, b.1982

Shania Twain, singer, b.1965

Johann W. von Goethe, writer, b.1749

---

29 TUESDAY · AUGUST 29 · 2006

☽ R. 12:30pm S. 10:00pm
☉ R. 6:32am S. 7:56pm

♃△♅ 4:13am
☽△♅ 4:54pm
☽☌♃ 5:05pm

1839: Amistad seized

Beheading of John the Baptist, *Christian*

The actions of men are the best interpreters of their thoughts.
— *John Locke*

Michael Jackson, entertainer, b.1958

Charlie "Bird" Parker, musician, b.1920

Ingrid Bergman, actor, b.1915

John Locke, philosopher, b.1632

---

30 WEDNESDAY · AUGUST 30 · 2006

☽ R. 1:39pm S. 10:27pm
☉ R. 6:33am S. 7:54pm

Santa Rosa de Lima, *Peru*

When Fascism comes to America, it will come wrapped in an American flag.
— *Huey Long*

Andy Roddick, tennis player, b.1982

Cameron Diaz, actor, b.1972

Roy Wilkins, civil rights leader, b.1901

Huey Long, politician, b.1893

Mary Shelley, writer, b.1797

---

31 THURSDAY · AUGUST 31 · 2006

☽ R. 2:49pm S. 11:03pm
☉ R. 6:34am S. 7:52pm

First Quarter
5:57 pm

♃☌♆ 4:53am
☉☌☿ 11:49pm

1896: Gold discovered, *Klondike*

Debbie Gibson, singer, b.1970

Richard Gere, actor, b.1949

William Shawn, editor, b.1907

William Saroyan, writer, b.1908

Maria Montessori, educator, b.1870

Good people are good because they've come to wisdom through failure.
— *William Saroyan*

Drawing by Craig Holdrege

Nature Note: **BATS IN THE DUSK**

When you are sitting outside on a balmy summer evening, you may see airborne creatures with rapidly beating wings flying back and forth. They are not birds. They are bats, the only flying mammal. On the wing at dusk, they feed on mosquitoes, and capture as many as 1,000 in an hour or two, orienting not with their eyes but with their own sonar (echolocation). We should rejoice in these inexhaustible insect predators—they are harmless to human beings. —*CH*

© Jupiter Images

BIRTHDAY: August 30, 1797

MARY SHELLEY, Writer

Mary Wollstonecraft Godwin Shelley who wrote *Frankenstein* at age 18, was the love child of two great English thinkers—William Godwin, a political philosopher, and Mary Wollstonecraft, author of the first feminist treatise, *The Vindication of the Rights of Women*. Both decried the confinement of marriage, but married when Wollstonecraft became pregnant. Eleven days after Mary's birth, her mother died. Her father raised her among the intellectual elite and she and her half sister Fanny once hid under a table to listen to Samuel Coleridge recite *The Rime of the Ancient Mariner*.

At 16, she met Percy Bysshe Shelley (see *Cosmo Doogood's 2005 Almanac*, page 206). They declared their love, ran away to France, and later married. Of her five pregnancies between the ages of 17 and 24, only one child survived. She was widowed, at 24, when Percy drowned while sailing. Although her husband had been an outspoken advocate of free love, it appears that Mary was devoted exclusively to him. She never remarried nor formed any lasting liaisons. For the remainder of her life, she cared for her father and her son, wrote six more novels, and a body of criticism of Percy's work. Mary had her husband's heart removed before his body was cremated on the shores of Italy, and she kept it with her until her death on February 1, 1851, at the age of 54.

– KM

"We will each write a ghost story," said Lord Byron; and his proposition was acceded to. There were four of us . . . Have you thought of a story? I was asked each morning, and each morning I was forced to reply with a mortifying negative. . . On the morrow I announced that I had thought of a story . . . At first I thought but of a few pages—of a short tale; but [Percy Bysshe] Shelley urged me to develop the idea at greater length.

Introduction to Frankenstein ed. 3, 1831

SEPTEMBER

AUG 23 - SEPT 22

SEPT 23 - OCT 22

Virgo

SEPTEMBER BIRTHSTONE
Sapphire

Libra

SEPTEMBER FLOWER
Aster

COURTESY Becomes Tact of Heart
Challenges: exploitation / carelessness

Summer wanes, autumn approaches. Swallows swoop and gather in the sky. The air smells of fallen apples. Goldenrod is everywhere. The sunlight, too, is golden, like the stubble in the fields. Liquid and tender, now it warms our backs, not our heads. Amid the late ripeness, nature begins the process of withering and fading away. At night, a chill is in the air. Flies die. Outer growth turns inward and an inner sun replaces the outer one. Self-consciousness rises, filling us with courage, initiative, and will. The future lies before us, requiring a sensitive, respectful heart. Therefore, at the equinox, when the days and nights are again of equal length, we celebrate Michaelmas, the feast of Michael and the Archangels. As St. Michael overcomes the dragon, we, too, may overcome all that hardens us – our past, our habits, our fixed ways of thinking and feeling – so as to become free to create a truly human, earth-caring, loving future. – *CB*

WEST COAST / PACIFIC MARITIME

No other sound announces the end of summer so dramatically as the eerie cries of bugling elk in mountain and coastal forests. Sounding part agony, and part fervent desire, this cry announces the beginning of fierce combat between males. Conifer trees across the region are fully laden with the weight of rusty brown seeds this month. Coastal waves may be tinged with red tide, a phenomenon that makes it temporarily unsafe to eat shellfish.

MOUNTAIN REGION / BASIN & RANGE

In the mountains of N. Utah, landlocked salmon known as kokanee leave the lakes they have inhabited all summer and move up into streams to spawn. Spawning males take on a brilliant red and green coloration. The mountain forests begin echoing with the bugling calls of amorous bull elks. The high sharp ridges near Salt Lake City are famous for attracting many thousands of migrating raptors this month. The fine specks of golden eagles, red-tailed hawks, sharp-shinned hawks, and other species can be observed.

Venus, Saturn and the Moon meet in the morning sky.

Saturn

Moon

Regulus

LEO

Venus

E   Sept 15, 6:15 a.m.

The waxing Moon and Jupiter meet after sunset.

SCORPIO

LIBRA

Jupiter

Moon

SW   Sept 27, 8 p.m.

LOOK UP:

1 Mercury at superior conjunction (not visible)

7 Full Moon, 1:43 PM Partial lunar eclipse favoring Asia and central and eastern Africa and Europe; greatest eclipse occurs at 1:51 PM

14 Last quarter Moon, 6:16 AM

22 Annular solar eclipse; greatest eclipse at 6:40 AM; The path of annularity arcs through the South Atlantic and makes landfall only on Guyana, Suriname, and French Guiana; New Moon, 6:46 AM

23 Autumnal equinox, 11:04 PM

30 First quarter Moon, 6:04 AM

SEPTEMBER						
S	M	T	W	T	F	S
					1	2
3	4	5	6	7	8	9
10	11	12	13	14	15	16
17	18	19	20	21	22	23
24	25	26	27	28	29	30

SEPTEMBER IS THE MONTH FOR:

BABY SAFETY · BEING KIND TO EDITORS & WRITERS · UPDATING YOUR RESUME · GOOD MANNERS · COLLEGE SAVINGS · FALL HATS · GAY SQUARE DANCING · METAPHYSICAL AWARENESS · BISCUITS · CHICKEN · HONEY · LITTLE LEAGUE · ORGANIC HARVESTING · WAFFLES · PIANOS · POTATOES · SCHOOL SUCCESS

MID-CONTINENT / CORN BELT & GULF

Near the mountains keep an eye out for the broad-winged hawk migration. Hawk Mountain in Pennsylvania and the hills around Little Rock are excellent vantage points. Forests are lively with squirrels collecting acorns and hickory nuts. Northerners savor the onset of fall colors as aspens and other deciduous trees turn fiery red and orange. Wild rice ripens and is harvested by waterfowl. Loons gather into large flocks in preparation for their journey south. Up to 250,000 sandhill cranes can be seen in fields of the Texas panhandle.

EAST COAST / ATLANTIC SEABOARD

Tens of thousands of swallows migrate past Cape May. Peak hawk migration along mountain crests and the seashore. Monarch butterflies are on the move. Late summer wildflowers like Queen Anne's lace and black-eyed Susans put on a good showing along roadsides. Spider webs are evident everywhere. The last purple martins wander south. Rainy days bring out mushrooms in great numbers. This month you can expect to find bottlenosed dolphins moving through estuaries. Watch out, this is the peak season for hurricanes. – DL

Notes

© iStockPhoto

BEING A PERSON / *William Stafford*

Be a person here. Stand by the river, invoke / the owls. Invoke winter, then spring. / Let any season that wants to come here make its own call. / After that sound goes away, wait. / A slow bubble rises through the earth / and begins to include sky, stars, all space, / even the outracing, expanding thought. / Come back and hear the little sound again. / Suddenly this dream you are having matches / everyone's dream, and the result is the world. / …How you stand here is important. / How you listen for the next things to happen. / How you breathe.

Ecclesiastical Year begins, *Orthodox Christian*	*Ann Richards, politician, b.1933*	☾ R. 3:57pm S. 11:51pm ☉ R. 6:35am S. 7:50pm	**FRIDAY · SEPTEMBER 1 · 2006**	**1**
1939: World War II begins	*Edgar Rice Burroughs, writer, b.1875*			
Gloria Estefan, singer, b.1957 *Lily Tomlin, comic actor, b.1939*	Why is it when we talk to God we're praying - but when God talks to us, we're schizophrenic? — *Lily Tomlin*	♀△♅ 6:10am ☽△♄ 11:54am ☽☌♆ 10:56pm		

1666: Great Fire of London	*Christa McAuliffe, astronaut, b.1948*	☾ R. 4:57pm ☉ R. 6:36am S. 7:48pm	**SATURDAY · SEPTEMBER 2 · 2006**	**2**
1864: Sherman enters Atlanta	*Henry George, economist, b.1839*			
Salma Hayak, actor, b.1966 *Keanu Reeves, actor, b. 1964* *Jimmy Connors, tennis player, b.1952*	Man is the only animal whose desires increase as they are fed; the only animal that is never satisfied. — *Henry George*	☽△♀ 12:39am		

1783: Treaty of Paris: ended the American Revolution.	*Charlie Sheen, actor, b.1965*	☾ R. 5:48pm S. 12:52am ☉ R. 6:37am S. 7:46pm	**SUNDAY · SEPTEMBER 3 · 2006**	**3**
	Mort Walker, cartoonist, b.1923			
It is better to offer no excuse than a bad one. — *George Washington*	*Kitty Carlisle, actor, b.1915* *Prudence Crandall, educator, b.1803*	☽△♅ 4:21am ☽△☉ 4:32am ☽△☿ 8:43am		

All times Central Time Zone, sun and moon rise and set Minneapolis, MN.

4 MONDAY · SEPTEMBER 4 · 2006

☽ R. 6:27pm S. 2:07am
☉ R. 6:39am S. 7:45pm

☽△♂ 9:23am
♆ 6:20pm

1781: City of Los Angeles founded

1957: Little Rock Nine turned away from school

Newspaper Carrier Day

Damon Wayans, actor, b.1960

Mitzi Gaynor, actor, b.1931

Paul Harvey, radio journalist, b.1918

Antonin Artaud, writer, b.1896

September tries its best to have us forget summer.
— Bern Williams

LABOR DAY

5 TUESDAY · SEPTEMBER 5 · 2006

☽ R. 6:59pm S. 3:29am
☉ R. 6:40am S. 7:43pm

☉♂♅ 5:54am
☽♂♆ 6:18pm
☽♂♄ 7:38pm

1774: First Continental Congress

Be Late for Something Day

I have noticed that the people who are late are often so much jollier than the people who have to wait for them
— E.V. Lucas

Raquel Welch, actor, b.1940

Bob Newhart, actor, b.1929

John Cage, composer, b.1912

Arthur Koestler, writer, b.1905

Jesse James, bank robber, b.1847

6 WEDNESDAY · SEPTEMBER 6 · 2006

☽ R. 7:24pm S. 4:55am
☉ R. 6:41am S. 7:41pm

☽♂♀ 3:05pm

1920: First radio broadcast of a prizefight

Jane Curtin, actor, b.1947

Robert Pirsig, writer, b.1928

Jane Addams, activist, b.1860

The truth knocks on the door and you say, "Go away, I'm looking for the truth," and so it goes away.
— Robert M. Pirsig

7 THURSDAY · SEPTEMBER 7 · 2006

☽ R. 7:46pm S. 6:20am
☉ R. 6:42am S. 7:39pm

Full Moon
1:42 pm

☽♂♅ 10:00am
☽△♃ 12:46pm
☽♂☉ 1:42pm

1822: Brazil Independence Day

1914: Opening of N.Y. Post Office

If I hadn't started painting, I would have raised chickens.
— Grandma Moses

Chrissie Hynde, singer/songwriter, b.1956

Buddy Holly, singer/songwriter, b.1936

Grandma Moses, painter, b.1860

Queen Elizabeth I, b.1533

Photo by Ed Purcell

IF BEES COULD VOTE / *Connie Wanek*

No doubt they'd vote en masse / like labor unions—or like gun enthusiasts: / for they carry concealed weapons / and would rather die than surrender them. / They'd vote like true conservatives / to keep every last thing they already have; / they'd vote stubbornly for their queen, / however rarely she travels the realm / or even shows herself. Most of all / they'd vote against the annual veil / of paralyzing smoke, the gray dream / during which half their goods vanish, / the vault door left wide open / in the pillager's haste.

Nativity of Mary, *Christian*	*Agnes de Mille, dancer, b.1905*	☾ R. 8:07pm S. 7:44am ☉ R. 6:43am S. 7:37pm	**FRIDAY · SEPTEMBER 8 · 2006**	**8**
1900: Galveston hurricane **1974:** Nixon pardoned	*Confucius, philosopher, b.551 BC*			
International Literacy Day *Patsy Cline, singer, b.1932* *Peter Sellers, actor, b.1925*	Reading is to the mind what exercise is to the body. — Sir Richard Steele	☽ ☌ ☿ 12:26am ☽ ☌ ♂ 2:00pm		
Lailat al Bara'a, *Islam*	*Leo Tolstoy, writer, b.1828*	☾ R. 8:28pm S. 9:07am ☉ R. 6:45am S. 7:35pm	**SATURDAY · SEPTEMBER 9 · 2006**	**9**
Chrysanthemum Day, *Japan* **490BC:** Battle of Marathon	*William the Conqueror, d.1087*			
Rachel Hunter, actor, b.1966 *Adam Sandler, actor, b.1966* *Hugh Grant, actor, b.1960*	What a strange illusion it is to suppose that beauty is goodness. — Leo Tolstoy	☽ △ ♃ 7:43pm		
Federal Lands Cleanup Day **Grandparents Day**	It does no harm just once in a while to acknowledge	☾ R. 8:51pm S. 10:30am ☉ R. 6:46am S. 7:33pm	**SUNDAY · SEPTEMBER 10 · 2006**	**10**
Stephen J. Gould, biologist, b.1941 *Mary Oliver, poet, b.1935* *Charles Kuralt, journalist, b.1934* *Arnold Palmer, golfer, b.1929*	that the whole country isn't in flames, that there are people in the country besides politicians, entertainers, and criminals. — Charles Kuralt	 ☽ △ ♆ 3:53am ☽ △ ♀ 11:52pm		

All times Central Time Zone, sun and moon rise and set Minneapolis, MN.

11 MONDAY · SEPTEMBER 11 · 2006

☾ R. 9:19pm S. 11:53am
☉ R. 6:47am S. 7:32pm

☽ ☌ ♃ 2:30pm
☽ △ ☉ 9:27pm

Patriot Day
2001: Terrorist attacks in New York & Wash. D.C.
Giostra della Quintana, *Italy*

Moby, musician, b.1965
Roger Maris, baseball player, b.1934

Jessica Mitford, writer, b.1917
D.H. Lawrence, writer, b.1885
O. Henry, writer, b.1862

Sorrow was like the wind. It came in gusts.
— *Marjorie Kinnan Rawlings*

---

12 TUESDAY · SEPTEMBER 12 · 2006

☾ R. 9:53pm S. 1:13pm
☉ R. 6:48am S. 7:30pm

☽ △ ☿ 3:58pm
☽ △ ♂ 9:32pm

Improve Your Home Offiic Week
Maria Muldaur, singer, b.1943
Jesse Owens, athlete, b.1913
Maurice Chevalier, singer/actor, b.1888
H.L. Mencken, critic, b.1880

An idealist is one who, on noticing that a rose smells better than a cabbage, concludes that it will also make better soup.
— *H. L. Mencken*

---

13 WEDNESDAY · SEPTEMBER 13 · 2006

☾ R. 10:36pm S. 2:29pm
☉ R. 6:49am S. 7:28pm

☽ △ ♆ 11:05pm

1814: Star-Spangled Banner inspired by the attack on Fort McHenry
Jacqueline Bisset, actor, b.1944
Judith "Miss Manners" Martin, advice columnist, b.1938
Roald Dahl, writer, b.1916

Claudette Colbert, actor, b.1903

There is hopeful symbolism in the fact that flags do not wave in a vacuum.
— *Arthur C. Clarke*

---

14 THURSDAY · SEPTEMBER 14 · 2006

☾ R. 11:29pm S. 3:34pm
☉ R. 6:51am S. 7:26pm

Last Quarter
6:15 am

☽ ☌ ♆ 11:01am

Holy Cross Day, *Christian*
Elevation of the Life-Giving Cross, *Orthodox*
Oliver Stone, director, b.1946
Tommy Lee Jones, actor, b.1946
Kate Millet, writer, b.1934

Margaret Sanger, feminist/advocate, b.1879
Dante Alleghieri, poet, d.1321

Autumn is the bite of the harvest apple.
— *Christina Petrowsky*

© Jupiter images

Nature Note: RAINY NIGHT LOVE

After a long dry summer, the sexual urges of slugs and snails awaken with the first soaking rains of autumn. Wander out on a rainy night and you will likely spot the amorous embraces of these wonderfully slow moving mollusks. Each individual has both male and female sex organs, so after an elaborate courtship of circling, biting, lunging, and in some species, shooting a kind of calcified "Cupid's arrow" to help the sperm's chances, a pair gets down to the serious business of lining up to fertilize each other. —DL

SEPTEMBER / *Louis Jenkins*

One evening the breeze blowing in the window turns cold and you pull the blankets around you. The leaves of the maples along Wallace Avenue have already turned and whoever it was you loved does not come around anymore, It's all right. Things change with the cycle of the seasons and evolve. A mistake, a wrong turn takes one elsewhere. But perhaps there are forces other than chance at work here....

1940: Battle of Britain Day

1971: Greenpeace founded

Curious things, habits. People themselves never knew they had them.
— *Agatha Christie*

Roy Acuff, musician, b.1903

Agatha Christie, writer, b.1890

James Fenimore Cooper, writer, b.1789

Francois de la Rochefoucauld, writer, b.1613

☽ S. 4:28pm
☉ R. 6:52am S. 7:24pm

☿☌♂ 2:00pm
☽☉♅ 9:05pm

FRIDAY · SEPTEMBER 15 · 2006 15

1620: Mayflower Day: Pilgrims deported from England

1810: Mexican Independence Day

Molly Shannon, comic actor, b.1964

B.B.King, musician, b.1925

Lauren Bacall, actor, b.1924

Francis Parkman, writer, b.1823

Anne Bradstreet, poet, d.1672

The love of truth lies at the root of much humor.
— *Robertson Davies*

☽ R. 12:31am S. 5:09pm
☉ R. 6:53am S. 7:22pm

♀☌♅ 12:01am
☽△♃ 3:47am

SATURDAY · SEPTEMBER 16 · 2006 16

Constitution Week

1920: Nat'l Football League formed

1862: Battle of Antietam, 25,000 killed

Hank Williams, Sr, singer/ song-writer, b.1923

Ken Kesey, writer, b.1935

Anne Bancroft, actor, b.1931

William Carlos Williams, poet, b.1883

Take what you can use and let the rest go by.
— *Ken Kesey*

☽ R. 1:38am S. 5:40pm
☉ R. 6:54am S. 7:20pm

SUNDAY · SEPTEMBER 17 · 2006 17

PARTIAL LUNAR ECLIPSE
1:05PM

All times Central Time Zone, sun and moon rise and set Minneapolis, MN.

---

18 MONDAY · SEPTEMBER 18 · 2006

☽ R. 2:47am S. 6:05pm
☉ R. 6:55am S. 7:18pm

☽ ☌ ♆ 5:53pm
☽ ☌ ♄ 11:10pm

Respect for the Aged Day, *Japan*

1851: *New York Times* first published

1947: U.S. Air Force established

Lance Armstrong, bicyclist, b.1971

Greta Garbo, actor, b.1905

Samuel Johnson, essayist, b.1707

One thing about the school of experience is that it will repeat the lesson if you flunk the first time.
— *Author unknown*

---

19 TUESDAY · SEPTEMBER 19 · 2006

☽ R. 3:54am S. 6:25pm
☉ R. 6:57am S. 7:16pm

☽ △ ♆ 7:17am

1985: Mexico City earthquake, 10,000 killed

Twiggy, model, b.1949

"Mama" Cass Elliot, singer, b.1943

Mike Royko, columnist, b.1932

William Golding, writer, b.1911

Nature's peace will flow into you as sunshine flows into trees. The winds will blow their own freshness into you, and the storms their energy, while cares will drop away from you like the leaves of Autumn.
— *John Muir*

---

20 WEDNESDAY · SEPTEMBER 20 · 2006

☽ R. 5:00am S. 6:42pm
☉ R. 6:58am S. 7:14pm

☽ ☌ ♅ 7:44pm

1884: Equal Rights Party founded

1973: Billie Jean King beats Bobby Riggs in tennis

Sophia Loren, actor, b.1934

Red Auerbach, coach, b.1917

Upton Sinclair, writer, b.1878

Alexander the Great, conqueror, b.356BC

Nothing makes a woman more beautiful than the belief that she is beautiful.
— *Sophia Loren*

---

21 THURSDAY · SEPTEMBER 21 · 2006

☽ R. 6:04am S. 6:57pm
☉ R. 6:59am S. 7:12pm

☽ ☌ ♀ 9:47am

Religious Freedom Week

Faith Hill, singer, b.1967

Ethan Coen, director, b.1957

Bill Murray, comic actor, b.1950

Stephen King, writer, b.1947

Leonard Cohen, singer, b.1934

Chief Joseph, leader Nez Perce, d.1904

H.G. Wells, writer, b.1866

Hear me, my chiefs! I am tired. My heart is sick and sad. From where the sun now stands, I will fight no more forever.
— *Chief Joseph*

© iStockPhoto

CIVILIZING IDEA:

WALKABOUT INTERNATIONAL

For the past 27 years, perfect strangers in San Diego have been meeting day and night to take a walk together through Walkabout International, which offers more than 100 walks each month. Walkabout promotes the idea of living well in the city by sponsoring walks to intriguing neighborhoods like the historic Gaslight District downtown or through the famed Del Mar Horseracing Track, taking walkers behind the scenes of thoroughbred racing. Oh, yes, and there's walking for exercise. Pick a pace from half speed (one to two miles an hour) to very brisk (over four miles an hour) and walk along places such as the urban San Diego River, La Jolla Shores beach, or into the wilderness. People also gather for walks to socialize on the Saturday Night Live walk through downtown, followed by the option for dinner, or for the TWEEB (Tuesday Walking Ethnic Eating Bunch). The 100 percent volunteer organization got its start when a young couple moved from Boston to San Diego and realized they had moved to a wonderful walking city. They put an ad in a local reader, people showed up, and the concept gained momentum. All the local walks are free and for all ages. Walkabout International also offers day trips and international excursions, all centered on the congenial activity of walking.

– KM

To contact Walkabout International,
go to *www.sandiego-online.com/forums/walk*
or e-mail *walkabout-int@bigfoot.com.*

© Photo from RayCharles.com

BIRTHDAY: September 23, 1930

RAY CHARLES, Singer

Born in the segregated South and, by his own reckoning, on the bottom rung of the ladder, Ray Charles gave the world more than 50 years of jazz, blues, R & B, country, and gospel.

At the age of three, he showed an interest in the piano, which a local café owner encouraged. Charles recalled his early childhood as a happy time until witnessing the drowning death of his younger brother in a washtub. He began going blind after the accident and was completely blind by seven. After that, his mother enrolled him in the St. Augustine School for the Deaf and Blind where he learned to read, write, and arrange music in Braille. Charles continued to play piano and also learned clarinet and saxophone before leaving school at 15. He was working as a professional musician in Florida, but at 17, he took his savings of $600 and moved to Seattle. There he met Quincy Jones, who was 14 at the time, and began a friendship that lasted a lifetime.

In a Boston airport on October 31, 1964, Charles was busted for possession of heroin, a habit he'd taken up early in his career. After a year of treatment, he stayed clean and went on to take the musical risks that defied the establishment and established him as the Genius of Soul.

– KM

What is soul? It's like electricity—we don't really know what it is, but it's a force that can light a room.

I was born with music inside me. Music was one of my parts. Like my ribs, my kidneys, my liver, my heart. Like my blood. It was a necessity for me like food or water.

You better live every day like your last because one day you're going to be right.

© iStockPhoto

HERĖ / *Lawrence Joseph*

…Now it is September / and I am there, between / the silhouette of broken fences / and weeds with yellow hair / seizing their own piece of buried sun. / Rain streams down my face, / A poplar breathes, / Over the only house I can see, / Burned and gutted…

1862: Emancipation Proclamation, Lincoln frees slaves	*Tommy Lasorda, baseball coach, b.1927*	☾ R. 7:07am S. 7:12pm ☉ R. 7:00am S. 7:11pm	**FRIDAY · SEPTEMBER 22 · 2006 22**
	Michael Faraday, scientist, b.1791		
Ronaldo, soccer player, b.1976	*Lord Chesterfield, statesman, b.1694*	New Moon 6:45 am	
Joan Jett, singer, b.1960	[Common sense] is the best sense I know of.	☽ ☌ ☉ 6:45am	
Debbie Boone, singer, b.1956	— Lord Chesterfield		

ANNULAR SOLAR ECLIPSE 4:52AM
FALL EQUINOX 11:03PM

Ramadan begins, through Oct. 24, *Islam*	*Bruce Springsteen, singer, b.1949*	☾ R. 8:10am S. 7:28pm ☉ R. 7:01am S. 7:09pm	**SATURDAY · SEPTEMBER 23 · 2006 23**
Rosh Hashanah, 9/23-9/24, *Jewish*	*Ray Charles, singer, b.1930*		
Navaratra Dashara, 9/23–10/1, *Hindu*	*John Coltrane, musician, b.1926*	☽ ☌ ♂ 4:13am ☿ △ ♆ 8:43am	
1846: Neptune discovered	*Euripides, play-wright, b.480BC*	☽ △ ♆ 7:24pm ☽ ☌ ☿ 9:00pm	
Ani DiFranco, singer, b.1970	Waste not fresh tears over old griefs. — Euripides		

1734: Schwenkfelder: Thanksgiving, *Pennsylvania-Dutch*	*F. Scott Fitzgerald, writer, b.1896*	☾ R. 9:14am S. 7:45pm ☉ R. 7:03am S. 7:07pm	**SUNDAY · SEPTEMBER 24 · 2006 24**
Nia Vardalos, actor, b.1962	At 18 our convictions are hills from which we look; At 45 they are caves in which we hide. — F. Scott Fitzgerald		
Phil Hartman, comic actor, b.1948			
Jim Henson, muppet creator, b.1936			

All times Central Time Zone, sun and moon rise and set Minneapolis, MN.

---

25 MONDAY · SEPTEMBER 25 · 2006

☽ R. 10:20am S. 8:05pm
☼ R. 7:04am S. 7:05pm

☽ △ ♅ 8:48pm

St.Sergius of Radonezh, *Russ. Orthodox*

1676: Greenwich Mean Time established

Catherine Zeta-Jones, actor, b.1969

Will Smith, actor, b.1968

Christopher Reeve, actor, b.1952

Dmitri Shostakovich, composer, b.1906

Wm. Faulkner, writer, b.1897

The past is not dead. In fact, it's not even past.
— *William Faulkner*

---

26 TUESDAY · SEPTEMBER 26 · 2006

☽ R. 11:29am S. 8:30pm
☼ R. 7:05am S. 7:03pm

☽ ☌ ♃ 8:06am

1960: First televised Presidential debate

Jane Smiley, writer, b.1949

Olivia Newton John, singer, b.1948

George Gershwin, composer, b.1898

T.S. Eliot, poet, b.1888

Johnny Appleseed, farmer, b.1774

We shall not cease from our exploration, and at the end of all our exploring, we shall arrive where we started and know the place for the first time.
— *T.S. Eliott*

---

27 WEDNESDAY · SEPTEMBER 27 · 2006

☽ R. 12:38pm S. 9:02pm
☼ R. 7:06am S. 7:01pm

Cosme e Damiao, *Brazil*

1964: Warren Report issued

Ancestor Appreciation Day

Cheryl Tiegs, model, b.1947

Arthur Penn, filmmaker, b.1922

Thomas Nast, artist, b.1840

Sam Adams, patriot, b.1722

It is certainly desirable to be well descended, but the glory belongs to our ancestors.
— *Plutarch*

---

28 THURSDAY · SEPTEMBER 28 · 2006

☽ R. 1:45pm S. 9:44pm
☼ R. 7:07am S. 6:59pm

1542: Cabrillo Day, Discovery of California

National Hunting & Fishing Day

Gwyneth Paltrow, actor, b.1973

Janeane Garofalo, comic actor, b.1964

Brigitte Bardot, actor, b.1934

Marcello Mastroianni, actor, b.1924

Al Capp, cartoonist, b.1909

Success is following the pattern of life one enjoys most.
— *Al Capp*

Nature Note: WHY LEAVES CHANGE COLOR

Though autumn is blessed with warm sunny days, the chilled nights produce a most remarkable change in leaves—turning them a kaleidoscope of reds, oranges, and yellows. Sugars produced in the leaves during the day become trapped because the cold nights prevent the trees from absorbing the molecules, this causes the sugars to break down into colorful pigments called anthocyanins. Some of these colors already exist in leaves, but are hidden by green chlorophyll during the summer. —*DL*

© Misummer Night Stamps

© iStockPhoto

THE AMERICA VERSE / *Rudolf Steiner*

May our feeling penetrate
Into the center of our heart
And seek, in love, to unite itself
With human beings seeking the same goal…

Michaelmas, St. Michael's Day,

1899: VFW Established

Lech Walesa, Solidarity leader, b.1943

Anita Ekberg, actor, b.1931

Enrico Fermi, physicist, b.1901

Horatio Nelson, naval hero, b.1758

Miguel de Cervantes, writer, b.1547

Our greatest foes, and whom we must chiefly combat, are within.
— *Miguel de Cervantes*

☽ R. 2:47pm S. 10:39pm
☉ R. 7:09am S. 6:57pm

☽△♄ 12:41am
☽☌♆ 6:22am

FRIDAY · SEPTEMBER 29 · 2006 29

1955: James Dean killed in auto collision

1962: James Meredith enrolls at Ole Miss

1452. Gutenberg Bible published

Elie Wiesel, activist, b.1928

Truman Capote, writer, b.1924

Deborah Kerr, actor, b.1921

God made man because He loves stories.
— *Elie Wiesel*

☽ R. 3:40pm S. 11:46pm
☉ R. 7:10am S. 6:55pm

First Quarter
6:04 am

SATURDAY · SEPTEMBER 30 · 2006 30

Festival of Penha, *Rio de Janiero, Brazil*

1890: Yosemite Nat'l Park est.

The greatest obstacle to discovery is not ignorance – it is the illusion of knowledge.
— *Daniel J. Boorstin*

Julie Andrews, actor, b.1935

Jimmy Carter, 39th President, b.1924

Daniel Boorstin, historian, b.1914

Fletcher Knebel, writer, b.1911

Vladimir Horowitz, pianist, b.1903

☽ R. 4:23pm
☉ R. 7:11am S. 6:54pm

SUNDAY · OCTOBER 1 · 2006 1

All times Central Time Zone, sun and moon rise and set Minneapolis, MN.

OCTOBER

SEPT 23 - OCT 22

OCT 23 - NOV 21

Libra

OCTOBER BIRTHSTONE
Opal

Scorpio

OCTOBER FLOWER
Coneflower

CONTENTMENT BECOMES EQUANIMITY
Challenges: foolishness, complaining, dissatisfaction

Green becomes gold. Orange pumpkins appear on the porches. Tasseled, colored corn hangs mysteriously on the doorframe. The world is on fire—it is becoming a sun! The maples redden. The poplars become flaming torches. Leaves drift weightlessly across the lawn and city parks. Twilight echoes with crows cawing. It is time to turn over a new leaf. Within us, summer's gift of sun becomes a yearning to find ourselves. No longer immersed in nature's greenness, we find ourselves detached from her. We want to think again, to find meaning in experience. Thought-life seems to strengthen. We want to understand. Perhaps the dead can help us. The month ends with Celtic Samhain, Christian All Souls and All Saints—Hallowe'en—when the veil between the worlds is thinnest and the spirits of the ancestors come with their gifts. *– CB*

WEST COAST / PACIFIC MARITIME

Fall is now in full swing. Tinged red like incandescent flames, salmon surge upstream into the streams of their birth, fighting swift currents and leaping small waterfalls with an instinctive impulse that leaves the human imagination speechless. Squirrels everywhere run hither and thither in search of newly fallen acorns to stash away for winter, stuffing their cheeks until they look utterly ridiculous, then making mad dashes to hiding places. Deciduous trees begin their transitions from greens to yellows and reds. Swallows reputedly leave Mission San Juan Capistrano on October 23, the feast day of St. John (San Juan).

MOUNTAIN REGION / BASIN & RANGE

In a giant sweep through west Texas, more than a hundred million migrating monarch butterflies from across the eastern United States funnel southbound toward their Mexican wintering grounds. Numbers can reach as high as an estimated 300 butterflies per minute in some areas, literally filling the air like a firestorm of fierce orange autumn leaves. But the real fall colors belong to cottonwoods and aspens that line wet areas throughout the western mountain region. Drier slopes in the Southwest offer a harvest of piñon pine nuts this fall, a delicious food that humans have treasured for 10,000 years.

Cosmic roulette: with binoculars, and luck you might find Mercury at greatest eastern elongation, sitting beneath Jupiter just above the horizon.

Jupiter

Mercury

Oct 17, 6:45 p.m.   WSW

Moon

Saturn

LEO

Regulus

Saturn meets the waning Moon.

E   Oct 27, 6 a.m.

LOOK UP:

6 Full Moon, 9:13 PM

13 Last quarter Moon, 6:27 PM

17 Mercury at greatest eastern elongation (24° 49')

21 Orionid meteor shower peaks

21 New Moon, 11:15 PM

23 Mars in conjunction with the sun (not visible).

27 Venus at superior conjunction (not visible)

29 First quarter Moon, 3:26 PM

OCTOBER IS FOR:

DENTAL HYGIENE · SHELTER DOG ADOPTION · STAMP COLLECTING · COUNTRY HAM · TEXAS PEANUTS · ORTHODONTIA · ROLLER SKATING · SERVICE DOGS · ALTERNATE HISTORIES · AUTO BATTERY SAFETY · COMPUTER LEARNING · DIVERSITY · EAT BETTER, EAT TOGETHER · GAY & LESBIAN HISTORY · LUPUS

OCTOBER

S	M	T	W	T	F	S
1	2	3	4	5	6	7
8	9	10	11	12	13	14
15	16	17	18	19	20	21
22	23	24	25	26	27	28
29	30	31				

MID-CONTINENT / CORN BELT & GULF

As cold creeps down from the north, the fiery band of fall colors retreats southward with the show, changing from aspens to maples, oaks, and ashes. Once the leaves turn and fall, and it becomes apparent that the songbirds have left as well, the effervescent northern cardinal becomes more apparent than ever. Juncos arrive from the north, and overhead anxious flocks of ducks and geese can be heard calling as they migrate in long formations. Crisp, sunny days can be the most beautiful of the entire year, though most people are outside raking leaves.

EAST COAST / ATLANTIC SEABOARD

Sharp-shinned hawks now dominate the river of migrating hawks. The final push of songbirds leaving the area may bunch up in coastal areas, making this a great time for birdwatchers. Fall colors abound—oaks, maples, hickories, and many others. Native brook trout begin spawning in the southern Appalachians. Acorns of the white oak ripen and are quickly eaten by black bears. Squirrels are in constant activity harvesting nuts. Robins flock to fruiting trees and bushes. Strong winds return to the Florida coast, and this is the time that southern bald eagles begin their courtship. —DL

2 · MONDAY · OCTOBER 2 · 2006

☽ R. 4:56 pm S. 1:03 am
☉ R. 7:12 am S. 6:52 pm

☽△♀ 2:27AM
☽△☉ 2:32PM

Dasera, *Hindu*

Yom Kippur, *Jewish*

1950: "Peanuts" comic strip debut

1968: Redwood Nat'l Park est.

Sting, singer, b.1951

Jan Morris, writer, b.1926

Graham Greene, writer, b.1904

Groucho Marx, comedian, b.1890

Mahatma Gandhi, Indian leader, b.1869

Whatever you do will be insignificant, but it is very important that you do it.
— Mahatma Gandhi

3 · TUESDAY · OCTOBER 3 · 2006

☽ R. 5:23 pm S. 2:24 am
☉ R. 7:14 am S. 6:50 pm

☽△♂ 2:10AM
☽☌♆ 3:31PM
☽☍♄ 10:50AM

1990: German Re-Unification

Tangun Day, *Korea*

Ashlee Simpson, singer, b.1984

Stevie Ray Vaughan, musician, b.1954

Chubby Checker, singer, b.1941

Gore Vidal, writer, b.1925

Thomas Wolfe, writer, b.1900

The secret of joy in work is contained in one word — excellence. To know how to do something well is to enjoy it.
— Pearl Buck

4 · WEDNESDAY · OCTOBER 4 · 2006

☽ R. 5:46 pm S. 3:47 am
☉ R. 7:15 am S. 6:48 pm

☽△☿ 5:34AM
♂△♆ 7:22AM
☽☌♅ 7:19PM

Susan Sarandon, actor, b.1946

Bernice Reagon, musician, b.1942

Anne Rice, writer, b.1941

Christopher Alexander, architect, b.1936

Buster Keaton, comedian, b.1895

St. Francis of Assisi, b.1181

Nearly all men can stand adversity, but if you want to test a man's character, give him power.
— Abraham Lincoln

5 · THURSDAY · OCTOBER 5 · 2006

☽ R. 6:07 pm S. 5:11 am
☉ R. 7:16 am S. 6:46 pm

☽△♃ 7:41AM

Nuzul alQur'an, *Islam*

1877: Chief Joseph surrender

Kate Winslet, actor, b.1975

Bob Geldof, singer/activist, b.1951

Vaclav Havel, Czech president, b.1936

Tecumseh, Shawnee chief, d.1813

Denis Diderot, encyclopedist, b.1713

Jonathan Edwards, theologian, b.1703

Life shrinks or expands in proportion to one's courage.
— Anais Nin

Nature Note: CRY OF THE HONKER

Long after the more delicate songbirds of summer have departed for southern climes, long skeins of noisily honking Canada Geese can be heard passing overhead in the evening sky. As anyone who uses a down pillow or jacket can attest, the soft feathers of geese are very warm, so warm in fact that it allows geese to remain on their northern breeding grounds until the bitter storms of early winter arrive to encourage them to head south. —DL

THE FIRST BIRDS / *Thorsten Bacon*

Sure, it's easy to say forget her / You're not the one hurting. She's a flirt, /
It's true, and probably has another lover by now. / But I wonder—what could
I have done differently? / The turning earth drains the curtains again; /
Men come hurtling our trash onto trucks at sunrise. / Do we ever learn?
The cat purrs and purrs. / The first birds are chirping at the feeder.

1981: Anwar El-Sadat assassinated	*Shana Alexander, writer, b.1925*	☾ R. 6:28 pm S. 6:34 am ☉ R. 7:17 am S, 6:44 pm	**FRIDAY · OCTOBER 6 · 2006** **6**
1876: American Library Ass'n founded	*Le Corbusier, architect, b.1887*		
Intergeneration Day	Imagination was given man to compensate for what he is not, and a sense of humor to console him for what he is. — Author unknown	Full Moon 10:13 pm	
Rebecca Lobo, basketball player, b.1973		☽ ☌ ♀ 1:02PM ☽ ☌ ☉ 10:13PM	
Britt Ekland, actor, b.1942			
Sukkot, *Jewish (through Oct. 12)*	*R.D. Laing, psychiatrist, b.1927*	☾ R. 6:51 pm S. 7:58 am ☉ R. 7:19 am S. 6:43 pm	**SATURDAY · OCTOBER 7 · 2006** **7**
Nat'l Metric Week	*Niels Bohr, mathematician, b.1885*		
Yo-Yo Ma, cellist, b.1955	Between two evils, I always pick the one I never tried before. — Mae West	☽ ☌ ♂ 6:51AM ☽ △ ♄ 11:22AM ☽ △ ♆ 3:04PM	
Vladimir Putin, Russ. President, b.1952			
Desmond Tutu, S. African leader, b.1931			
1871: Great Chicago Fire	*R.L. Stine, writer, b.1943*	☾ R. 7:16 pm S. 9:23 am ☉ R. 7:20 am S. 6:41 pm	**SUNDAY · OCTOBER 8 · 2006** **8**
1871: Peshtigo, Wisc. Forest Fire	*Jesse Jackson, civil rts. leader, b.1941*		
	Frank Herbert, writer, b.1920		
The people I distrust most are those who want to improve our lives but have only one course of action. — Frank Herbert	*John W. Gardner, writer, b.1912* *Heinrich Schütz, composer, b.1585*	☽ ☌ ♀ 2:11PM	

All times Central Time Zone, sun and moon rise and set Minneapolis, MN.

9 MONDAY · OCTOBER 9 · 2006

☽ R. 7:48 pm S. 10:47 am
☉ R. 7:21 am S. 6:39 pm

☽ ☌ ♃ 8:47AM

Health & Sports Day, *Japan*

Hangal Nal: Alphabet Day, *Korea*

Cirio de Nazare, *Brazil*

National Children's Day

Columbus Day

John Lennon, singer, b.1940

Helene Deutsch, psychoanalyst, b.1884

Amy Semple McPherson, evangelist, b.1840

Life is what happens to you while you're busy making other plans.
— John Lennon

10 TUESDAY · OCTOBER 10 · 2006

☽ R. 8:29 pm S. 12:09 pm
☉ R. 7:22 am S. 6:37 pm

☉ △ ♆ 9:04AM
☿ △ ♅ 6:07PM

1973: Spiro Agnew resignation

1845: U.S. Naval Academy established

UN World Mental Health Day

Autumn is a second spring when every leaf is a flower.
— Albert Camus

Dale Earnhardt Jr., race driver, b.1974

Tanya Tucker, singer, b.1958

Ben Vereen, actor, b.1946

Helen Hayes, actor, b.1900

Giuseppi Verdi, composer, b.1813

11 WEDNESDAY · OCTOBER 11 · 2006

☽ R. 9:20 pm S. 1:21 pm
☉ R. 7:24 am S. 6:35 pm

☽ △ ♀ 12:06AM
☽ △ ♆ 6:26AM
☽ △ ☉ 8:08AM
☽ △ ♂ 3:09PM
☽ ☌ ♆ 7:23PM

World Egg Day

National Coming Out Day

1975: "Saturday Night Live" premieres

Joan Cusack, actor, b.1962

Eleanor Roosevelt, writer, 1st Lady, b.1884

Do what you feel in your heart to be right — for you'll be criticized anyway. You'll be damned if you do, and damned if you don't.
— Eleanor Roosevelt

12 THURSDAY · OCTOBER 12 · 2006

☽ R. 10:20 pm S. 1:21 pm
☉ R. 7:25 am S. 6:34 pm

1999: World population reaches 6 billion

Luciano Pavarotti, singer, b.1935

Dick Gregory, comedian, b.1932

Jean Nidetch, nutritionist, founded "Weight Watchers," b.1923

Riches do not delight us so much with their possession, as torment us with their loss.
— Dick Gregory

© Jupiter Images

Notes

Ginkgo biloba

Classification: *Ginkgo forms its own unique group of plants. Like mosses and ferns it has motile spermatophytes for fertilization, and its leaves resemble those of maidenhair fern. Like conifers, it produces seeds that are not embedded in a fruit (Gymnosperms).*

Medicinal Uses: *In traditional oriental medicine, the seeds are used for a variety of respiratory and cardiovascular ailments. In the West today, ginkgo leaf extracts are used as antioxidants and to enhance memory and mental clarity.*

Name: *The word ginkgo refers to the seeds, meaning "silver apricot" (gin: silver; kyo: apricot) in Chinese; biloba means two-lobed in Latin and refers to the leaf form.*

Ginkgo
Prehistoric urban tree

Often planted along streets in cities or in urban parks, the ginkgo is an exotic tree in more ways than one. It's the only living species of a large group of plants that flourished around the globe before the dinosaurs roamed the earth. When you see a ginkgo, you have a lens into a past world.

Its fan-shaped leaves take you into a world unlike that of any other tree. Each leaf has two lobes that reveal the underlying pattern of simple two-fold (dichotomous) branching in its vein structure. This is a kind of elemental vegetative growth one finds in some seaweed, liverworts, and ferns. Ginkgo's vitality is also seen in its remarkable resistance to diseases and air pollution, allowing it to grow most everywhere.

Ginkgo produces flowers and seeds, but it usually takes up to 30 years of vegetative growth before a tree flowers for the first time. And after waiting so long, ginkgo provides us with another botanical surprise: some trees only form the pollen-bearing flowers, while others form only seed-producing flowers. If you live in a city and are waiting to see the cherry-sized seeds dangling from the branches, you won't have much luck. The ripening seeds have a fetid odor, so seed-bearing trees are usually not cultivated in our cities.

Native to China, ginkgo was planted by the Chinese in and around temples in the Middle Ages. Later it reached Europe and America. The ethereal beauty of its leaves, its vitality, and its cooling shade make Gingko a welcome companion in the urban world.

– CH

© iStockPhoto

OCTOBER / *Robert Frost*

O hushed October morning mild,
Thy leaves have ripened to the fall;
Tomorrow's wind, if it be wild,
Should waste them all…

Nancy Kerrigan, ice skater, b.1969

Jerry Rice, football great, b.1962

Paul Simon, singer, b.1941

Lenny Bruce, comic, b.1925

Yves Montand, actor, b.1921

Men never do evil so completely and cheerfully as when they do it from a religious conviction.
— Blaise Pascal

☾ R. 11:27 pm   S. 3:08 pm
☉ R. 7:26 am   S. 6:32 pm

Last Quarter
7:26 pm

☽△♅ 2:14ᴀᴍ
☽△☿ 7:59ᴀᴍ
☽△♃ 8:30ᴘᴍ
♀△♆ 9:34ᴘᴍ

FRIDAY · OCTOBER 13 · 2006 13

Shemini Atzeret, *Jewish*

1964: Martin Luther King, Jr. awarded the Nobel Peace Prize

1960: Peace Corps Proposed

Hannah Arendt, political scientist, b.1906

e.e. cummings, poet, b.1894

Dwight Eisenhower, 34th US Pres., b.1890

William Penn, founded PA, b.1644

The most wasted of all days is one without laughter.
— e.e. cummings

☾ S. 3:43 pm
☉ R. 7:27 am   S. 6:30 pm

SATURDAY · OCTOBER 14 · 2006 14

Simhat Torah, *Jewish*

1917: Mata Hari executed

Duchess Sarah Ferguson, b.1959

John K. Galbraith, economist, b.1908

C.P. Snow, writer, b.1905

P.G. Wodehouse, writer, b.1881

Friedrich Nietzsche, philosopher, b.1844

Helen Hunt Jackson, writer/ Indian rights advocate, b.1830

Virgil, epic poet, b.70 BC

If you rest, you rust.
— Helen Hayes

☾ R. 12:37 am   S. 4:09 pm
☉ R. 7:29 am   S. 6:28 pm

☽☌♆ 11:17ᴘᴍ

SUNDAY · OCTOBER 15 · 2006 15

All times Central Time Zone, sun and moon rise and set Minneapolis, MN.

16 MONDAY · OCTOBER 16 · 2006

☾ R. 1:45 am S. 4:31 pm
☼ R. 7:30 am S. 6:27 pm

☾☌♄ 10:48AM
☾△Ψ 2:14PM

World Food Day

1853: Crimean War
1859: John Brown's Raid
1793: Marie Antoinette executed

Tom Robbins, actor, b.1958

Suzanne Somers, actor, b.1946

Eugene O'Neill, playwright, b.1888

Oscar Wilde, celebrity/playwright, b.1854

Noah Webster, lexicographer, b.1758

I am not young enough to know everything.
— Oscar Wilde

17 TUESDAY · OCTOBER 17 · 2006

☾ R. 2:51 am S. 4:49 pm
☼ R. 7:31 am S. 6:25 pm

1989: San Francisco earthquake

Eminem, singer, b.1972

Rita Hayworth, actor, b.1918

Arthur Miller, writer, b.1915

Pope John Paul I, b.1912

Jupiter Hammon, poet, b.1711

Everybody likes a kidder, but nobody lends him money.
— Arthur Miller

18 WEDNESDAY · OCTOBER 18 · 2006

☾ R. 3:55 am S. 5:05 pm
☼ R. 7:33 am S. 6:23 pm

☾☌♅ 12:07AM

Persons Day, *Canada*

Martina Navratilova, tennis player, b.1956

Laura Nyro, singer/songwriter, b.1947

Chuck Berry, singer, b.1926

Melina Mercouri, actor, b.1925

A.J. Liebling, journalist, b.1904

Fannie Hurst, writer, b.1889

Under conditions of tyranny it is far easier to act than to think.
— Hannah Arendt

19 THURSDAY · OCTOBER 19 · 2006

☾ R. 4:59 am S. 5:20 pm
☼ R. 7:34 am S. 6:21 pm

Lailat al Kadir, *Islam*

Battara-Ichi: Pickle Market Day, *Japan*

1987: Stock Market Crash: Drops 23%

Evander Holyfield, prizefighter, b.1962

John Le Carre, writer, b.1931

Patricia Ireland, pres. NOW, b.1945

Lewis Mumford, writer, b.1895

Marsilio Ficino, philosopher, b.1433

Our national flower is the concrete cloverleaf.
— Lewis Mumford

© Jupiter Images

Nature Note: HOW TO LAY A FIRE IN A FIREPLACE

For a proper fire you need dry fuel and air. **1)** Make sure the fireplace flue is open (lets air up the chimney). **2)** Stuff lightly crumpled newspapers under the grate—but don't pack them in. **3)** Put plenty of dry kindling on the newspapers. **4)** Put on two dry logs, but don't weigh down the whole pile—air needs to circulate. **5)** If you have a wood-burning stove or fireplace doors, be sure the damper is open. **6)** Light the newspaper. **7)** Once the fire gets going well, add a third log. You need at least three to sustain a good fire. **8)** Fuss with it. The only fires worth having demand your attention to keep them at their best and brightest. —MC

© iStockPhoto

THE LIFE OF A DAY / *Tom Hennen*

We examine each day before us with barely a glance and say, no, this isn't one I've been looking for, and wait in a bored sort of way for the next, when, we are convinced, our lives will start for real. / Meanwhile, this day is going by perfectly well-adjusted, as some days are, with the right amounts of sunlight and shade, and a light breeze scented with a perfume made from the mixture of fallen apples, corn stubble, dry oak leaves, and the faint odor of last night's meandering skunk.

Qud Day, *Islam* **Birth of the Bab,** *Baha'i* Snoop Dogg, rapper, b.1972 Art Buchwald, columnist, b.1925 Mickey Mantle, baseball player, b.1931 Arlene Francis, actor, b.1908	Arthur Rimbaud, writer, b.1854 John Dewey, educator, b.1859 Christopher Wren, architect, b.1632 We can have facts without thinking but we cannot have thinking without facts. – John Dewey	☽ R. 6:02 am S. 5:35 pm ☉ R. 7:35 am S. 6:20 pm	**FRIDAY · OCTOBER 20 · 2006 20**
Diwali "Deepevali" *Hindu* **1967:** Vietnam War protesters storm Pentagon **1879:** Incandescent Lamp Demo Ursula Le Guin, writer, b.1929 Dizzy Gillespie, musician, b.1917	Alfred Nobel, est'd Nobel Prize, b.1833 S.T. Coleridge, poet, b.1772 Give me the children until they are seven and anyone may have them afterwards. – St. Francis Xavier	☽ R. 7:06 am S. 5:52 pm ☉ R. 7:37 am S. 6:18 pm ☽△♆ 12:54AM ☽♂♀ 9:05PM	**SATURDAY · OCTOBER 21 · 2006 21**
1962: Cuban Missile Crisis Deepak Chopra, physician, b.1946 Annette Funicello, actor, b.1942 Catherine Deneuve, actor, b.1942 Timothy Leary, LSD advocate, b.1920	Doris Lessing, writer, b.1919 Sarah Bernhardt, actor, b.1844 Franz Liszt, composer, b.1811 Think wrongly if you please, but in all cases think for yourself. – Doris Lessing	☽ R. 8:11 am S. 6:11 pm ☉ R. 7:38 am S. 6:16 pm New Moon 12:14 am ☽♂☉ 12:58AM ☽♂♂ 10:19AM	**SUNDAY · OCTOBER 22 · 2006 22**

All times Central Time Zone, sun and moon rise and set Minneapolis, MN.

23 MONDAY · OCTOBER 23 · 2006

☾ R. 9:19 am S. 6:35 pm
☼ R. 7:39 am S. 6:15 pm

☾△♅ 1:01AM
☾♂♂ 1:45AM

1956: Hungarian Revolution

1989: Hungarian Independence

Departure of the Swallows, *Capistrano, Calif*

Tiffeny Milbrett, soccer player, b.1972

Pelé, soccer player, b.1940

Johnny Carson, TV host, b.1925

Gertrude Ederle, swimmer, b.1906

The only real prison is fear, and the only real freedom is freedom from fear.
— *Aung San Suu Kyi*

---

24 TUESDAY · OCTOBER 24 · 2006

☾ R. 10:29 am S. 7:05 pm
☼ R. 7:41 am S. 6:13 pm

☾♂♃ 12:43AM
☾♂☿ 1:57AM

Eid al Fitr: Ramadan ends, *Islam*

1929: Stock Market Panic: Black Thursday

1945: United Nations Day founded

Kweisi Mfume, NAACP Pres., b.1948

Kevin Kline, actor, b.1947

Brenda Ueland, writer, b.1891

Sarah Hale, women's rts. advocate, b.1788

America is not merely a nation but a nation of nations.
— *Lyndon B. Johnson*

---

25 WEDNESDAY · OCTOBER 25 · 2006

☾ R. 11:37 am S. 7:43 pm
☼ R. 7:42 am S. 6:12 pm

♀♂♂ 1:10AM

St. Crispin's Day, *England, France*

Anne Tyler, writer, b.1941

Helen Reddy, singer/songwriter, b.1941

Minnie Pearl, comedienne, b.1912

Pablo Picasso, artist, b.1881

Geoffrey Chaucer, writer, d.1400

A great marriage is not when the 'perfect couple' comes together. It is when an imperfect couple learns to enjoy their differences.
— *Dave Meurer*

---

26 THURSDAY · OCTOBER 26 · 2006

☾ R. 12:41 pm S. 8:34 pm
☼ R. 7:43 am S. 6:10 pm

☾△♄ 10:50AM
☾♂♆ 1:02PM

1785: Mule Day: First mules enter U.S.

Natalie Merchant, singer, b.1963

Jaclyn Smith, actor, b.1948

Hillary Rodham Clinton, senator, b.1947

Mahalia Jackson, singer, b.1911

Leon Trotsky, revolutionary, b.1879

I believe that a worthwhile life is defined by a kind of spiritual journey and a sense of obligation.
— *Hillary Rodham Clinton*

© iStockPhoto

BIRTHDAY: *September 21, 1929*
URSULA K. LE GUIN,
Writer

© Marian Wood Kolisch

Ursula Le Guin submitted her first story for publication to the magazine *Astounding Science Fiction* at the age of 11. It was rejected. But nearly 20 years later, her novel *Left Hand of Darkness* won both the Hugo and Nebula awards, making Le Guin one of the brightest stars of science fiction.

As a writer, Le Guin plumbs the depth of what it means to be human—even with her nonhuman characters—drawing on the possibilities of the heart and the mind rather than technology and speculative science.

A self-proclaimed Taoist and translator of Lao Tzu, Le Guin is a prolific writer and has published novels, poetry, children's books, essays, short stories, and memoirs. Le Guin received the Science Fiction and Fantasy Writers of America Grand Master Award in 2003.

– KM

We are volcanoes. When we women offer our experience as our truth, as human truth, all the maps change. There are new mountains.

The unread story is not a story; it is little black marks on wood pulp. The reader, reading it, makes it live: a live thing, a story.

To me the "female principle" is, or at least historically has been, basically anarchic. It values order without constraint, rule by custom not by force. It has been the male who enforces order, who constructs power structures, who makes, enforces, and breaks laws.

My imagination makes me human and makes me a fool; it gives me all the world and exiles me from it.

Love does not just sit there, like a stone; it had to be made, like bread, remade all the time, made new.

The creative adult is the child who has survived.

What sane person could live in this world and not be crazy?

© Nova Development

Procyon lotor

Description: *Highly variable color, with an easily recognizable black facial mask and ringed tail.*

Habitat: *Varied, including seashores, farmland, prairies, wooded areas, and suburban and urban neighborhoods.*

Diet: *Omnivorous.*

Adult length: *2 to 4 ft. from nose to tail tip.*

Adult weight: *5 to 40 pounds.*

Activity: *Generally, but not strictly, nocturnal.*

Birthing season: *From March to May; however, in southern U.S., may occur year-round.*

Age when independent: *Between 6 and 12 months.*

Raccoons
Masked trickster, urban success story

Clever and charismatic, the raccoon—from the Algonquin *arukun*, "he who scratches with his hands"— is as at home in the city as in the country. A recent study of raccoons in Washington D.C.'s Rock Creek Park found the densest populations of the animal ever recorded, except for a study of Missouri River bottomlands done more than 50 years ago.

In Native cultures, raccoon is the Trickster who uses his wits to lead enemies astray, leaving them stranded and bewildered. The Cheyenne call him *macho-on*, "one who makes magic," and his bandit's mask lends him an aura of mischievousness and wily intelligence. His scientific name, *Procyon lotor*, refers to the washing behavior thought to be instinctive. In reality, what raccoons really like to do is experience their food, handling it as much as possible and dunking and soaking it in water when available. Maybe it's that human like behavior and their five-fingered "hands" that have always made raccoons seem subtly akin to us, or at least akin to the lost wild in ourselves.

Next time you catch sight of a raccoon scuttling along with his humpbacked, flat-footed walk before agiley slipping his big body down the nearest storm drain, give a nod to his great survival skills—raccoons lived on our continent, virtually unchanged, for more than a million years.

– *MC*

With help from the Humane Society of the United States

AIMLESS LOVE / *Billy Collins*

This morning as I walked along the lakeshore, / I fell in love with a wren / and later in the day with a mouse / the cat had dropped under the dining room table. / In the shadows of an autumn evening, / I fell for a seamstress / still at her machine in the tailor's window, / and later for a bowl of broth, / steam rising like smoke from a naval battle. / This is the best kind of love, I thought, / without recompense, without gifts, / or unkind words, / without suspicion, / or silence on the telephone…

1787: Federalist Papers published

Maxine Hong Kingston, writer, b.1940

John Cleese, actor, b.1939

Sylvia Plath, poet, b.1932

Dylan Thomas, poet, b.1914

Marlene Dietrich, actor, b.1901

Theodore Roosevelt, 26th US Pres., b.1858

Do what you can, with what you have, where you are.
— *Theodore Roosevelt*

☾ R. 1:36 pm S. 9:36 pm
☉ R. 7:45 am S. 6:09 pm

☉ ♂ ♀ 12:49ᴘᴍ

FRIDAY · OCTOBER 27 · 2006 **27**

1636: Harvard Univ. founded

St. Jude's Day

Julia Roberts, actor, b.1967

BillGates, founder of Microsoft, b.1955

Erasmus, writer, b.1467

No matter how rich you become, how famous or powerful, when you die the size of your funeral will still pretty much depend on the weather.
— *Michael Pritchard*

☾ R. 2:21 pm S. 10:48 pm
☉ R. 7:46 am S. 6:07 pm

☿ 2:15ᴘᴍ

SATURDAY · OCTOBER 28 · 2006 **28**

1929: Stock Market crash

1969: Internet created: Between Stanford & UCLA

Winona Ryder, actor, b.1971

Richard Dreyfuss, actor, b.1947

Fanny Brice, comedienne, b.1891

James Boswell, biographer, b.1740

Men are wise in proportion, not to their experience, but to their capacity for experience.
— *James Boswell*

☾ R. 1:56 pm S. 11:05 pm
☉ R. 6:47 am S. 5:06 pm

First Quarter 3:25 pm

♆ 2:55ᴀᴍ

SUNDAY · OCTOBER 29 · 2006 **29**

All times Central Time Zone, sun and moon rise and set Minneapolis, MN.

30 MONDAY · OCTOBER 30 · 2006

☾ R. 2:24 pm
☿ R. 6:49 am S. 5:04 pm

☾ ☌ ♆ 11:04AM
☿ ☌ ♃ 10:02PM
☾ ☌ ♄ 10:49PM

Los Angelitos, *Mexico*

Grace Slick, singer, b.1939

Ruth Gordon, actor, b.1896

Ezra Pound, poet, b.1885

Emily Post, writer, b.1872

Fyodor Dostoievski, writer, b.1821

John Adams, 2nd US Pres., b.1735

Children should be educated and instructed in the principles of freedom.
— *John Adams*

DAYLIGHT SAVINGS TIME ENDS
2:00AM

31 TUESDAY · OCTOBER 31 · 2006

☾ R. 2:28 pm S. 12:25 am
☿ R. 6:50 am S. 5:03 pm

☾ △ ♂ 6:36PM

Samhain: Wiccan New Year

Reformation Day: *Christian*

Peter Jackson, director, b.1961

Dan Rather, TV journalist, b.1931

Lee Grant, actor, b.1927

Helmut Newton, photographer, b.1920

Ethel Waters, singer, b.1896

John Keats, poet, b.1795

October's poplars are flaming torches lighting the way to winter.
— *Nova Bair*

HALLOWE'EN

1 WEDNESDAY · NOVEMBER 1 · 2006

☾ R. 3:09 pm S. 1:45 am
☿ R. 6:51 am S. 5:01 pm

☾ △ ☿ 1:42AM
☾ ☌ ♅ 3:32AM
♀ △ ♅ 10:32PM

All Saints Day, *Christian*

1993: European Union est.

Toni Collette, actor, b.1972

Kinky Friedman, singer/song-writer, b.1944

Betsy Palmer, actor, b.1929

Stephen Crane, writer, b.1871

People that are really very weird can get into sensitive positions and have a tremen-dous impact on history.
— *Dan Quayle*

2 THURSDAY · NOVEMBER 2 · 2006

☾ R. 2:29 pm S. 3:05 am
☿ R. 6:53 am S. 5:00 pm

☾ △ ☿ 12:24AM
☾ △ ♃ 2:55AM

All Souls Day, *Roman Catholic*

Day of the Dead, *Mexico*

k.d. lang, singer, b.1961

Shere Hite, sex researcher, b.1942

Burt Lancaster, actor, b.1915

Marie Antoinette, Queen Consort of Louis XVI of France, b.1755

Daniel Boone, frontiersman, b.1734

I don't like that man. I must get to know him better.
— *Abraham Lincoln*

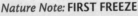

Nature Note: FIRST FREEZE

Watch closely as winter approaches for the first touch of frost gracing the landscape. The earliest sign is likely to be a white dusting of delicate crystals on the fringes of dried leaves or brown grasses. But it'll take weeks more before air and ground temperatures drop low enough for ice to form along the perimeter of small puddles or on the soil. On particularly cold nights dewdrops freeze as they coat the surface of windows, cars, and mailboxes. —DL

© PhotoDisc

CELEBRATE: November 2

DAY OF THE DEAD
(Día de los Muertos)

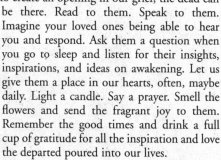

Marigolds splash orange on homemade shrines. Cemeteries glow at night with luminaria and lively visiting families. Tantalizing aromas of food prepared for the Mexican Day of the Dead rise up to entice the living and those in spirit. Street vendors hawk grinning candy skeletons playing guitars or driving lowrider cars.

Most of us believe that the spirit lives on after death, but we don't do much about it. But celebrating the dead is good medicine for the soul, filling that space with family, remembrance, place, community, and continuity.

For all those same good reasons, more people are caring for their own at death. Those who do this consider it a natural transition, and claim their right to bathe and dress a loved one, to build the casket, or hold a blessing vigil at home. Such loving care and funeral ritual (it is legal), brings completion and deep connectedness at life's greatest threshold.

But what if our loved ones die suddenly or far away? Can we still connect? It is time to know again what the ancients knew—the spirit lives on. Love never dies. When we are able to create an opening in our grief, the dead can

be there. Read to them. Speak to them. Imagine your loved ones being able to hear you and respond. Ask them a question when you go to sleep and listen for their insights, inspirations, and ideas on awakening. Let us give them a place in our hearts, often, maybe daily. Light a candle. Say a prayer. Smell the flowers and send the fragrant joy to them. Remember the good times and drink a full cup of gratitude for all the inspiration and love the departed poured into our lives.

– Nancy Poer
www.nancyjewelpoer.com

NOVEMBER

OCT 23 - NOV 21

NOV 22 - DEC 21

Scorpio

NOVEMBER BIRTHSTONE
Topaz

Sagittarius

NOVEMBER FLOWER
Chrysanthemum

PATIENCE BECOMES INSIGHT
Challenges: prideful, mean-spirited

The last red berries shrivel. Night comes early, dawn late. The sun is weaker. Ice is on the birdbath, frost on the car. Perhaps it is already snowing. Certainly, it's damp and raw. Rain is forecast. Now is the time to act, to begin. As Ishmael says in Moby Dick, "whenever it is a damp, drizzly November in my soul...I account it high time to get to sea as soon as I can." He means it's time for human deeds. Without our contribution, nothing will happen, life will have no meaning. Without our experience, the world cannot evolve, life on earth cannot become more abundant. "We have it in our power to begin the world over again," said Tom Paine. "Start by doing what's necessary; then do what's possible; and suddenly you are doing the impossible," said St. Francis of Assisi. All it takes is patience, grace, intention, and the right moment. – *CB*

WEST COAST / PACIFIC MARITIME

With the first full rains of the year soaking the forest litter, this is the season when lichens, mosses, and fungi awaken from their long dusty sleep. The addition of water allows lichens and mosses to begin photosynthesizing, giving them bright green or otherwise colorful surfaces. Fungi of diverse form begin to sprout from layers of needles and leaves on the forest floor. Sandhill cranes arrive from the north with loud bugling calls – standing five-feet tall they are most impressive birds.

MOUNTAIN REGION / BASIN & RANGE

Pushed out of northern regions by the growing threat of winter, snow geese and sandhill cranes arrive on their wintering grounds throughout the Southwest. Most famous of all are the huge flocks that pass Albuquerque en route to Bosque del Apache National Wildlife Refuge. Along with the same movement rough-legged hawks from Canada arrive to begin feeding on voles in open fields. Elk descend from the mountains into their lower elevation wintering grounds. Despite the cold, it is still possible to find roadrunners sunning themselves on rocky perches around Phoenix on warmer days.

As Mercury climbs the morning sky it will meet the waning Moon on November 18.

Spica

Moon
11/18

11/22
11/18   11/26
Mercury   11/30
11/14

ESE   Nov 14 to 30, 6:30 a.m.

The Leonides : Out of the heart of Leo up to 150 meteorites per hour are predicted on Nov 19 in the early morning hours.

LEO   *Regulus*

Saturn

S   Nov 19, after midnight

LOOK UP:

5 Full Moon, 6:59 AM Southern Taurid meteor shower peaks; Moon interferes

8 Mercury at inferior conjunction; Normally this means that Mercury is not visible, but beginning at 1:13 PM the planet can be seen transiting the sun; Mid-transit occurs at 3:42 PM and the transit ends at 6:11 PM; This is a telescopic event and requires eye protection

12 Last quarter Moon, 11:46 AM

17 Leonid meteor shower peaks, 3:00 PM

18 Leonid meteor shower outburst predicted, 100 to 120 per hour, from 10:00 PM to 11:00 PM

20 New Moon, 4:19 PM

21 Jupiter in conjunction with the sun (not visible)

25 Mercury at greatest western elongation (19° 54').

28 First quarter Moon, 12:29 AM

NOVEMBER						
S	M	T	W	T	F	S
				1	2	3	4
5	6	7	8	9	10	11
12	13	14	15	16	17	18
19	20	21	22	23	24	25
26	27	28	29	30		

NOVEMBER IS THE MONTH FOR: AVIATION HISTORY · FIGS · FAMILY STORIES · BEING THANKFUL · FAMILY CAREGIVERS · GEORGIA PECANS · HEALTHY SKIN · HOSPICES · LIFEWRITING · PEANUT BUTTER LOVERS · VEGANS · AIDS AWARENESS

MID-CONTINENT / CORN BELT & GULF

Newly bare trees reveal for the first time the year's crop of bird nests; you may be surprised how many there are. Cold weather drives eastern bluebirds to the warmer southern states. This is usually the time of the first snowfalls and enough accumulation that it's possible to ski or snowshoe. Lakes in the north start to ice over. White-tailed deer begin to court, but it's also the opening of the deer-hunting season. After a summer of being brown, snowshoe hares begin to turn white.

EAST COAST / ATLANTIC SEABOARD

In the woodlands of New York, bucks have rubbed the velvet off their antlers and are ready to mate. Taking advantage of ice-free water, ducks and geese gather in large numbers, heading south only as ice begins to form. Raccoons and opossums may visit feeders at night to steal suet. Most deciduous leaves have fallen. Moths gather around porch lights at night until the first hard freeze. Witch hazel is in bloom. Winter preparations are finalized; most animals have migrated south or moved underground. Sandhill cranes arrive on their southern wintering grounds around Okefenokee Swamp and Gainesville. —DL

BIRTHDAY: *November 5, 1857*

IDA TARBELL,
Journalist and Author

Journalist and author Ida Minerva Tarbell was one of the most well known women of her day. An imposing six feet tall, she revealed the fraud of the Standard Oil monopoly in a series of articles that appeared in *McClure's Magazine* in 1902. A celebrated muckraker, she devoted much of her life to uncovering waste and corruption in both the public and private sector.

Born in a log farmhouse in Pennsylvania, Tarbell moved with her family at 13 into a Philadelphia mansion when her father's business prospered. Ironically, given his daughter's future exposé, he made his fortune building giant wooden containers for oil. By 14, Tarbell was praying for deliverance from marriage in favor of the freedom she already knew she needed. Tarbell was the only woman in her undergraduate class at Allegheny College and later earned a Master's degree. After two years of teaching, she retired and began writing for *The Chautauquan*, which championed the reformist causes of the day. In 1891, she moved to Paris, studied at the Sorbonne, wrote articles to meet her expenses, and interviewed Emile Zola, Alexander Dumas, and Louis Pasteur. In her later years, she wrote books, including a biography of Abraham Lincoln and her autobiography. Tarbell died on January 6, 1944, at the age of 86.

– KM

Sacredness of human life! The world has never believed it! It has been with life that we settled our quarrels, won wives, gold and land, defended ideas, imposed religions. We have held that a death toll was a necessary part of every human achievement, whether sport, war or industry. A moment's rage over the horror of it, and we have sunk into indifference.

Imagination is the only key to the future. Without it none exists—with it all things are possible.

Rockefeller and his associates did not build the Standard Oil Co. in the boardrooms of Wall Street banks. They fought their way to control by rebate and drawback, bribe and blackmail, espionage and price cutting, by ruthless ... efficiency of organization.

UNTITLED / *Emily Dickinson*

Morns are meeker than they were- / The nuts are getting brown- /
The berry's cheek is plumper- / The Rose is out of town. / The maple
wears a gayer scarf- / The field a scarlet gown- / Lest I should be
old fashioned / I'll put a trinket on.

National Culture Day, *Japan*	*Stephen Austin, founder of Texas, b.1793*	☾ R. 3:50 pm S. 4:26 am ☉ R. 6:54 am S. 4:59 pm **FRIDAY · NOVEMBER 3 · 2006** **3**
First edition of *Cosmo Doogood's Urban Almanac* published, 2005	*Generosity is giving more than you can, and pride is taking less than you need.* — *Kahlil Gibran*	☉△♅ 7:01AM
Roseanne Barr, comedian, b.1952		
William Cullen Bryant, poet, b.1794		

Mischief Night, *England*	*Art Carney, actor, b.1918*	☾ R. 4:14 pm S. 5:49 am ☉ R. 6:56 am S. 4:57 pm **SATURDAY · NOVEMBER 4 · 2006** **4**
1946: UNESCO founded	*Walter Cronkite, Jr., journalist, b.1916*	
1922: King Tut's tomb found	*Will Rogers, humorist, b.1879*	☽△♄ 1:41AM ☽△♆ 3:03AM
Sean "Puffy" Combs, rapper, b.1969	*Diplomacy is the art of saying 'Nice doggie' until you can find a rock.* — *Will Rogers*	
Loretta Swit, actor, b.1937		

Guy Fawkes Day, *England*	*Irene Dunne, actor, b.1904*	☾ R. 4:43 pm S. 7:14 am ☉ R. 6:57 am S. 4:56 pm **SUNDAY · NOVEMBER 5 · 2006** **5**
Sadie Hawkins Day: girls invite the boys	*Eugene V. Debs, socialist, b.1855*	
	Will Durant, historian, b.1885	**Full Moon** 6:58 am
Sam Shepard, actor, playwright, b.1943	*Civilization exists by geological consent, subject to change without notice.* — *Will Durant*	☽☌♂ 12:47AM ☽☌☉ 7:59AM ☽☌♀ 11:55AM ☽☌☿ 7:25PM
Art Garfunkel, singer, b.1941		
Elke Sommers, actor, b.1940		

All times Central Time Zone, sun and moon rise and set Minneapolis, MN.

6 · MONDAY · NOVEMBER 6 · 2006

☾ R. 5:19 pm S. 8:38 am
☉ R. 6:58 am S. 4:55 pm

☽ ☌ ♃ 5:17AM

St. Leonard's Day, *Roman Catholic*

Gustavus Adolphus Day; Swedish king killed in 1632

Maria Shriver, TV reporter, b.1955

Sally Field, actor, b.1946

James Naismith, basketball creator, b.1861

John P. Sousa, composer, b.1854

Adolphe Sax, saxophone inventor, b.1814

Music is what feelings sound like.
— Author Unknown

7 · TUESDAY · NOVEMBER 7 · 2006

☾ R. 6:06 pm S. 9:58 am
☉ R. 7:00 am S. 4:53 pm

☿ ☌ ♀ 11:51AM
☽ △ ♆ 4:21PM

1917: Russian Revolution, Bolsheviks depose Czar Nicholas II

Joni Mitchell, singer, b.1943

Mary Travers, singer, b.1937

Billy Graham, evangelist, b.1918

Marie Curie, physicist, b.1867

Albert Camus, existentialist, b.1913

Too many have dispensed with generosity in order to practice charity.
— Albert Camus

8 · WEDNESDAY · NOVEMBER 8 · 2006

☾ R. 7:04 pm S. 11:06 am
☉ R. 7:01 am S. 4:52 pm

☽ ☌ ♇ ♆ 6:16AM
♂ △ ♅ 11:23AM
☉ ☌ ☿ 4:30PM

1519: Cortes conquers Mexico

Ricki Lee Jones, singer, b.1954

Bonnie Raitt, singer, b.1949

Margaret Mitchell, writer, b.1900

Dorothy Day, humanitarian, b.1897

Edmund Halley, astronomer, b.1656

In democracy it's your vote that counts;
In feudalism it's your count that votes.
— Mogens Jallberg

9 · THURSDAY · NOVEMBER 9 · 2006

☾ R. 8:11 pm S. 12:00 pm
☉ R. 7:02 am S. 4:51 pm

☽ △ ♅ 10:06AM
☽ △ ♂ 11:22AM
☽ △ ☿ 5:34PM
☽ △ ☉ 10:23PM

1989: Berlin wall opened

1938: Kristallnacht, *"Crystal Night"* pogrom against Jews in Germany

1965: East Coast blackout

Carl Sagan, astronomer, b.1934

Anne Sexton, writer, b.1928

Dorothy Dandridge, singer, b.1922

Stanford White, architect, b.1853

Benjamin Banneker, almanac maker, b.1731

A generation which ignores history has no past and no future.
— Robert Heinlein

© iStockPhoto

WOLF LOVE / *Victory Lee Schouten*

I read, / most whales / and most wolves / choose life mates, / loving
ferociously forever. / I see / some men / and some women / choose pain
and blame, / loving gingerly at best. / I want wolf love / with you. /
Wolf love, with you.

1871: Stanley finds Livingstone	*Friedrich von Schiller, poet, b.1759*	☾ R. 9:22 pm S. 12:40 pm ☉ R. 7:04 am S. 4:50 pm	FRIDAY · NOVEMBER 10 · 2006 **10**
1983: Microsoft releases Windows	*Martin Luther, theologian, b.1483*		
1951: Area codes introduced	It does not prove a thing to be right	☾△♀ 5:18ᴀᴍ ☾△♃ 3:59ᴘᴍ	
Ann Reinking, dancer, b.1949	because the majority say it is so.		
Richard Burton, actor, b.1925	— *Friedrich von Schiller*		

Martinmas, *Canada, U.K., France, U.S.*	*Jonathan Winters, comedian, b.1925*	☾ R. 10:32 pm S. 1:11 pm ☉ R. 7:05 am S. 4:49 pm	SATURDAY · NOVEMBER 11 · 2006 **11**
1918: Armistice Day, World War I ends	*Gen. George S. Patton, war hero, b.1885*		
Demi Moore, actor, b.1962	We are what we pretend to be, so we must be care-	☿♂♂ 10:15ᴀᴍ	
Carlos Fuentes, writer, b.1928	ful what we pre- tend to be.		
Kurt Vonnegut Jr., writer, b.1922	— *Kurt Vonnegut*		

Vᴇᴛᴇʀᴀɴs Dᴀʏ

Birth of Baha'u'llah, *Baha'i*	*Auguste Rodin, sculptor, b.1840*	☾ R. 11:40 pm S. 1:35 pm ☉ R. 7:07 am S. 4:47 pm	SUNDAY · NOVEMBER 12 · 2006 **12**
	Elizabeth Cady Stanton, suffragist, b.1815		
Nadia Comaneci, gymnast, b.1961		Last Quarter 11:45 am	
Neil Young, singer/ song- writer, b.1945	At the height of laughter, the universe is flung	☾♂♆ 6:37ᴀᴍ ☾♂♄ 9:28ᴘᴍ	
Grace Kelly, actor, b.1929	into a kaleido- scope of new possibilities. — *Jean Houston*	☾☉♆ 10:52ᴘᴍ	

All times Central Time Zone, sun and moon rise and set Minneapolis, MN.

13 MONDAY · NOVEMBER 13 · 2006

☾ S. 1:54 pm
☉ R. 7:08 am S. 4:46 pm

☿△♆ 12:26PM

1927: Holland Tunnel opened, *New York City*

World Kindness Day

Whoopi Goldberg, actor, b.1949

Louis Brandeis, jurist, b.1856

Robert Louis Stevenson, writer, b.1850

Saint Augustine, b.354

The world is a great book; he who never stirs from home reads only a page.
— *Saint Augustine*

---

14 TUESDAY · NOVEMBER 14 · 2006

☾ R. 12:45 am S. 2:10 pm
☉ R. 7:09 am S. 4:45 pm

☽♂♅ 6:11AM

1666: First blood transfusion

Prince Charles, Prince of Wales, b.1948

Veronica Lake, actor, b.1922

Aaron Copland, composer, b.1900

Claude Monet, painter, b.1840

To stop the flow of music would be like the stopping of time itself, incredible and inconceivable.
— *Aaron Copland*

---

15 WEDNESDAY · NOVEMBER 15 · 2006

☾ R. 1:48 am S. 2:26 pm
☉ R. 7:11 am S. 4:44 pm

♀♂♃ 3:35PM

Shichi-Go-San: "seven-five-three", *Japan*

1943: Gypsies condemned by Himmler, up to 500,000 killed

America Recycles Day

Petula Clark, singer, b.1934

J.G. Ballard, writer, b.1930

Marianne Moore, writer, b.1887

Georgia O'Keefe, painter, b.1887

Felix Frankfurter, jurist, b.1882

To some lawyers all facts are created equal.
— *Felix Frankfurter*

---

16 THURSDAY · NOVEMBER 16 · 2006

☾ R. 2:51 am S. 2:41 pm
☉ R. 7:12 am S. 4:43 pm

1885: Louis Riel hanged, led North West Rebellion, *Manitoba, CA*

Lisa Bonet, actor, b.1967

Chinua Achebe, writer, b.1930

Alice Adams, sculptor, b.1930

George S. Kaufman, writer, b.1889

William Handy, composer, b.1873

I respect faith, but doubt is what gets you an education.
— *Wilson Mizner*

To Do: **CLEMENTINE CANDLES**

Place your clementine in an upright position; cut off the top half of the peel and set aside. Carefully remove the fruit, taking care to leave the center nub in place—this will become your wick. Allow the peel to dry (20 to 30 minutes). Pour one to two tablespoons of olive oil into the bottom half. Be sure to saturate the "wick" well. Light the wick, cut a small hole in the peel's top half, and carefully place it on top of the bottom "candle" for a natural, mellow glow. —*D. M.*

© PhotoDisc

CONTEMPLATE:

THE PARADOXICAL COMMANDMENTS / Kent M. Keith

Kent Keith wrote *The Paradoxical Commandments* in 1968 when he was a sophomore at Harvard as part of a handbook for high school student leaders. They've appeared on the Web in various guises. It's reported that Mother Teresa put a version called *Anyway* on the wall of her children's home in Calcutta. And another version called *The Final Analysis* is often, wrongly, attributed to Mother Teresa. Here is the original.

The Paradoxical Commandments

1. People are illogical, unreasonable, and self-centered.
   Love them anyway.

2. If you do good, people will accuse you of selfish ulterior motives.
   Do good anyway.

3. If you are successful, you win false friends and true enemies.
   Succeed anyway.

4. The good you do today will be forgotten tomorrow.
   Do good anyway.

5. Honesty and frankness make you vulnerable.
   Be honest and frank anyway.

6. The biggest men and women with the biggest ideas can be shot down by the smallest men and women with the smallest minds.
   Think big anyway.

7. People favor underdogs but follow only top dogs.
   Fight for a few underdogs anyway.

8. What you spend years building may be destroyed overnight. Build anyway.

9. People really need help but may attack you if you do help them.
   Help people anyway.

10. Give the world the best you have and you'll get kicked in the teeth.
    Give the world the best you have anyway.

 *Notes*

NATURE POETRY / *Meg Kearney*

Concrete, glass, steel—
Meaning limestone, silica, gypsum, sand,
Manganese, sodium, sulfur, ore—
Anything unnatural here?

Danny DeVito, actor, b.1944	Of course I've got lawyers. They are like nuclear weapons: I've got em coz everyone else has. But as soon as you use them they screw everything up. — *Danny DeVito*	☾ R. 3:55 am S. 2:58 pm ☉ R. 7:13 am S. 4:42 pm
Lorne Michaels, producer, b.1944		
Lauren Hutton, actor, b.1944		☽△♆ 8:00PM ☿ 7:25PM
Martin Scorsese, director, b.1942		
August Mobius, astronomer, "Mobius Strip," b.1790		

FRIDAY · NOVEMBER 17 · 2006 17

1978: Jonestown Massacre, more than 900 followers committed mass suicide

Margaret Atwood, writer, b.1939

Mickey Mouse, b.1928

Alan Shepard, astronaut, b.1923

Johnny Mercer, songwriter, b.1909

Sojourner Truth, abolitionist, b.1797

Louis Daguerre, inventor, b.1789

Let not thy will roar, when thy power can but whisper.
— *Dr. Thomas Fuller*

☾ R. 5:00 am S. 3:16 pm
☉ R. 7:15 am S. 4:41 pm

SATURDAY · NOVEMBER 18 · 2006 18

1863: Lincoln's Gettysburg Address

1493: Puerto Rico Discovery Day

Jodie Foster, actor, b.1962

Meg Ryan, actor, b.1961

Ted Turner, media mogul, b.1938

Indira Gandhi, Indian politician, b.1917

Peter F. Drucker, management guru, b.1909

You cannot shake hands with a clenched fist.
— *Indira Gandhi*

☾ R. 6:07 am S. 3:38 pm
☉ R. 7:16 am S. 4:41 pm

☽☌☿ 4:01AM
☽△♅ 7:08AM
☽☌♂ 10:39PM

SUNDAY · NOVEMBER 19 · 2006 19

All times Central Time Zone, sun and moon rise and set Minneapolis, MN.

20 MONDAY · NOVEMBER... ...2006

☾ R. 7:17 am S. 4:06 pm
☉ R. 7:17 am S. 4:40 pm

New Moon
4:18 pm

⛢ 1:08ᴀᴍ
☽☌☉ 5:18ᴘᴍ
☽☌♃ 6:54ᴘᴍ

1910: Mexico
Revolution Day

*Robert F.
Kennedy,
senator, b.1925*

*Nadine Gordimer,
writer, b.1923*

*Gene Tierney,
actor, b.1920*

*Edwin Hubble,
American
astronomer,
b.1889*

Each time
someone stands
up for an ideal,
or acts to
improve the
lot of others,
or strikes out
against injustice,
he sends forth
a tiny ripple
of hope.
— *Robert F.
Kennedy*

---

21 TUESDAY · NOVEMBER 21 · 2006

☾ R. 8:27 am S. 4:43 pm
☉ R. 7:19 am S. 4:39 pm

☽☌♀ 6:07ᴀᴍ
☉☌♃ 6:15ᴘᴍ

**World Hello
Day**

1783: Man's
first flight in a
balloon

1995: Dow
Jones tops 5,000
for the first time

*Bjork,
singer/songwriter,
b.1965*

*Goldie Hawn,
actor, b.1945*

*Marlo Thomas,
actor, b.1937*

*Henry Purcell,
composer, d.1695*

*Voltaire, philoso-
pher, b.1694*

Those who can
make you believe
absurdities can
make you commit
atrocities.
— *Voltaire*

---

22 WEDNESDAY · NOVEMBER 22 · 2006

☾ R. 9:33 am S. 5:30 pm
☉ R. 7:20 am S. 4:38 pm

☿△⛢ 9:50ᴀᴍ
☽△♄ 7:03ᴘᴍ
☽☌♆ 8:20ᴘᴍ

1963: John F.
Kennedy
assassinated

1859:
*On The Origin
Of Species* pub-
lished, Charles
Darwin

*Scarlett
Johansson,
actor, b.1984*

*Jamie Lee Curtis,
actor, b.1958*

*Hoagie
Carmichael,
composer, b.1899*

*Charles
DeGaulle, French
leader, b.1890*

*George Eliot,
writer, b.1819*

One must be
poor to know the
luxury of giving.
— *George Eliot*

---

23 THURSDAY · NOVEMBER 23 · 2006

☾ R. 10:32 am S. 6:30 pm
☉ R. 7:21 am S. 4:37 pm

**Labor
Thanksgiving
Day,** *Japan*

1936:
Life magazine
premiered

*Harpo Marx,
comic actor,
b.1888*

*Boris Karloff,
actor, b.1887*

*Billy the Kid, out-
law, b.1859*

It is impossible
to defeat an
ignorant man
in argument.
— *William G.
McAdoo*

Tʜᴀɴᴋsɢɪᴠɪɴɢ Dᴀʏ

© iStockPhoto

THERE IS SOME KISS WE WANT / *Rumi, translated by Coleman Barks*

There is some kiss we want / with our whole lives, / the touch of Spirit on the body. / Seawater begs the pearl / to break its shell. / And the lily, how passionately / it needs some wild Darling! / At night, I open the window / and ask the moon to come / and press its face against mine. / Breathe into me. / Close the language-door / and open the love window. / The moon won't use the door, / only the window.

You're Welcome-giving Day

Candy Darling, actor, b.1944

Dale Carnegie, writer, b.1888

Scott Joplin, composer, b.1868

Henri Toulouse-Lautrec, painter, b.1864

Benedict de Spinoza, philosopher, b.1632

One thing you will probably remember well is any time you forgive and forget.
— Franklin P. Jones

☾ R. 11:20 am   S. 7:39 pm
☉ R. 7:22 am   S. 4:37 pm

FRIDAY · NOVEMBER 24 · 2006 **24**

St. Catherine's Day, *Canada, France*

Amy Grant, singer, b.1960

Joe DiMaggio, baseball player, b.1914

Lewis Thomas, physician/ writer, b.1913

Carry Nation, temperance advocate, b.1846

Andrew Carnegie, financier, b.1835

Dreams come a size too big so that we may grow into them.
— Josie Bisset

☾ R. 11:58 am   S. 8:55 pm
☉ R. 7:24 am   S. 4:36 pm

SATURDAY · NOVEMBER 25 · 2006 **25**

Christ the King, *Christian*

Day of Covenant, *Baha'i*

Tina Turner, singer, b.1938

Charles M. Schultz, creator of "Peanuts," b.1922

John Harvard, Harvard Univ. founder, b.1607

Sojourner Truth, former slave, d.1883

I have a new philosophy. I'm only going to dread one day at a time.
— Charles M. Schulz

☾ R. 12:28 pm   S. 10:13 pm
☉ R. 7:25 am   S. 4:36 pm

☽ ☌ ♆ 5:09ᴘᴍ

SUNDAY · NOVEMBER 26 · 2006 **26**

All times Central Time Zone, sun and moon rise and set Minneapolis, MN.

27 MONDAY · NOVEMBER 27 · 2006

☾ R. 12:52 pm S. 11:31 pm
☼ R. 7:26 am S. 4:35 pm

☽ ☌ ♄ 6:41ᴀᴍ

Jimi Hendrix, guitarist, b.1942

Bruce Lee, actor, b.1940

Gail Sheehy, writer, b.1937

James Agee, poet, b.1909

If a man does not keep pace with his companions, perhaps it is because he hears a different drummer. Let him step to the music which he hears, however measured or faraway.
— Henry David Thoreau

---

28 TUESDAY · NOVEMBER 28 · 2006

☾ R. 1:13 pm
☼ R. 7:27 am S. 4:34 pm

First Quarter 12:29 am

☽ ☌ ♅ 10:00ᴀᴍ
☽ △ ☿ 9:07ᴘᴍ

Jon Stewart, comedian, b.1962

Rita Mae Brown, writer, b.1944

Berry Gordy, Jr., cofounder of Motown, b.1929

Friedrich Engels, philosopher, b.1820

William Blake, poet, b.1757

When the doors of perception are cleansed, man will see things as they truly are, infinite.
— William Blake

---

29 WEDNESDAY · NOVEMBER 29 · 2006

☾ R. 1:32 pm S. 12:48 am
☼ R. 7:29 am S. 4:34 pm

☽ △ ♂ 10:44ᴀᴍ
☽ △ ♃ 8:41ᴘᴍ

1989: Czechoslovakia ends Communist rule

Joel Coen, filmmaker, b.1954

Madeline L'Engle, writer, b.1918

C.S. Lewis, writer, b.1878

Louisa May Alcott, writer, b.1832

Under capitalism, man exploits man. Under communism, it's just the opposite.
— John Kenneth Galbraith

---

30 THURSDAY · NOVEMBER 30 · 2006

☾ R. 1:52 pm S. 2:05 am
☼ R. 7:30 am S. 4:34 pm

☽ △ ☉ 8:14ᴀᴍ
☽ △ ♀ 11:33ᴘᴍ

St. Andrew's Day, Christian

Elisha Cuthbert, actor, b.1982

Ben Stiller, comic actor, b.1965

Abbie Hoffman, activist, b.1936

Gordon Parks, photographer, b.1912

Winston Churchill, statesman, b.1874

Mark Twain, writer, b.1835

Jonathan Swift, writer, b.1667

Always do right. This will gratify some people and astonish the rest.
— Mark Twain

Recipe: PARSNIPS

That funny-looking, pale, carroty thing is a parsnip, and it's loaded with natural sweetness. One great way to cook parsnips is to roast them in a hot oven along with onions, carrots, potatoes, whole garlic cloves, and a liberal dose of olive oil. Another swell way is to peel, slice, and steam them until just tender and then drain. Next pour on some melted butter and put them in a nonstick skillet with a generous amount of fresh breadcrumbs. Toss them around over medium-high heat until both breadcrumbs and parsnips turn golden brown. Throw in some fresh parsley or thyme before serving. Lovely with roast chicken or even tossed with pasta. —MC

CONTEMPLATE:

THANKSGIVING FEAST / James P. Lenfestey

We gather together
to feast, to fatten, to unite
with holiday birds and grains.

Old Gobbler,
you American birthright,
born wildly hungry,
eating out of Indian hands for
centuries,
impressive in the pan
even without your thick feather suit
and your head like a stoplight,
impressive with huge breasts and
thighs,
white meat and dark meat.

Old gabbler, the goose,
you snide one hissing
from your pricked breast,
fatter, oilier, slicker,
dripping from the roaster,
dripping out of northern lakes.

Old yeast, you breeder of bread.

Old cranberry, you sauce bog.

Old corn, you silky pudding,
you whistling huskface mask,
you rustling stubble in the snow.

Old squash, you hot steaming slide
of running butter.

Old spinach, you fat leaves of grass,
potherb, family Goosefoot,
crusted over with cheeses.

Old family and friends,
tribal and civilized,
earth and air,
water and sun,
fathers and daughters,
grandmothers, grandsons,

Harvested here
on the eyebrow of winter,
spread around the table,
tasting—ahh—each other.

DECEMBER

© PhotoDisc

NOV 22 - DEC 21

Sagittarius

DECEMBER BIRTHSTONE
Lapis Lazuli

DEC 22 - JAN 19

Capricorn

DECEMBER FLOWER
Poinsettia

CONTROL OF SPEECH BECOMES FEELING FOR TRUTH
Challenges: gossip, moralizing, dogmatism, subjectivity of opinion

Silence slips peacefully over the black-and-white world. The wind moans. The Earth is hard as iron. Mist and cold penetrate to the bone. The days grow shorter, the snowfalls heavier. Bare trees and hunched figures in overcoats and heavy jackets dot the streets. But inside it is warm, and the kitchen windows are steamed up. People gather in expectation of the rebirth of the light. There is almost the sense that the Sun will break forth again from the interior of the Earth – or from within our own souls. Christmas and Hanukkah, among other celebrations, hold forth the promise that, by our dedication and self-sacrifice a new green world of meaning, love, and compassion can be born. At the solstice, the heavens show us the rebirth of the light, Dies Natalis Solis Invicti – the Birthday of the Unconquerable Sun. May the power of the world's being grow strong! May life's power to act blossom forth! May the past bear what is to come! – *CB*

WEST COAST / PACIFIC MARITIME

After a few weeks of rain, slugs and snails sally forth from their hiding places. Stroll outside on a wet night with a flashlight and you will be truly impressed by the great numbers and many types you can find. Rainfall reaches its peak in parts of the Pacific Northwest. Along the southern California coast, find thousands of monarch butterflies in the restful sanctuary of old eucalyptus groves. Take time this month to sign up for a Christmas Bird Count – a 100-year tradition of counting birds for one day that is sponsored by the National Audubon Society.

MOUNTAIN REGION / BASIN & RANGE

Winter activity is best shown by the eager energy of male mule deer sharpening their antlers in preparation for battles in which the bucks fight for access to females. Deep snow and iced-over lakes settle in for the winter at higher elevations. Both bears and squirrels are ensconced in their warm dens. Steller's jays make a noisy appearance at backyard bird feeders, often chasing away hungry mountain chickadees or purple finches.

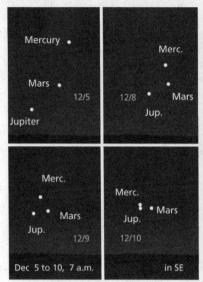

An extraordinary convergence of three planets climaxes on December 10. The waning Moon pays a visit on December 18.

Mercury · Mars · Jupiter — 12/5
Merc. · Mars · Jup. — 12/8
Merc. · Mars · Jup. — 12/9
Merc. · Jup. · Mars — 12/10
Dec 5 to 10, 7 a.m. — in SE

Jupiter · Mars · Mercury — SCORPIO
Dec 18, 7:15 a.m. — SE

LOOK UP:

4 Full Moon, 6:26 PM; Mercury stands out amid the faint stars of Libra this morning; Try locating dim, ruddy Mars and bright Jupiter below it in the hour before dawn

12 Last quarter Moon, 8:33 PM

14 Geminid meteor shower peaks, 12:00 AM, Moon interferes

20 New Moon, 8:01 AM

21 Winter solstice, 6:23 PM

27 First quarter Moon, 8:48 AM

DECEMBER IS THE MONTH FOR:

BINGO'S BIRTHDAY · COOKIE CUTTERS · DRUNK DRIVING PREVENTION · STRESS-FREE FAMILY HOLIDAYS · CELEBRATING · GIFT WRAP · SAFE TOYS AND GIFTS · UNIVERSAL HUMAN RIGHTS · U.N. WORLD AIDS AWARENESS · JINGLE BELLS

DECEMBER

S	M	T	W	T	F	S
					1	2
3	4	5	6	7	8	9
10	11	12	13	14	15	16
17	18	19	20	21	22	23
24/31	25	26	27	28	29	30

MID-CONTINENT / CORN BELT & GULF

During bouts of fierce cold, squirrels retreat into their cozy leafy nests high in the treetops. Animals everywhere, from mice to bears, are asleep in their cozy niches. Snows deepen, and ice on lakes starts to crack and boom as it shifts. Along the Gulf Coast, however, hundreds of thousands of birds enjoy milder weather. From New Orleans it's possible to see giant congregations of wintering ducks. In forested areas, look for freshly shed deer antlers.

EAST COAST / ATLANTIC SEABOARD

Deep snows settle in across New England and higher ranges in the south. Waxwing flocks gather in berry bushes. Northern species like crossbills, hawk owls, or snowy owls may show up. Bird feeders become very active with chickadees, towhees, cardinals, and blue jays, plus many other species. Leafy squirrel nests in the trees are exposed among the bare branches. This is one of the few months in Florida that's relatively free of mosquitoes. Walk the beaches in search of washed-up shells. Keep an eye out for flocks of wintering waterfowl and white pelicans. – DL

© From *The Worst Case Survival Handbook: The Holidays*

URBAN SURVIVAL STRATEGY:
HOW TO MAKE AN IMPROMPTU TOAST

Be brief. No one is really listening.

1. Keep it simple.

A toast made in front of a large or mixed crowd should be brief and safe.

2. Follow the "Past, Present, Future" (PPF) rule.

Acknowledge past successes, present situations, and future objectives. For example: "We've been through some difficult times together, but we've made it through. I'm so lucky to know all of you. Here's to the future."

3. Avoid problems.

Stay away from mistakes and setbacks. If the last year has been truly horrible, refer to it in a neutral, ambiguous way: "It's been quite a year..." or, "As this extraordinary year comes to an end..." If the problems are continuing and you don't want to lie, say something emphatic but meaningless: "What an amazing, talented group of people!" or, "I continue to be inspired by each and every one of you!" The future is the easiest portion of the toast, since you can hope and wish without regard to reality. Nonetheless, moderation is best: "The coming year promises to be astonishing" or, "The sky's the limit in the year ahead."

4. Focus on the people.

Your toast should be about people in general—about spirit, creativity, and bonding—rather than about specific events or challenges. All of the partygoers are hoping you don't mention them by name, and they really want to get back to eating and drinking.

5. Use humor judiciously.

A little levity may be appreciated, but jokes can slow down your toast and breed restlessness. Depending upon your condition, you may be in no position to gauge what is funny. Attempts at humor could backfire and insult people, open wounds, or just be incomprehensible. If a remark or joke bombs, keep going. Pausing will only call attention to it and add to the audience's discomfort.

6. Smile, nod, and look proud as you are speaking.

Keep your glass raised and lift it even higher as you conclude the toast. Remember, no one is really listening, anyway.

– From *The Worst Case Survival Handbook: Work*

ATMOSPHERE / *Susan Griffin*

Learning to / draw tenderness, the / sky is full of / snow for her, / and she knows the / road curves around / her and the chill / of the air has no / fear, and she / sees her sorrow / gleaming in the / hardening river, she is / learning to take / tenderness from the / atmosphere.

World AIDS Day	*Woody Allen, actor/filmmaker, b.1935*	☾ R. 2:14 pm S. 3:24 am ☉ R. 7:31 am S. 4:33 pm	**FRIDAY · DECEMBER 1 · 2006** **1**
1955: Rosa Parks arrested	*Lou Rawls, singer, b.1935*		
1891: Basketball created			
Bette Midler, singer, b.1945	How to make God laugh:	☽△♄ 12:15PM	
Richard Pryor, comedian, b.1940	Tell him your future plans. — Woody Allen	☽△♅ 1:41PM	

1823: Monroe Doctrine declared	*Britney Spears, singer, b.1981*	☾ R. 2:39 pm S. 4:46 am ☉ R. 7:32 am S. 4:33 pm	**SATURDAY · DECEMBER 2 · 2006** **2**
1859: John Brown executed	*Julie Harris, actor, b.1925*		
	Nikos Kazantzakis, writer, b.1885		
I expect nothing. I fear no one. I am free. — *Nikos Kazantzakis*	*George Seurat, painter, b.1859*		

Advent, *Christian* (also Dec. 10, 17, 24)	*Maria Callas, singer, b.1923*	☾ R. 3:12 pm S. 6:09 am ☉ R. 7:33 am S. 4:32 pm	**SUNDAY · DECEMBER 3 · 2006** **3**
1984: Bhopal poison gas disaster	*Sven Nykvist, cinematographer, b.1922*		
	Carlos Montoya, guitarist, b.1903		
Julianne Moore, actor, b.1961	*Joseph Conrad, writer, b.1857*	☽☌☿ 11:10AM	
Darryl Hannah, actor, b.1961	All a man can betray is his conscience. — *Joseph Conrad*	☽☌♂ 7:31PM	

All times Central Time Zone, sun and moon rise and set Minneapolis, MN.

4 MONDAY · DECEMBER 4 · 2006

☾ R. 3:53 pm S. 7:30 am
☉ R. 7:34 am S. 4:32 pm

Full Moon
6:25 pm

☽ ☌ ♃ 1:50AM
☽ ☌ ⊙ 7:25PM

1867: National Grange founded

Marisa Tomei, actor, b.1964

Cassandra Wilson, singer, b.1955

Rainer Maria Rilke, poet, b.1875

Wassily Kandinsky, artist, b.1866

Samuel Butler, writer, b.1835

Thomas Carlyle, essayist, b.1795

When words leave off, music begins.
— Thomas Carlyle

---

5 TUESDAY · DECEMBER 5 · 2006

☾ R. 4:46 pm S. 8:44 am
☉ R. 7:35 am S. 4:32 pm

☽ △ ♆ 3:23AM
☽ ☌ ♀ 1:09PM
☽ ☌ ♆ 6:12PM
♄ 11:06PM

1955: AFL-CIO founded

Jose Carreras, singer, b.1946

Little Richard, singer, b.1935

Calvin Trillin, writer, b.1935

Joan Didion, writer, b.1934

Walt Disney, animator, b.1901

Christina Rossetti, poet, b.1830

Phyllis Wheatley, poet, d.1784

Work while you have the light. You are responsible for the talent that has been entrusted to you.
— Henri-Frédéric Amiel

---

6 WEDNESDAY · DECEMBER 6 · 2006

☾ R. 5:50 pm S. 9:46 am
☉ R. 7:36 am S. 4:32 pm

☽ △ ♅ 8:12PM

St. Nicholas Day, *Europe*

1865: 13th Amendment ratified, slavery abolished

Macy Gray, singer, b.1969

Dave Brubeck, jazz musician, b.1920

Alfred Eisenstaedt, photographer, b.1898

Ira Gershwin, lyricist, b.1896

Whenever I hear anyone arguing for slavery, I feel a strong impulse to see it tried on him personally.
— Abraham Lincoln

---

7 THURSDAY · DECEMBER 7 · 2006

☾ R. 7:01 pm S. 10:33 am
☉ R. 7:37 am S. 4:32 pm

♀ △ ♅ 2:17AM
♀ △ ♄ 10:51PM

1941: Japanese attack Pearl Harbor

Larry Bird, basketball great, b.1956

Tom Waits, singer/songwriter, b.1949

Ellen Burstyn, actor, b.1932

Noam Chomsky, linguist, public citizen, b.1928

Willa Cather, writer, b.1873

Do not dwell in the past, do not dream of the future, concentrate the mind on the present moment.
— Buddha

ESSENTIAL PLACE :: PPG PLAZA, PITTSBURGH, PENNSYLVANIA :: To learn more, see pg. 274

WE ARE THE DECISIVE ELEMENT / *Johann Wolfgang von Goethe*

I have come to the frightening conclusion that I am the decisive element. /
It is my personal approach that creates the climate. / It is my daily mood
that makes the weather. / I possess tremendous power to make life miserable
or joyous. / I can be a tool of torture or an instrument of inspiration. /
I can humiliate or humor, hurt or heal. / In all situations, it is my response
that decides whether a crisis is escalated or de-escalated, and a / person is
humanized or de-humanized....

Feast of the Immaculate Conception, *Roman Catholic*

Bodhi Day, *Buddhist Rohatsu*

Sinead O'Conor, singer, b.1966

Kim Basinger, actor, b.1953

Jim Morrison, singer, b.1943

James Thurber, writer, b.1894

Diego Rivera, painter, b.1886

Mary, Queen of Scots, b.1542

Horace, writer, b.65 BC

He knows all about art, but he doesn't know what he likes.
— James Thurber

☾ R. 8:14 pm   S. 11:08 am
☉ R. 7:38 am   S. 4:32 pm

☾△☿ 7:39ᴀᴍ
☾△♂ 10:03ᴀᴍ
☾△♃ 12:53ᴘᴍ

FRIDAY · DECEMBER 8 · 2006   8

John Malkovich, actor, b.1953

Joan Armatrading, singer, b.1950

Redd Foxx, comedian, b.1922

Jean de Brunhoff, writer, b.1899

Emmett Kelly, clown, b.1898

John Milton, poet, b.1608

I am a part of all that I have met.
— John Milton

☾ R. 9:24 pm   S. 11:35 am
☉ R. 7:39 am   S. 4:32 pm

☾☌♆ 4:04ᴘᴍ
☾△☉ 4:22ᴘᴍ
☿☌♂ 9:27ᴘᴍ

SATURDAY · DECEMBER 9 · 2006   9

Since 1901: Nobel Prize Ceremony, *Oslo and Stockholm*

Susan Dey, actor/humanitarian, b.1952

Kenneth Branagh, actor, b.1960

Dorothy Lamour, actor, b.1914

Emily Dickinson, poet, b.1830

Alfred Nobel, d.1896

Red Cloud, Lakota chief, d.1909

We turn not older with years, but newer every day.
— Emily Dickinson

☾ R. 10:31 pm   S. 11:57 am
☉ R. 7:40 am   S. 4:32 pm

☾☌♄ 6:46ᴀᴍ
☾△♆ 9:05ᴀᴍ
☿△♃ 11:58ᴀᴍ
☾△♀ 3:36ᴘᴍ

SUNDAY · DECEMBER 10 · 2006   10

All times Central Time Zone, sun and moon rise and set Minneapolis, MN.

11 MONDAY · DECEMBER 11 · 2006

☾ R. 11:36 pm S. 12:15 pm
☉ R. 7:41 am S. 4:32 pm

♂ ☌ ♃ 11:11 AM
☾ ☍ ♅ 2:30 PM

1946: UNICEF founded

1936: Edward VIII abdicates to marry Wallis Simpson

Terri Garr, actor, b.1949

Brenda Lee, singer, b.1944

John F. Kerry, U.S. senator, b.1943

Tom Hayden, activist, b.1939

Alfred de Musset, writer, b.1810

Hector Berlioz, composer, b.1803

Be to her virtues very kind. Be to her faults a little blind.
— Matthew Prior

12 TUESDAY · DECEMBER 12 · 2006

☾ S. 12:31 pm
☉ R. 7:42 am S. 4:32 pm

Last Quarter
8:32 am

La Virgen De Guadalupe, *Mexico*

Our ignorance of history makes us libel our own times. People have always been like this.
— Gustave Flaubert

Jennifer Connelly, actor, b.1970

Sheila E(scovedo), entertainer, b.1959

Dionne Warwick, singer, b.1941

Frank Sinatra, singer, b.1915

Gustave Flaubert, writer, b.1821

13 WEDNESDAY · DECEMBER 13 · 2006

☾ R. 12:39 am S. 12:46 pm
☉ R. 7:43 am S. 4:32 pm

Luciadagen: Lucia's Day, *Sweden*

Jamie Foxx, actor, b.1967

Steve Buscemi, actor, b.1957

Christopher Plummer, actor, b.1929

Laurens van der Post, writer, b.1906

Mary Todd Lincoln, 1st Lady, b.1818

Human beings are perhaps never more frightening than when they are convinced beyond doubt that they are right.
— Laurens Van der Post

14 THURSDAY · DECEMBER 14 · 2006

☾ R. 1:42 am S. 1:02 pm
☉ R. 7:44 am S. 4:32 pm

☾ △ ♆ 4:51 PM

1911: Amundsen reaches the South Pole

Patty Duke, actor, b.1946

Stewart Brand, cataloger, b.1938

Lee Remick, actor, b.1935

Margaret Chase Smith, politician, b.1897

Tycho Brahe, astronomer, b.1546

Nostrodamus, astronomer, b.1503

The highest courage is to dare to appear to be what one is.
— John Lancaster Spalding

To Do: DECORATING CANDLES

Gather candles of all shapes, sizes, and colors. Next buy special decorating wax sheets made by Stockmar. If you can't find them locally, you can order them on-line at www.peanutbutterkisses.com/art_wax.html. Using _a sharp knife or little cookie or aspic cutters, create shapes from the wax to press into the sides of the candles. There is no end to the designs you can make, and even the youngest child can take part. These candles are great for gift giving or to burn in your own home, a reminder of when you slowed down and just enjoyed being together. —MC

© iStockPhoto

OUTLOOK / *Crystal Bacon*

I've begun to love the cold, the slick, bitter seed / of this life: brittle, brilliant. Even the bare trees / have embraced the ice: arms and fingers shelled / in diamond, in glass, and still they wave and click, / bend and freeze in the chill kiss of the wind…

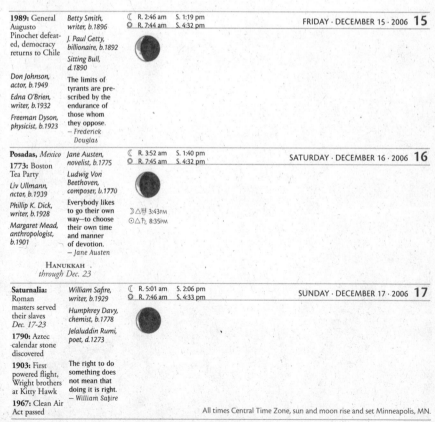

1989: General Augusto Pinochet defeated, democracy returns to Chile

Don Johnson, actor, b.1949

Edna O'Brien, writer, b.1932

Freeman Dyson, physicist, b.1923

Betty Smith, writer, b.1896

J. Paul Getty, billionaire, b.1892

Sitting Bull, d.1890

The limits of tyrants are prescribed by the endurance of those whom they oppose.
– Frederick Douglas

☾ R. 2:46 am   S. 1:19 pm
☉ R. 7:44 am   S. 4:32 pm

FRIDAY · DECEMBER 15 · 2006   15

Posadas, *Mexico*
1773: Boston Tea Party

Liv Ullmann, actor, b.1939

Phillip K. Dick, writer, b.1928

Margaret Mead, anthropologist, b.1901

HANUKKAH
through Dec. 23

Jane Austen, novelist, b.1775

Ludwig Von Beethoven, composer, b.1770

Everybody likes to go their own way—to choose their own time and manner of devotion.
– Jane Austen

☾ R. 3:52 am   S. 1:40 pm
☉ R. 7:45 am   S. 4:32 pm

☽△⛢ 3:43PM
☉△♄ 8:35PM

SATURDAY · DECEMBER 16 · 2006   16

Saturnalia: Roman masters served their slaves Dec. 17-23

1790: Aztec calendar stone discovered

1903: First powered flight, Wright brothers at Kitty Hawk

1967: Clean Air Act passed

William Safire, writer, b.1929

Humphrey Davy, chemist, b.1778

Jelaluddin Rumi, poet, d.1273

The right to do something does not mean that doing it is right.
– William Safire

☾ R. 5:01 am   S. 2:06 pm
☉ R. 7:46 am   S. 4:33 pm

SUNDAY · DECEMBER 17 · 2006   17

All times Central Time Zone, sun and moon rise and set Minneapolis, MN.

18 MONDAY · DECEMBER 18 · 2006

☾ R. 6:11 am S. 2:39 pm
☼ R. 7:46 am S. 4:33 pm

☉☌♆ 9:39AM
☾☌♃ 2:23PM
☾☌♂ 9:24PM

Misa de Aguinaldo, *Venezuela*

Christina Aguilera, singer, b.1980

Katie Holmes, actor, b.1978

Brad Pitt, actor, b.1964

Steven Spielberg, filmmaker, b.1947

Paul Klee, painter, b.1879

Joseph Grimaldi, mime, b.1778

Antonio Stradivari, violin maker, b.1737

A single day is enough to make us a little larger
— Paul Klee

---

19 TUESDAY · DECEMBER 19 · 2006

☾ R. 7:20 am S. 3:23 pm
☼ R. 7:47 am S. 4:33 pm

☾☌☿ 12:38PM

Jennifer Beals, actor, b.1963

Kevin McHale, basketball player, b.1957

Cicely Tyson, actor, b.1939

Edith Piaf, singer, b.1915

William Parry, explorer, b.1790

Any intelligent fool can make things bigger, more complex, and more violent. It takes a touch of genius — and a lot of courage — to move in the opposite direction.
— E. F. Schumacher

---

20 WEDNESDAY · DECEMBER 20 · 2006

☾ R. 8:23 am S. 4:19 pm
☼ R. 7:48 am S. 4:34 pm

New Moon
8:01 am

☾△♄ 2:23AM
☾☌♆ 5:30AM
☾☌☉ 9:01AM

Alyssa Milano, actor, b.1972

Uri Geller, psychic, b.1946

David Levine, caricaturist, b.1926

Susanne K. Langer, philosopher, b.1895

Sacagawea, interpreter, d.1812

What is life? It is a flash of a firefly in the night. It is the breath of a buffalo in the wintertime. It is the little shadow which runs across the grass and loses itself in the sunset.
— Crowfoot (last words)

---

21 THURSDAY · DECEMBER 21 · 2006

☾ R. 9:16 am S. 5:27 pm
☼ R. 7:48 am S. 4:34 pm

☾☌♀ 11:06AM

Yule, *Christian*
1620: Pilgrims land at Plymouth, Mass.

Chris Evert, tennis player, b.1954

Samuel L. Jackson, actor, b.1948

Jane Fonda, actor, b.1937

Frank Zappa, musician, b.1940

Joseph Stalin, dictator, b.1879

Christmas, children, is not a date. It is a state of mind.
— Mary Ellen Chase

WINTER SOLSTICE
1:35PM

© iStockPhoto

Notes

*"When we first started seeing each other,
we would always use the same word for snow."*

CELEBRATE:

CHRISTMAS CARDS & CHRISTMAS TREES

The Christmas card didn't start with Hallmark. A stressed-out peer of the realm, Sir Henry Cole asked John Calcott Horsley in 1843 to design some cards for him so he wouldn't have to compose individual letters to his family and friends. As with anything associated with the royals, Christmas cards became the rage in England. In the US, a German lithographer named Louis Prang began producing cards and by the end of the century, millions were being sold as a substitute for gift giving. Today, we have a new time-saving custom to contend with, one which Sir Henry would have surely embraced—the dreaded family Christmas letter.

Although decorating with evergreens has long been a Christmas holiday tradition (and a winter pagan one before that), Christmas trees didn't gain popularity until the reign of Queen Victoria. Her German husband, Prince Albert, decorated a tree for his family in 1848 and the practice took off, easily crossing the ocean to America. Each year, nearly 33 million real Christmas trees are sold in the US, and a whopping 30 million Christmas cards, some of which aren't mailed until February.

TO DO:

MAKE AN ICE LUMINARIA

Candle flames glowing in snow and ice cast a magical winter spell. Build a hollow cairn of snowballs and nestle a candle inside (pictured). Or for a more elegant, longer-lasting luminaria, take an ice cream bucket and a slightly smaller container. Put rocks in the bottom of the ice cream bucket, put in the smaller container, and make sure the tops of the containers are level with each other. Weight down the smaller container with a few more rocks. Pour water into the space between the containers and put the bucket outside or in your freezer. When the ice is solid, place the bucket in the sink and run some warm water into the smaller container. Lift it out. Turn the bucket over, run warm water over it, and slide it off the ice. Put outside, place a candle in the bottom, and light it as the early winter darkness falls. – *MC*

© iStockPhoto

SOLSTICE FIRE / *Will Winter*

…Suddenly, it is December and it is dark. / In July I had so much; / remember how I squandered it, / going to a movie that sunny afternoon? / What was I thinking?… / …This year, if I am lucky, / and if this fire works, / the Night Thief will begin restitution. / Tomorrow a minute is back, maybe two. / Before long, I'm thinking that my gold / will be returned to its rightful owner. / And, as for me, / I will be more careful next time.

Ralph Fiennes, actor, b.1962	Children are likely to live up to you believe of them. — Lady Bird Johnson	☾ R. 9:58 am S. 6:43 pm ☉ R. 7:49 am S. 4:35 pm	**FRIDAY · DECEMBER 22 · 2006 22**
Diane Sawyer, journalist, b.1946			
Lady Bird Johnson, 1st Lady, b.1912			
Giacomo Puccini, composer, b.1858			

Night of the Radishes, *Mexico*	Yousuf Karsh, photographer, b.1908	☾ R. 10:30 am S. 8:02 pm ☉ R. 7:49 am S. 4:35 pm	**SATURDAY · DECEMBER 23 · 2006 23**
Eddie Vedder, singer, b.1965	Harriet Monroe, poet, b.1860		
Akihito, Japanese Emperor, b.1933			
Robert Bly, poet, b.1926	When the character of a man is not clear to you, look at his friends. — Japanese Proverb	☽ ☌ ♆ 11:51PM	

Howard Hughes, industrialist, b.1905	Juan Ramon Jimenez, poet, b.1881	☾ R. 10:56 am S. 9:21 pm ☉ R. 7:49 am S. 4:36 pm	**SUNDAY · DECEMBER 24 · 2006 24**
I.F. Stone, writer, b.1907	Kit Carson, American frontiersman, b.1809		
Ava Gardner, actor, b.1922	The cowards never start and the weak die along the way. — Kit Carson	☿ △ ♄ 7:18AM ☽ ☍ ♄ 11:42AM	

CHRISTMAS EVE

All times Central Time Zone, sun and moon rise and set Minneapolis, MN.

---

25 MONDAY · DECEMBER 25 · 2006

☾ R. 11:18 am S. 10:38 pm
☉ R. 7:50 am S. 4:37 pm

☿ ☌ ♆ 2:47PM
☾ ☌ ♅ 4:10PM

Feast of the Nativity, *Orth. Christian*

Annie Lennox, singer, b.1954

Anwar Sadat, Egyptian Pres., b.1918

Cab Calloway, singer, b.1907

Rebecca West, writer, b.1892

Clara Barton, Red Cross founder, b.1821

Sir Isaac Newton, scientist, b.1642

May Peace be your gift at Christmas and your blessing all year through!
— *Author Unknown*

CHRISTMAS DAY

26 TUESDAY · DECEMBER 26 · 2006

☾ R. 11:38 am S. 11:55 pm
☉ R. 7:50 am S. 4:37 pm

Boxing Day, *England*

Zarathosht Diso, *Zoroastrian*

Kwanzaa, through Jan. 1

Susan Butcher, dogsled driver, b.1954

Steve Allen, comedian, b.1921

Mao Tse-Tung, Chinese leader, b.1893

Henry Miller, writer, b.1881

Our own physical body possesses a wisdom which we who inhabit the body lack.
— *Henry Miller*

27 WEDNESDAY · DECEMBER 27 · 2006

☾ R. 11:57 am
☉ R. 7:50 am S. 4:38 pm

First Quarter
8:48 am

☾ △ ♃ 12:32PM

Marlene Dietrich, actor, b.1901

Louis Pasteur, chemist, b.1822

Johannes Kepler, astronomer, b.1571

Let me tell you the secret that has led me to my goal. My strength lies solely in my tenacity.
— *Louis Pasteur*

28 THURSDAY · DECEMBER 28 · 2006

☾ R. 12:17 pm S. 1:11 am
☉ R. 7:51 am S. 4:39 pm

☾ △ ♂ 2:57AM
☾ △ ♄ 5:57PM
☾ △ ♆ 9:54PM

1733: "Poor Richard's Almanack" published

1973: Endangered Species Act est.

Denzel Washington, actor, b.1954

Maggie Smith, actor, b.1934

Mortimer Adler, philosopher, b.1902

You have to allow a certain amount of time in which you are doing nothing in order to have things occur to you, to let your mind think.
— *Mortimer Adler*

© Jupiter Images

To Do: WALKING MEDITATION

Here are two ways to practice walking meditation to refresh your soul.
1) Put your attention on the placement of your feet as they meet the ground. Focus on the physical sensation of walking. Let all your thoughts float on by. 2) As you walk purposefully and relatively slowly, let your thoughts go and turn up your senses. Let what you hear, smell, feel on your skin wash over and through you, taking with it all stress and all discomfort. To learn more about walking meditation, see *Peace Is Every Step: The Path of Mindfulness in Everyday Life* by Thich Nhat Hanh. —MC

© iStockPhoto

LATE FRAGMENT / *Raymond Carver*

And did you get what / you wanted from this life even so? /
I did. / And what did you want? / To call myself beloved,
to feel myself / beloved on the earth.

1890: Massacre
at Wounded
Knee

*Jude Law,
actor, b.1972*

*Marianne
Faithful,
singer, b.1946*

*Pablo Casals,
cellist, b.1876*

*Grigori Rasputin,
mystic, b.1916*

Give not over
thy soul to sor-
row; and afflict
not thyself in thy
own counsel.
Gladness of
heart is the life
of man and the
joyfulness of
man is length
of days.
— *Ecclesiastes*

☾ R. 12:41 pm S. 2:30 am
☉ R. 7:51 am   S. 4:40 pm

☾△☿ 7:33AM
☾△☉ 4:50PM

FRIDAY · DECEMBER 29 · 2006 **29**

Day of Hajj,
Pilgrimage,
Islam

*Tiger Woods,
golfer, b.1975*

*Patti Smith,
singer/song-
writer, b.1946*

*Tracey Ullman,
actor, b.1959*

*Sandy Koufax,
baseball pitcher,
b.1935*

Bo Diddley,
singer, b.1928

*Rudyard Kipling,
writer, b.1865*

He wrapped
himself in
quotations —
as a beggar
would enfold
himself in
the purple
of Emperors.
— *Rudyard
Kipling*

☾ R. 1:09 pm S. 3:50 am
☉ R. 7:51 am S. 4:40 pm

☾△♀ 9:37PM

SATURDAY · DECEMBER 30 · 2006 **30**

Eid-Al-Adha:
Feast of the
Sacrifice, *Islam*

Hogmanay,
Scotland

**First Night
Celebrations:**
U.S. and CAN

*Paul Westerberg,
singer, b.1959*

*Donna Summer,
singer, b.1948*

John Denver,
singer, b.1943

*Henri Matisse,
painter, b.1869*

All that really
belongs to us
is time; even he
who has nothing
else has that.
— *Baltasar
Gracian*

☾ R. 1:46 pm S. 5:10 am
☉ R. 7:51 am S. 4:41 pm

SUNDAY · DECEMBER 31 · 2006 **31**

NEW YEAR'S EVE

All times Central Time Zone, sun and moon rise and set Minneapolis, MN.

2006

ESSENTIAL MISCELLANY

In the realm of Nature there is nothing purposeless, trivial, or unnecessary :: Maimonides

es-sen-tial \ĭ-sĕn′chəl\ **1:** of, relating to, or constituting essence: INHERENT **2:** of the utmost importance: BASIC, INDISPENSABLE, NECESSARY

mis-cel-la-ny \mĭs′ə-lā′nē\ **1:** a mixture of various things **2 a** *pl*: separate writings collected in one volume **b:** a collection of writings on various subjects

URBAN ALMANAC

ur \ûr\ **1:** original : primitive (*Ur*-form) **2:** original version of (*Ur*-Hamlet)

banal \bə′năl\ [possessed in common, commonplace] (1840)

mana \măn′ə\ [of Melanesian & Polynesian origin: akin to Hawaiian & Maori *mana*] (1843) **1 a:** the power of the elemental forces embodied in an object or person **2:** moral authority : PRESTIGE

c – capacitance [capacity] (1909) \sē\ the property of an electric nonconductor that permits the storage of energy as a result of electric displacement when opposite surfaces of the nonconductor are maintained at a difference of potential

Cosmo Doogood's **Urban Almanac**
[The original] [power of the elemental forces] [that permits the storage of energy] to be [possessed in common]

The following pages are offered for your amusement and delectation. Savor them in solitude or use them as gambits to start a conversation. What is essential is really much better when shared.

—*Cosmo*

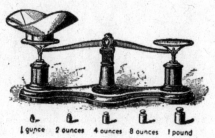

½ ounce 2 ounces 4 ounces 8 ounces 1 pound

WEIGHTS

Pint Quart Peck Half-Bushel Bushel

DRY MEASURES

Gill Pint Quart Gallon

LIQUID MEASURES

FAHRENHEIT

-40	-31	-22	-13	-4	5	14	23	32	41	50	59	68	77	86	95	104
-40	-35	-30	-25	-20	-15	-10	-5	0	5	10	15	20	25	30	35	40

CELSIUS

TEMPERATURE

MPH

0	20	30	40	50	60	70	80	90	100
0	32	48	64	80	96	112	128	144	160

KMPH

SPEED

MEASUREMENT CONVERSIONS

TEMPERATURE
Centigrade to Fahrenheit multiply by 1.8 and add 32
Fahrenheit to Centigrade subtract 32 and multiply by 0.5555

LENGTH, DISTANCE, AND AREA	*multiply by*
inches to centimeters	2.54
centimeters to inches	0.39
feet to meters 0.30	
meters to feet 3.28	
yards to meters	0.91
meters to yards	1.09
miles to kilometers	1.61
kilometers to miles	0.62
acres to hectares	0.40
hectares to acres	2.47

WEIGHT	*multiply by*
ounces to grams	28.35
grams to ounces	0.035
pounds to kilograms	0.45
kilograms to pounds	2.21
British tons to kilograms	1016
U.S. tons to kilograms	907

A British ton is 2,240 pounds
A U.S. ton is 2,000 pounds

VOLUME	*multiply by*
imperial gallons to liters	4.55
liters to imperial gallons	0.22
U.S. gallons to liters	3.79
liters to U.S. gallons	0.26

5 imperial gallons equal 6 U.S. gallons
1 liter is slightly more than a U.S. quart,
slightly less than 1 British quart.

THE WIND

THE BEAUFORT SCALE FOR WIND SPEEDS

0 (Calm): less than 1 mph; calm, smoke rises vertically

1 (Light Air): 1–3 mph; direction of wind shown by smoke but not by wind vanes

2 (Light Breeze): 4–7 mph; wind felt on face, leaves rustle, ordinary vane moved by wind

3 (Gentle Breeze): 8–12 mph; leaves and small twigs in constant motion, wind extends light flag

4 (Moderate Breeze): 13–18 mph; raises dust and loose paper, small branches are moved

5 (Fresh Breeze): 19–24 mph; small trees in leaf begin to sway, crested wavelets form on inland waters

6 (Strong Breeze): 25–31 mph; large branches in motion, telegraph wires whistle, umbrellas used with difficulty

7 (Moderate Gale or Near Gale): 32–38 mph; whole trees in motion, inconvenience in walking against the wind

8 (Fresh Gale or Gale): 39–46 mph; breaks twigs off trees, generally impedes progress

9 (Strong Gale): 47–54 mph; slight structural damage occurs, chimney pots and slates removed

10 (Whole Gale or Storm): 55–63 mph; trees uprooted, considerable structural damage occurs

11 (Storm or Violent Storm): 64–72 mph; very rarely experienced, accompanied by widespread damage

12 (Hurricane): 73–136 mph; devastation occurs

BOREAS—The North Wind

NOTOS—The South Wind

APELIOTES—The East Wind

ZEPHYROS—The West Wind

© Dover Books

DAYS OF THE WEEK

SUNDAY—Sun's day, from Latin *Dies solis*

THURSDAY—After Thor, Teutonic god of war

MONDAY—Moon's day, from Latin *Dies lunae*

TUESDAY—After Tiw, Teutonic god of law

THE NAMES OF DAYS in English have a mixed ancestry. All were inherited from Teutonic tribes, but the Teutons had borrowed some names from the Romans. Thus, Sunday, Monday, and Saturday are Roman; The other days are from the gods honored by the Teutons. Other languages have divine inspiration for the weekday names also—in French and Italian, Wednesday's *mercredi* or *mercoledi* is named after the Roman god Mercury.

FRIDAY—After Fria, Teutonic goddess of love

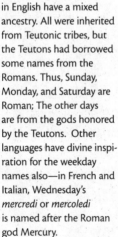

SATURDAY—After Saturn, Roman god of agriculture

WEDNESDAY—After Woden, prinicipal Teutonic god

DISTANCES BETWEEN MAJOR CITIES (SM)

	Delhi	Hong Kong	Lagos	London	Mexico City	Montreal	Moscow	New York	Paris	Rome	Sydney	Tokyo
Amsterdam	3954	5772	3161	217	5724	3422	1338	3639	261	809	10342	5788
Auckland	7838	5687	12853	11404	8085	9004	10161	8844	11893	11492	1343	5493
Bangkok	1815	1065	7988	5919	9812	10731	4394	8669	5863	5491	4687	2868
Brussels	3981	5888	3063	206	5822	3452	1391	3662	170	734	10452	5873
Buenos Aires	9823	11478	4916	6915	4592	5640	8382	5302	6892	6931	7326	11591
Cairo	2738	5057	2442	2187	7695	5403	1770	5609	1995	1329	8950	5958
Delhi	-	2345	5022	4169	9119	70121	2698	7299	4089	3679	6495	3656
Frankfurt	3804	5698	3030	396	5935	3610	1250	3851	289	598	10262	5797
Geneva	3990	5985	2745	466	6261	3684	1499	3859	250	439	10588	6094
Hong Kong	2345	-	7351	5979	8794	7736	4443	8050	5987	5773	4586	1807
Istanbul	2833	4980	2859	1552	7095	4784	1089	5009	1394	852	9281	5560
Johannesburg	4996	8718	3422	5640	9207	9595	6280	7967	5422	4802	7601	8409
Karachi	665	2980	4378	3931	9235	6976	2597	7293	3810	3307	6840	4319
Lagos	5022	7351	-	3115	6875	5266	3875	5257	2922	2497	9634	8371
London	4169	5979	3115	-	5543	3252	1550	3458	220	898	10565	5956
Madrid	4515	6556	2380	765	5633	3455	2126	3588	649	836	10985	6704
Manila	3047	702	7915	6681	8830	8180	5130	8505	6689	6476	3892	1879
Mexico City	9119	8794	6875	5543	-	2307	6671	2086	5714	6366	8053	7014
Montreal	7012	7736	5266	3252	2307	-	4393	338	3434	4102	9952	6470
Moscow	2698	4443	3875	1550	6671	4393	-	4669	1540	1476	8997	4668
New York	7299	8050	5357	3458	2086	338	4669	-	3628	4280	9957	6737
Paris	4089	5987	2922	220	5714	3434	1540	3628	-	688	10550	6029
Rio de Janeiro	8747	11002	3742	5767	4766	5082	7162	4816	5697	5707	8398	11553
Rome	3679	5773	2497	898	6366	4102	1476	4280	688	-	10149	6146
Stockholm	3456	5115	3753	908	5965	3665	771	3917	963	1256	9684	5091
Sydney	6495	4586	9634	10565	8053	9952	9193	9957	10550	10149	-	4863
Tehran	1578	3836	3642	2738	8167	5859	1526	6119	2610	2121	8057	4760
Tel Aviv	3350	6164	3224	2216	7752	5506	2148	5666	2039	1404	9975	7565
Tokyo	3656	1807	8371	5956	7014	6470	4668	6737	6029	6146	4863	-

ACKNOWLEDGMENTS:
CREDITS AND RESOURCES,
CITED WORKS, ILLUSTRATIONS

CREDITS

Left-hand page weather quotes, top: www.docweather.com

Left-hand page love quotes, bottom: from Perugina' Baci Italian chocolates

Monthly Sky Charts created by Michael Bader. www.bbcommunication.ch

Pages 104, 124, 250
Urban Survival Strategies from *The Worst-Case Scenario Survival Handbook* by Joshua Piven and David Borgericht. Published by Chronicle Books

POEMS

Poetry (Calendar full pages)

Frontispiece "Maybe," by Kirsten Bergh, from *She Would Draw Flowers*. Available through Steiner Books at www.anthropress.com

Page 168
"Bewilderment," by Rumi. From *The Essential Rumi*, translated by Coleman Barks. © 1997, Coleman Barks. Published by Harper San Francisco.

Page 184
"The Summer Day," by Mary Oliver. From *New and Selected Poems*. © 2004, Mary Oliver. Published by Beacon Press.

**Poetry
(Calendar right-hand pages)**

Page 87
"Prayer," by His Holiness the Fourteenth Dalai Lama.

Page 89
Lines from "Change," by Louis Jenkins. From *The Winter Road*. © 2000, Louis Jenkins. Published by Holy Cow! Press.

Page 93
Lines from "January, Anchorage," by Linda McCarriston. From *Little River*. © 2002, Linda McCarriston. Published by Northwestern University Press.

Page 95
"Early Darkness," by D. Patrick Miller. © 1987. From *Instructions of the Spirit*. Published by Fearless Books, 2004.

Page 99
Lines from "Kindness," by Naomi Shihab Nye. From *Words Under the Words*. © 1995, Naomi Shihab Nye. Published by Eighth Mountain Press.

Page 105
Lines from "The Modern Things," by Bjork. From *Post*, Elektra Records, 1995.

Page 107
"The Minute I Heard My First Love Story," by Rumi. From *The Essential Rumi*, translated by Coleman Barks. © 1997, Coleman Barks. Published by Harper San Francisco.

Page 111
"Is My Soul Asleep?" by Antonio Machado. From *Times Alone*, translated by Robert Bly. © 1983, Robert Bly. Published by Wesleyan University Press.

Page 113
Lines from "Possibility," by Charles Coe. From *Picnic on the Moon*. © 1999, Charles Coe. Published by Leapfrog Press.

Page 119
Lines from "A Valley Like This," by William Stafford. From *Even in Quiet Places*. © 1996, William Stafford. Published by Confluence Press.

Page 121
Lines from "The Man in the Moon," by Billy Collins. From *Questions About Angels*. © 1999, Billy Collins. Published by University of Pittsburgh Press.

Page 125
Lines from "The Man Watching," by Rainer Maria Rilke. From *Selected Poems of Rainer Maria Rilke*, translated by Robert Bly. © 1981, Robert Bly. Published by Harper & Row.

Page 127
Lines from "Horses in Spring," by Connie Wanek. From *Hartley Field*. © 2002, Connie Wanek. Published by Holy Cow! Press.

Page 133
Lines from "Warmer," by Martha Collins. From *The Arrangement of Space*. © 1991, Martha Collins. Published by Peregrine Smith.

Page 135
Lines from "On Commonwealth Avenue and Brattle Street," by Diana Der-Hovanessian. From *Any Day Now*. © 1999, Diana Der-Hovanessian. Published by Sheep Meadow Press.

Page 139
"April Chores," by Jane Kenyon. From *Let Evening Come*. © 1990, the estate of Jane Kenyon. Published by Graywolf Press.

Page 141
Lines from "Our Mother," by
Susan Griffin. From
Unremembered Country. ©
1987, Susan Griffin. Published
by Copper Canyon Press.

Page 145
Lines from "I Think That I Shall
Never See…" by Jim Heynen.
From Standing Naked New
and Selected Poems.
© 2001, Jim Heynen.
Published by Confluence Press.

Page 151
"Lingering in Happiness," by
Mary Oliver. From Why I Wake
Early. © 2004, Mary Oliver.
Published by Beacon Press.

Page 153
"A Patch of Old Snow," by Louis
Jenkins. From Just Above Water.
© 1997, Louis Jenkins.
Published by Holy Cow! Press.

Page 155
Lines from "So Like Her Father,"
by Connie Wanek. From Hartley
Field. © 2002, Connie Wanek.
Published by Holy Cow! Press.

Page 157
Lines from "Leaves of Grass," by
Walt Whitman. From Leaves of
Grass, preface.

Page 163
Lines from "Throw Yourself Like
Seed," by Miguel de Unamuno,
translated by Robert Bly. From
Rag and Bone Shop of the Heart,
ed. Robert Bly, James Hillman,
and Michael Meade. © 1992,
Robert Bly. Published by
HarperCollins.

Page 165
Lines from "Touch Me," by
Stanley Kunitz. From The
Collected Poems of Stanley
Kunitz. © 2000, Stanley Kunitz.
Published by Norton.

Page 169
Lines from "When Death
Comes," by Mary Oliver. From
New and Selected Poems. ©
2004, Mary Oliver. Published by
Beacon Press.

Page 171
"Awakening Gatha," by Deena
Metzger. From Looking for
the Faces of God. © 1989, Deena
Metzger. Published
by Parallax Press.

Page 177
Lines from "Secret," by Dorothea
Tanning. From A Table of
Content. © 2004, Dorothea
Tanning. Published by Graywolf
Press.

Page 179
Lines from "Children Near the
Water," by Connie Wanek.
From Hartley Field. © 2002,
Connie Wanek. Published by
Holy Cow! Press.

Page 181
Lines from "Moist Moon People,"
by Carl Sandburg. From The
Complete Poems of Carl
Sandburg. © 2003, Carl Sandburg.
Published by Harcourt Books.

Page 185
Lines from "From Blossoms,"
by Li-Young Lee. From Rose.
© 1986, Li-Young Lee.
Published by BOA Editions.

Page 187
"So Where Is It?" by James P.
Lenfestey. Reprinted with
permission of the author.

Page 191
"In the Grove The Poet at Ten,"
by Jane Kenyon. From Let
Evening Come. © 1990, the
estate of Jane Kenyon.
Published by Graywolf Press.

Page 195
"Telescope," by Ted Kooser.
From Delights and Shadows.
© 2004, Ted Kooser. Published
by Copper Canyon Press.

Page 197
"Sour, Doughy, Raw, and
Numb," by Rumi, from The
Essential Rumi, translated by
Coleman Barks. © 1997,
Coleman Barks. Published
by Harper San Francisco.

Page 201
"Untitled," by Emily Dickinson.

Page 207
"Being a Person," by William
Stafford. From The Way It is.
© 1998, the William Stafford
Archives. Published by
Graywolf Press.

Page 209
"If Bees Could Vote," by Connie
Wanek. From Hartley Field.
© 2002, Connie Wanek.
Published by Holy Cow! Press.

Page 211
Lines from "September," by
Louis Jenkins. From Just Above
Water. © 1997, Louis Jenkins.
Published by Holy Cow! Press.

Page 215
Lines from "Here," by Lawrence
Joseph. From Codes, Precepts,
Biases, and Taboos Poems
1973-1993. © 1983, 2005,
Lawrence Joseph. Published
by Farrar, Straus and Giroux.

Page 217
Lines from "The Amercia
Verse," by Rudolf Steiner.

Page 221
"The First Birds," by Thorsten
Bacon. Reprinted with permis-
sion of the author.

Page 225
Lines from "October," by Robert Frost. From *The Poetry of Robert Frost*, edited by Edward Connery Lathem. © 1923, 1969, Henry Holt and Company. © 1951, 1962, Robert Frost.

Page 227
"The Life of a Day," by Tom Hennen. From *Crawling Out the Window*. © 1998, Tom Hennen. Published by Black Hat Press.

Page 231
Lines from "Aimless Love," by Billy Collins. From *Nine Horses*. © 2003, Billy Collins. Published by Random House.

Page 237
"Untitled," by Emily Dickinson.

Page 239
"Wolf Love," by Victory Lee Schouten. From *Wolf Love*. © 2000, Victory Lee Schouten. Published by Great Path Publishing.

Page 241
"The Paradoxical Command-ments," by Kent M. Keith. © 1968, 2001, Kent M. Keith.

Page 243
"Nature Poetry," by Meg Kearney. From *Urban Nature Poems About Wildlife in the City*, edited by Laure-Anne Bosselaar. © 2000, Meg Kearney. Published by Milkweed Editions.

Page 245
"There Is Some Kiss We Want," by Rumi, from *Like This 43 Odes*, translated by Coleman Barks. © 1990, Coleman Barks. Published by Maypop Books.

Page 247
"Thanksgiving Feast," by James P. Lenfestey. Reprinted with permission of the author.

Page 251
"Atmosphere," by Susan Griffin. From *Unremembered Country*. © 1987, Susan Griffin. Published by Copper Canyon Press.

Page 253
Lines from "We Are the Decisive Element," by Johann Wolfgang von Goethe.

Page 255
Lines from "Outlook," by Crystal Bacon. From *Elegy With a Glass of Whiskey*. © 2004, Crystal Bacon. Published by BOA Editions, Ltd.

Page 259
Lines from "Solstice Fire," by Will Winter. Reprinted with permission of the author.

Page 261
"Late Fragment," by Raymond Carver. From *All of Us: The Collected Poems*. © 2000, Raymond Carver. Published by Vintage Books.

CITED WORKS

Moon Time: The Art of Harmony with Nature and Lunar Cycles, Johanna Paungger and Thomas Poppe, Rider, UK.

Guided by the Moon, Johanna Paungger and Thomas Poppe, Marlowe & Company, New York.

If You Want to Write. © 1938, 1987, Brenda Ueland. Published by Graywolf Press.

Sky Phenomena: A Guide to Naked-eye Observation of the Stars by Norman Davidson. © 1993, 2004, Norman Davidson. Revised 2004. Published by Lindisfarne Press, Great Barrington, MA 01230, www.lindisfarne.org.

Celestial Delights: The Best Astronomical Events Through 2010 by Francis Reddy and Greg Walz-Chojnacki. Published by Celestial Arts/Ten Speed Press, Berkeley, CA.

Benjamin Franklin: An American Life, by Walter Isaacson. Published by Simon & Schuster, New York.

L'almanach de la maison résonances, l.e.c. édition 24, rue Feydeau 75002 Paris LEC@wanadoo.fr

Making Maple Syrup by Noel Perrin. Storey Communications, Inc., 1980 ISBN 0-88266-226-0

Backyard Sugarin' by Rink Mann. The Countryman Press, PO Box 748, Woodstock, VT ISBN 0-88150-216-2

Winter World: The Ingenuity of Animal Survival by Bernd Heinrich, ecco/HarperCollins, 2003, ISBN 0-06095-737-9

REFERENCES

Birthdays, holidays, festivals, historic events, etc.:

Chase's 2004 Calendar of Events edited by Holly McGuire and Kathy Keil. © 2004, The McGraw-Hill Companies, Inc., New York.

The Book of Holidays Around the World by Alice van Straalen. © 1986, Book-of-the-Month Club, Inc. Published by E.P. Dutton, New York.

Weather and Cosmos, by Dennis Klocek, Rudolf Steiner College Press, Fair Oaks, CA 95628.

Extreme Weather by Christopher C. Burt. W.W. Norton & Co., New York.

Seasonal Guide to the Natural Year (entire series). Various authors. Published by Fulcrum Publishing, Golden, CO. (800) 992-2908.

The Autobiography and Other Writings, by Benjamin Franklin, Penguin Books, New York.

Wild Neighbors: The Humane Approach to Living with Wildlife, The Humane Society of the United States, Washington, D.C., Fulcrum Publishing.

Start Now! A Book of Soul and Spiritual Exercises by Rudolf Steiner, translated and edited by Christopher Bamford. Published by Steiner Books, Great Barrington, MA 01230. (800) 856-8664

Urban Nature Poems About Wildlife in the City, edited by Laure-Anne Bosselaar. Published 2000 by Milkweed Editions, Minneapolis, MN. (800) 520-6455.

Good Poems, selected and introduced by Garrison Keillor. Published by Penguin Books, New York.

Prayers for a Thousand Years, edited by Elizabeth Roberts & Elias Amidon. Published by HarperCollins Publishers, Inc., New York.

WEBSITES

The UK Phenology Network
www.phenology.org.uk.

ATTRA – National Sustainable Agriculture Information Service
www.attra.org/attra-pub/phenology.html.

Biodynamics Now
www.igg.com/bdnow.

Biodynamic Farming and Gardening Association
www.biodynamics.com.

www.poets.org

ILLUSTRATIONS

Page 17
Illustration from *Le Petit Prince* by Antoine de Saint-Exupery, copyright 1943 by Harcourt, Inc. and renewed 1971 by Consuelo de Saint-Exupery. Reproduced by permission of the publisher.

Pages 42-45
Illustrations by Nora Wildgen

Page 60
Charcoal Drawing by Alec Neal

CONTRIBUTORS

Christopher Bamford is editor at SteinerBooks and Lindisfarne Books. He is the author of *Voice of the Eagle: The Heart of Celtic Christianity* and *An Endless Trace The Passionate Pursuit of Wisdom in the West.* Recently he edited and introduced *Start Now! The Spiritual Exercises of Rudolf Steiner.*

Margaret Bossen is the principal of Bossenova, an award-winning graphic design and multimedia production group. In addition to developing high-end Web and Interactive projects, she works on print design, corporate identity, and logotype design. See www.bossenova.com

Martha Coventry is director of external publications for the University of Minnesota and writes for various periodicals about food, nature, and family. She is the mother of two daughters, Lizzie and Sally, and lives in Minneapolis in a house on a hill overlooking a city lake.

Norman Davidson writes, lectures, and consults at Sunbridge College in Spring Valley, New York. He is the author of *Sky Phenomena A Guide to Naked-eye Observation of the Stars* (Lindisfarne Press, Great Barrington, MA), and *Astronomy and the Imagination* (Penguin Books).

Maria Dolan is co-author of *Nature in the City Seattle* (Mountaineers Books) and author of *Outside Magazine's Urban Adventure Seattle* (W.W.Norton & Co.) Her writing on such topics as octopus love, urban owls, quirky birdwatchers, and snowboarding mishaps has been published in the *Seattle Times, Salon.com, Travelers Tales,* and elsewhere.

Craig Holdrege is the director of The Nature Institute in rural upstate New York, a center dedicated to holistic and phenomenological science (www.natureinstitute). A biologist and educator, he is keenly interested in the interconnectedness of things.

He also critically examines new developments in genetics and biotechnology and is the author of *Genetics and the Manipulation of Life: The Forgotten Factor of Context.*

Walter Isaacson, the president of the Aspen Institute, has been the chairman of CNN and the managing editor of *Time* magazine. He is the author of *Benjamin Franklin: An American Life*, and *Kissinger: A Biography* and the coauthor of *The Wise Men: Six Friends and the World They Made.* He lives in Washington, D.C., with his wife and daughter.

Lynn Jericho counsels individuals, speaks and leads workshops. Mother of two grown children, she co-founded a birthing center and a Waldorf school. She is the co-author of *Ground Zero and the Human Soul.* Her book, *Inner Christmas*, will be published in 2006. www.LynnJericho.com

Dennis Klocek (Doc Weather) is Director of the Consciousness Studies Program at Rudolf Steiner College, Fair Oaks, California, and founder of the Coros Institute. He is the author many books, including *Weather and Cosmos; Seeking Spirit Vision;* and *Knowledge, Teaching, and the Death of the Mysterious.* Dennis also writes and publishes a weather predictions newsletter www.WeatherWeek.com See also www.docweather.com

Elizabeth Larsen is a freelance writer living in Minneapolis whose writing has appeared in *Utne, Sierra, Child*, and *Travel and Leisure Family.* She only knows how to locate The Big Dipper in the night sky and is hoping her three young children will one day teach her the other constellations.

Roger Lewin, is a prize-winning author of twenty popular science books. His book *Complexity: Life at the Edge of Chaos* holds the honor of being voted one of the top 100 science books for the 20th century. For ten years he was news editor of *Science Magazine.* This article was adapted from his book, *Making Waves: Dr. Irving Dardik's SuperWave Principle,* published by Rodale Press in the fall of 2005.

David Lukas is a full-time naturalist, instructor, and author of *Wild Birds of California*, and other books. He lives in the Yuba watershed of California and is currently co-authoring a field guide to the birds of Sierra Nevada.

Andi MacDaniel has written about sustainable agriculture and environmental issues for *Utne, Ode,* and *Whole Life Times.* She currently works as a program associate for Renewing the Countryside, a non-profit rural advocacy organization based in Minneapolis.

Danielle Maestretti is a Bay Area native currently living in Minneapolis; her heart, however, resides in Buenos Aires, where she studied for several months. She enjoys puns, dill pickles, NPR, riding her bicycle, and planning future trips to Latin America.

Kathleen Melin has lived in Paris, London, Minneapolis, and Anchorage. She now lives on her ancestral farm in the country near Saint Croix Falls, Wisconsin, though she treasures the richness and variety of the city. She writes and teaches at the University of Wisconsin.

John Miller has worked with developmentally disabled adults (in the Camphill movement), and as a woodworker, gardener, farmer, and teacher. He has taught in Waldorf schools for 17 years, working primarily at Minneapolis' City of Lakes Waldorf School and Watershed High School. John and his wife Kerry have four adult children. John is currently in the early stages of co-founding a college inspired by the life of Albert Schweitzer.

Nancy Jewel Poer appears in the PBS documentary "A Family Undertaking" and is author of *Living Into Dying Spiritual and Practical Deathcare for Family and Community.* You can contact her at www.nancyjewelpoer.com.

Eric Utne has been an architecture student, natural foods merchant, acupuncturist, writer, editor, publisher, and middle school teacher, among other things. He co-founded *New Age Journal* in 1974 and founded *Utne* Reader in 1984. He is father of four sons and lives with his wife, Nina, and youngest son, Eli, in Minneapolis. He is a close personal friend of Cosmo Doogood.

Leif Utne is a Minneapolis-based Capricorn. In addition to his day job as an editor at *Utne* magazine, he plays flute and keyboards in a rock band, and has been frustratedly trying to learn the guitar for years.

ESSENTIAL PLACES AND URBAN SANCTUARIES

Our readers nominated the Essential Places and Urban Sanctuaries in this issue of the almanac. (Thank you!) Where possible, we have used their words to describe their choices.

ESSENTIAL PLACES INFORMATION

Page 106
Old Cutler Road (Miami, Florida)

"Old Cutler Road to Coconut Grove in Miami is a marvelous canopy insulating you from the polyglot chaos which is Miami, which I embrace, choose, and love, but from which I occasionally require respite. By day, the road's greeness envelops you, its coolness protects you. By night, it is a wonderland, dark, mysterious, entrancing." —*Dona Dailey*

Where: Old Cutler Road runs north and south, partly through Matheson Hammock County Park and Fairchild Tropical Garden, and west of Biscayne Bay.

Page 140
16th and Broadway (Sacramento, California)

"When Sacramentans make the long drive home late at night, we finally see the multi-colored neon lights atop the Tower Theater at 16th and Broadway. People come to the corner for foreign and art films, to browse through books and music at the first Tower Records and Books, to meet friends.... Broadway is a mixed street, filled with restaurants, auto supply stores, a fishing and gun firm, a gas station, and Target. Such a conglomeration keeps the corner from being just an entertainment spot, making it central to business as well as a neighborhood treasure." —*Virginia Kidd*

Where: 16th Avenue and Broadway

Page 166
Lagomarcino's (Moline, Illinois)

"Lagomarcino's is special because it's been in business in the same location for almost 100 years, still family owned and operated. And, the Lagomarcino family goes out of its way to find staff who are developmentally disabled, making a vital contribution to our local ARC's (formerly Association for Retarded Citizens) education programs. I love Lagomarcino's because it's the only place in town I can go where the interior is essentially the same as it was when my grandmother, who was born in 1897, sat in a cozy wooden booth and had a soda when she was a child." —*Vicki Graves*

Where: 1422 5th Avenue, near the John Deere Commons

Page 192
Gateway National Recreation Area (Brooklyn, New York)

"[It's an essential place]...because it has the nation's largest community garden, because it's where Amelia Earhart and Charles Lindbergh took off and landed, because it's where the cops practice high speed chases, and most importantly because at the beach south of the archery range, pieces of pottery wash up from when the whole area was Barren Island, New York City's first garbage dump." —*Rebecca Bloom*

Where: For directions and information on our only urban national park, see www.nps.gov/gate

Page 222
Fourth Avenue (Tucson, Arizona)

"In 1969, Fourth Avenue, between the downtown underpass and Speedway, was in a rotting stage with roaming hippies and decaying old businesses...Today, the trolley merrily clacks down the avenue, connecting the university to the restaurants, bars, and dozens of locally owned shops like The Native Seed Search, The Food Conspiracy, Antigone's Bookstore, and many renowned thrift stores. High-quality murals are kept up by artists who have galleries nearby and the sidewalk trees planted thirty years ago provide shade for all the strollers." —*Kevin Moodie*

Where: For more on Fourth Avenue, including a map, see www.fourthavenue.org

Page 252
The Plaza at PPG Place (Pittsburgh, Pennsylvania)

"Thanks to the generosity of the Hillman Family, the area fondly referred to as the 'Tomb of the UnKnown Bowler' now transforms itself every summer and winter. In the summer, a magnificent fountain appears as if from nowhere where kids can frolic and enjoy themselves for hours in a safe place (while the parents sit nearby reading, writing, or enjoying lunch). It's a swimming hole for the urban pioneer—no frills, no problems—all just plain fun. Come winter, an outdoor ice skating rink magically appears! A place where families can come to town and enjoy themselves." —*Darla Cravotta*

Where: For directions to and parking for the Plaza, see www.ppgplace.com

URBAN SANCTUARY INFORMATION

Page: 90
New York Public Library
Our readers nominated many libraries around the country; we chose New York City's public library as the composite of all that is wonderful about our unique library system (thank you, Andrew Carnegie). Not only can you borrow books for free, but you can sit in quiet company with other seekers of entertainment and enlightenment in pleasant or historic surroundings in cities and small towns all over America. As reader Darla Cravotta writes, "Libraries are essential urban sanctuaries—they are community anchors, community centers, and places of respite."

Where: For more on the New York Pubic Library and a map of its branches, see www.nypl.org

Page: 122
Wayfarer's Chapel (Rancho Palos Verdes, California)
"The setting of Wayfarer's Chapel is beautiful and peaceful, on a cliff above the Pacific Ocean—Catalina Island in the distance on a clear day surrounded by flowers and pepper trees and sage. The chapel itself is very small and intimate, designed, I think, by Frank Lloyd Wright or a disciple of his, all glass and wood cradled into the hillside, as if planted there by God herself." —*Arden Cody*

Where: For more information and directions, see www.wayfarerschapel.org

Page: 156
Alfred Caldwell Lily Pool (Chicago, Illinois)
"This oasis was designed by the landscape architect, Alfred Caldwell in the 1920s, I think. Over the years it deteriorated and at one point was a rookery for wild birds. In the late 1990s, the City and Friends of the Parks restored the pool to its original design—beautiful limestone, prairie grasses, waterfall, and, of course, lily pads. ...It's quiet at any time of day. If I listen carefully, I can hear traffic swooshing up and down Lake Shore Drive, but mostly I hear birds in the trees, ducks in the pond, and water rushing over the falls." —*Marcia Flick*

Where: Open at Fullerton Avenue (across from the Notebaert Nature Museum) and Stockton Drive, (the entrance to parking for the Lincoln Park Zoo). Also, see www.ci.chi.il.us/Landmarks/C

Page : 180
Mount Royal (Montreal, Quebec, Canada)
"Mount Royal is smack-dab in downtown Montreal...There are walkers, joggers, bikers, dog-walkers, and horse-back riders all sharing the winding paths; it's as if once you begin your ascent, everyone around you becomes a nicer person. There's a chalet at the 'peak' where you can buy ice cream and bottled water right next to an observation deck with a spectacular view of the city. A bit further along, is a man-made lake—great for picnics and pedal-boating in the summer and ice skating in winter." —*Kara Stahl*

Where: For more information and a map, see www.montreal.com/parks

Page: 208
Milwaukee lakefront (Milwaukee, Wisconsin)
"The Milwaukee lakefront 'begins' downtown, where high rises and the Art Museum meet the water... At the northern tip, the wilderness seems to take over, even though residences continue for another thirty miles. Some of this parkland has been civilized with the gleaming sand and the disciplined yacht club, yet stretches feel so windswept and elemental. The mood of Lake Michigan overwhelms the mood of the park (unlike the lakefront of Chicago, which is dominated by architecture). The urban condition seems miles away from the impact of this deep body of water." —*Andrew Kutchera*

Where: Along Lake Michigan, beginning downtown and going north

Page: 238
Josyln Art Museum (Omaha, Nebraska)
"Looking back on [the Joslyn's] Mediterranean-inspired courtyard, I am not quite sure what it was doing a mile and a half from the Missouri River. [As a young woman] the Joslyn courtyard gave me my first taste of the something I reluctantly call 'sacred time and sacred space'—not because it's not true but it just sounds a little grand. It was my first consciousness of how the beauty of a place can open one's heart, and that place can be a church or grove of redwoods or a Midwestern museum." —*J. Ruth Gendler*

Where: For more on the museum, including a map, see www.joslyn.org

The History of a Legendary Almanac

Cosmo Doogood has been admonishing people throughout recorded history to "Look up. Look out. Look in." For over twelve centuries he has provided farmers, navigators, astronomers, astrologers, artists, and poets essential information in the form of annual almanacs to help them connect with, understand, and celebrate Nature & Her Rhythms. King Arthur's wise counselor Merlin and Trevrizent, teacher of the Grail Knight Parzival, both relied on Cosmo's annual calculations to track the movements of the planets through the starry heavens. Leonardo da Vinci used his Cosmo's Almanac to sketch his observations and deepen his understanding of regional flora and fauna. Benjamin Franklin brought Cosmo's practical wit and star wisdom to the New World, sowing the seeds for democracy and making his *Poor Richard's Almanack* the most popular publication of its time. Henry David Thoreau and Walt Whitman carried their Cosmo's Almanacs with them wherever they went to jot down nature notes and capture fleeting inspirations. More recently, Sigmund Freud and Virginia Woolf recorded their dreams each morning in their Cosmo's. Today, Martha Stewart and Donald Trump use their Cosmo's to bring order to their busy schedules while maintaining an intimate connection to nature.

PROTECT YOUR COSMOS

These sturdy yet supple, removable covers have a timeless old-world feel. They're constructed of durable plant-based materials that will protect your almanacs for a lifetime. Simple, convenient, and handsomely designed, these almanac covers come in classic black with Cosmo's logo debossed and stamped in gold on the front. A built-in elastic band keeps your almanac safe and secure when not in use.

$14.95 US/ $17.95 CDN,
without almanac
$24.95 US/ $35.95 CDN,
2006 almanac included

Prices include shipping and handling. Send check or money order made out to Cosmo Doogood, in US funds drawn on a US bank, to: Cosmo's Covers, c/o Midwest Book Distributors, 1060 33rd Ave SE, Minneapolis, MN 55414. Please allow six to eight weeks for delivery. For expedited delivery call: Sonya at Midwest Book Distributors 1-877-430-0044.

Slip the back cover of your almanac into the slot on the inside back of the removable cover. Gently work back and forth until in place.